ABOUT THE AUTHORS

Dr. Paula Mayock is a Lecturer in Youth Research at the School of Social Work and Social Policy and Children's Research Centre, Trinity College, Dublin. Much of her research focuses on the lives and experiences of young people who are marginalised or "at risk", covering areas including drug use and drug problems, youth homelessness, sexual health and suicide risk. She has recently undertaken post-doctoral research funded by the NIDA (National Institute on Drug Abuse) INVEST Fellowship programme, USA. Paula is the author of several research reports, book chapters and articles and is a member of the editorial board of *Youth Studies Ireland*.

Dr. Eoin O'Sullivan lectures in Social Policy in the School of Social Work and Social Policy, Trinity College, Dublin. He is also a member of the European Observatory on Homelessness. Recent collaborative publications include *Crime and Punishment in Ireland 1922 to 2003: A Statistical Sourcebook* (IPA, 2005), *Crime, Punishment and the Search for Order in Ireland* (IPA, 2004), *Crime Control in Ireland: The Politics of Intolerance* (CUP, 2001) and *Suffer the Little Children: The Inside Story of Ireland's Industrial Schools* (NIB 1999, 2001).

LIVES IN CRISIS

Homeless Young People in Dublin

Paula Mayock *and* Eoin O'Sullivan

The Liffey Press

Published by
The Liffey Press
Ashbrook House 10 Main Street
Raheny, Dublin 5, Ireland
www.theliffeypress.com

A catalogue record of this book is
available from the British Library.

ISBN 978-1-905785-07-0

Printed in the Republic of Ireland by Colour Books

CONTENTS

LIST OF TABLES AND FIGURES

List of Tables

List of Figures

ACKNOWLEDGEMENTS

First and foremost, we want to thank the young people who participated in the study, who gave generously of their time and spoke openly about their life experiences. Each story was invaluable to this research and we recognise that it took great courage to share these experiences.

We want to extend our thanks to the Office of the Minister for Children for funding the research on which this book is based. Special thanks to Dr. Sinéad Hanafin for her encouragement and support.

Thanks to Professor Sheila Greene, Director, and Professor Robbie Gilligan, Associate Director, of the Children's Research Centre, Trinity College Dublin for their interest in this project and for their assistance in bringing this book to fruition.

The preparation of this book has depended on the support of a large number of individuals. Very special thanks to Križan Vekić, who conducted many of the interviews and assisted with the coding and analysis of data. Thanks also to Zosia Borska and Mary Louise Corr, both of the Children's Research Centre, for their help during various stages of the research process. We also want thank to our colleagues at the Children's Research Centre and the School of Social Work and Social Policy, Trinity College Dublin for their support. We would like to especially mention Jessica Breen, Helen Buckley, Shane Butler, Nicola Carr, Siobhán Connolly, Jennifer Cronly, Barry Cullen, Fiona Daly, Evelyn Mahon, Jarlath McKee and Padraic Whyte for their helpful comments on aspects of the text.

We are grateful for the editorial assistance and advice provided by Ger Mulgrew and we want to express particular thanks for the time and effort she invested in this publication. Thanks also to photographer Derek Speirs for the image for the cover.

Finally, we would like to thank our families and friends for their help and support throughout the completion of this work.

Dedicated to Ger Mayock

INTRODUCTION[1]

Gavin, 15 years

*Well I'm on the streets about six, seven months. I used to get
beatings at home an' all by my stepfather. My real father is dead
and, my mother, she's an alcoholic and she always drinks an' all.
And any time she gets drunk an' all and he gets drunk he always
beats me up. And that's how I ended up being on the streets.
Came into town and stayed on the streets, going into hostels, shit
like that an' all, you know what I mean.*

Aoife, 19 years

*I left my mother and, em, I started living with my partner and
now that's finished. That was a year and a half ago and so I came
to be homeless like. But before I went with my partner. I was with
my mother in my mother's house so then my mother got addicted
and left her house and then she was in B&Bs ... Now I've left my
partner. And now my mother is in one of the houses (operated by
a voluntary agency), maybe you know them? I know that like my
mother is in there with my two brothers and sister. My brothers
are fifteen and seventeen and my sister is fourteen and like they*

---

[1] All identifiers – respondents' names, their home neighbourhoods, the names of
family members, friends and professionals – have been removed or substituted
with pseudonyms to protect the identities of the study's participants and other
individuals mentioned by them during the course of conducting interviews. A
glossary of the more common colloquial terminology used by the study's participants can be found in Appendix 1.

*won't take me in like because I'm nineteen. I left my parents and
all and they said I'm old enough but my mother really does want
me in. And if I could get someone to help me get me in I'd love it
like because my mother does want me in with her and I want to be
with my mother ... I need to get someone to help me get in there.
I'd be grateful if they could like. I started to get on drugs because
I wasn't with me mother, I got on heroin because of what it could
do for me. I just don't want to be homeless but I'd nothing else to
do with me life so I got like to mix around in bad company and I
got on drugs like. I want to get off them now but it's actually too
late now at the moment to get off them. I'm gone too far ... Like if
I was with my mother you know it would work out but if I'm by
myself it won't because I want to be with my mother like. I miss
my mother to talk to me, to tell me like what's wrong and what's
right. There's no one there to help me, to tell me. Like the people
from the hostel, they can help me you know, but it's not the same
as your mother like, you know what I mean. I need to be staying
at home with me mother and then I'd like, then I'd be off the
drugs. But when I'm not with my mother like there's nothing else
for me to live for, do you know what I mean[2]. I just want to be
with my mother. Like if someone could help me get to be with my
mother.*

Lyndsey, 15 years

*I was living with my Mam like for a few years up 'till I was
turned fourteen, and then I, I chose to (pause) ... like my mam
kept on hitting me. The night before (leaving home) I went down
to my social worker and I went down again the next morning.
Like I just woke up early, I just washed myself and then I just got
myself dressed and went down to my social worker and I just told
her what happened. I had a different social worker then. Before
that I had Jane but she went on maternity leave and then I got
Ruth. I was in a foster place for four weeks I think it was and*

---

[2] "Do you know what I mean" is a phrase used repeatedly by the study's participants. For those not familiar with this colloquialism, it is a common tag used by
the speaker, largely to confirm what s/he has already stated.

then I moved to (a short-term residential setting/hostel) and I'm here a year. I came here in October and I'm still here.

Tony, 22 years

I'm originally from (North Dublin suburban locality) and I got fucked out of me home at the age of fifteen. I was robbing on me ma, I was, I gave her a terrible life I did, you know. And I ended up on drugs. Then that's how I got into the drug scene through me uncle, he started me on drugs, the hash and the E's and then the coke and then I ended up on gear. Then I ended up homeless from the drugs, you know. And then I ended up coming through the hostels. I went through the different hostels, the first one now, that was alright, the food was great, you can have a shower there. Then there was another hostel, that wasn't great, that's manky dirty up there, people wetting the bed right, horrible. And then where I am now, this is the best hostel, well I think it's the best, great food, shower, warm beds, you can come in at 6 and leave at half nine in the morning. It's the best hostel going.

Paul, 19 years

Well I was in foster care since I was one, you know, since I was a kid. All four of us, there was me and my two brothers and my sister got put in another foster care. I went to (suburban Dublin locality) with me sister and me brothers went to (other suburban locality). So we were sort of together, you know what I mean, me with me sister and me other brothers together. And we used to go on access visits every month. But then when I was thirteen, I started doin' drugs like, you know what I mean. It was more like I was only a kid, hanging around with older lads and smoking hash, and just, just acting the ball. I left school, was robbin' on me foster parents, and it all just built up and they had to throw me out, you know. I understand that they had to throw me out 'cos there was the other kids as well, you know, that they're bringing in fostering like. Now I wasn't leaving drugs in the house, it's just, I was just acting the bollocks you know like setting a bad example for the other kids. So they had to throw me out. Yeah, I was thirteen, and I was homeless then in [local sub-

urban area] for a year, stayin' in mates' houses and here and there, you know, everywhere like. And then like, I always knew about the hostels, but I'd always see pictures of them, you know dorms with loads of beds an' all. So then I went into, I got arrested one day and nobody would come and collect me from the Garda Station. It was for robbin' like, it was me first time robbin' in the shopping centre to try get money, you know, me first time robbin' outside of the (foster) family like to try to get money. So they left me in the hostel and I just, I thought it was alright like. I got on with the lads an' all in there so I just stayed in them then. That was from fourteen that I'm in the hostels.

Megan, 19 years

I was in school but I left school and I've been on the streets since I was fourteen. I was going to the Out of Hours, going through there. And when I was fifteen I went on drugs. I was back at home there a while ago but now I'm back here (hostel). I'm in drug treatment now, you know the clinic. So I'm doing well at the moment. That's really all, been on the streets.

Christian, 17 years

I've been in hostels for the last five years or something since 2000. Before that I was in foster home and supportive residence and before that I was at home. Sure I've been in care since about '97 so (pause) ... I was in a foster home. Then I went back home for a few days. Then I went to another supportive residence, no, I came here (hostel for under-eighteens) in '99, then I went to supportive lodgings for fifteen months out in (suburban Dublin area). Then I came back and lived here in 2000 'till 2001. Then I went to a place down (in the North inner-city), lived there for two or three year. Then I left in 2002. Then I was in the Out of Hours and I've been in a probation home, then lived back here and lived in an awful gaff, one of these hostels. That's it, and then back here (hostel for under-eighteens).

These are the accounts given by seven young people – Gavin, Aoife, Lyndsey, Tony, Paul, Megan and Christian – when asked to tell their "life story". Fragments of much lengthier and more complex life histories, they provide a useful introduction to this book's exploration of the experiences of homeless young people in Dublin. Whilst it would be remiss to describe the stories above as typical, they do nonetheless resonate with at least some aspects of the lives of the 40 young people whose experiences form the subject matter of this book.

The findings documented in later chapters are drawn from the *first phase* of a longitudinal study of homeless young people in Dublin city which set out to examine their pathways into and through homelessness.[3] Based on the first-hand accounts, a key aim was to present a picture of the lived experience of homelessness. Data collection commenced in September 2004 and involved the conduct of in-depth life history interviews with homeless young people recruited through a range of venues including emergency residential settings (hostels) for young people under the age of 18, drop-in centres, adult hostels and street-based settings.

The study's young people, aged between 14 and 22 years at the time of interview, gave rich and detailed accounts of their lives and experiences. Follow-up interviews have since been conducted with a large number of these but this publication deals *only* with the study's Phase I interviews. While this may be seen as a drawback, the study's Phase I accounts are sufficiently detailed and complex to merit separate attention and exploration.[4] This book's analysis of the narratives of 40 homeless young people reveals the multi-faceted nature of youth homelessness and tells us a great deal about the past and current experiences of this diverse group. It also challenges many taken-for-granted ideas about homelessness in general and youth homelessness, in particular. A substantial number of the young people interviewed have suffered multiple deprivations and yet they all spoke with remarkable openness and sincerity. There is much to be learned

---

[3] Some preliminary findings of the first phase of this research can be found in Mayock & Vekić (2006).

[4] The study's Phase II accounts will be dealt with in a separate publication.

from their accounts and it is our hope that this representation of their life stories captures the complexity of the problem we call "youth homelessness".

The book starts by tracing the emergence and development of services for homeless children and young people in Ireland (Chapter 1). Chapter 2 extends the discussion of youth homelessness by reviewing a broader range of national and international literature and discussing dominant explanations for homelessness among the young. This chapter also argues the merits of a pathways approach to researching youth homelessness. Chapter 3 provides a detailed account of the research methodology, including the sampling strategy, access and recruitment issues, data analysis and ethical considerations. The following five chapters present findings pertaining to young people's pathways into homelessness (Chapter 4), their experiences of living out of home (Chapter 5), their drug and criminal "careers" (Chapter 6), their health status (Chapter 7) and their relationship and responses to services (Chapter 8). Chapter 9 concludes by presenting an overview of the experiences of homeless young people in Dublin at the beginning of the twenty-first century; their pathways into and through homelessness; and the policies that shape responses to the vulnerabilities and crises evident in their young lives.

Chapter 1

YOUTH HOMELESSNESS IN IRELAND: THE EMERGENCE AND DEVELOPMENT OF SERVICES

This introductory chapter provides an overview of the emergence of youth homelessness as an issue of concern from the mid-1960s in Ireland and charts the development of services for homeless children and young people. It reviews how different agencies have shaped and re-shaped what we understand today as "youth homelessness" and outlines the evolution of the policy and legislative frameworks that currently govern responses to youth homelessness in Ireland. A key aim is to provide a historical and policy context for the detailed contemporary qualitative accounts of youth homelessness in Dublin presented in the body of the book. This orientation is consistent with Neale's (1997b: 59) view that "[e]xperiences of homelessness must be located within their broader social, historical, and cultural context, if they are to be understood as fully as possible".

This comprehensive overview demonstrates that what is commonly understood as "youth homelessness" is historically variable rather than an immutable fact. It is further suggested that youth homelessness, as a specific category of youth, has been subject to the same myriad of statutory and voluntary agencies that have governed marginal youth more generally over the past two hundred years. Most notably, from the second half of the twentieth century, homeless young people, like other categories of disadvantaged youth, were gradually viewed as "deprived" replac-

ing the portrayal of such young people as "depraved"
(O'Sullivan, 1979). However, elements of earlier thinking remain
and, as a consequence, contradictory images pervade discussions
and portrayals of homeless youth. While contemporary discussions generally understand youth homelessness to be a manifestation of deprivation, representations of young homeless people as
dangerous, as criminal and as drug abusing persist.

The Emergence of Youth Homelessness and the Demise of Industrial Schools

It was only from the mid-1960s that the issue of youth homelessness gained explicit attention either from voluntary or statutory
agencies. At that time, a number of services designed specifically
for such children began to develop. This is not to say that homeless
children did not exist prior to this period; rather, the various Industrial Schools[1] that dotted the country in large numbers absorbed
such categories of children. Clear (1993), for example, highlights the
decline of arrests for vagrancy for those children under 15 years
following the introduction of Industrial Schools to Ireland[2] (See
also Barnes, 1989, and Robins, 1980, for further details).

Industrial Schools effectively absorbed the mass of homeless
children that existed in mid-nineteenth century Ireland and maintained this role until the system gradually reshaped itself as small-

---

[1] Industrial Schools were legislated for in Ireland in 1868, based on the models
already in operation in England and Scotland. The objective of Industrial Schools
was to inculcate children into habits of "industry, regularity, self-denial, self-
reliance and self-control". Although the schools contained a small number of
children who had committed minor acts of delinquency, the majority were
placed in the schools due to the poverty of their parents. The first Industrial
school was established in 1869 and, by 1900, there were 70 industrial schools
certified with a capacity for nearly 8,000 children. By the 1950s, nearly 6,000 children were contained in Industrial Schools, but the numbers steadily declined
from this period (see O'Sullivan and O'Donnell, 2007, for further details).

[2] Many of the Industrial Schools were preceded by various private orphanages,
which had emerged from the mid-eighteenth century, but the Industrial School
system provided a stable and steady source of funding for those managing the
institutions (see O'Sullivan, 2001a, for further details).

scale residential care units some 100 years later in the 1970s. The decline in the number of children in Industrial Schools can be seen in Figure 1.1.[3]

Figure 1.1: Total Number of Children in Industrial Schools, 1922-1969

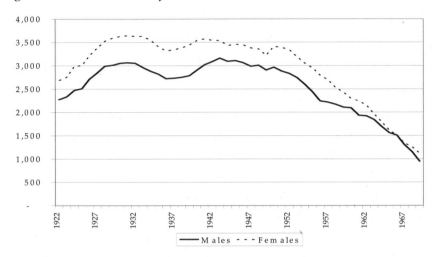

Source: Department of Education, Annual Reports, Various Years.

In 1966, 98 children "not having any home" were committed to Industrial Schools.[4] With the gradual demise of these institutions, homeless children became more visible on the streets of Dublin, and a number of voluntary agencies responded to their needs. In

---

[3] The nature and role of Industrial (and the less numerous Reformatory Schools) in twentieth century Ireland has been the subject of much debate. However, in a recent overview, Ferguson (2007: 124) has argued that "it is beyond question that the entire industrial and reformatory regime was an abusive and cruel one".

[4] It is difficult to accurately quantify the numbers of homeless children committed to Industrial Schools before 1966. Until 1966, no such category existed in the official data, and those who were homeless would have been included under the broad heading "Wandering and not having any home or settled place of abode (as amended)" or "begging". Between 1922 and 1960, 18,357 children (9,765 females and 8,592 males) were committed to Industrial Schools under these categories, representing nearly 56 per cent of all committals to Industrial Schools over that period. By the time homeless children were categorised separately, the Industrial Schools, as noted above, were in terminal decline.

1966 the Los Angeles Society was established following a survey conducted by a number of voluntary agencies which estimated that as many as 150 boys were sleeping rough in Dublin. The Society, after spending a year on various fundraising projects, set up its first hostel for homeless boys. The hostel aimed to provide accommodation, meals and the "security of a home" for 12 homeless boys between the age of 15 and 19 years (Dunne, 1979: 4.1).

In 1968, arising from the same movement which had led to the establishment of the Los Angeles Society, a group of people with a common belief in the need for the provision of hostel accommodation, especially for homeless girls in Dublin, formed the Homeless Girls Society and set about trying to raise sufficient funds to establish such an intervention. As a result, 1970 saw the opening of Sherrard House in the North Inner City. A limited after-care service had also been available in Dublin for those children exiting the Industrial School system since 1963, namely Our Lady's Hostel for Boys, operating under the patronage of the Archbishop of Dublin. By the mid-1960s, it had accommodation for 42 boys aged between 15 and 19 years (Tuairim, 1966).

Laudable as all these initiatives were, they were nowhere near the scale required to deal with the considerable number of children being discharged on an annual basis from the Reformatory and Industrial Schools. Between 1961 and 1970, an average of 780 children (477 boys and 303 girls) were being discharged per annum from these schools. The Reformatory and Industrial Schools Systems Report[5] published in 1970 noted that the question of releasing children who had no home to return to was particularly "difficult" and that there were few hostels in the State to meet this need (Report on Industrial Schools and Reformatories, 1970: 58).

Thus, the problem of youth homelessness was gradually emerging as an identifiable phenomenon from the late 1960s. Nonetheless, it remained a relatively marginal public policy issue

---

[5] In 1967, the Minister for Education at that time, Donagh O'Malley, established a committee, under the chairmanship of District Justice Eileen Kennedy to investigate the Reformatory and Industrial School System in Ireland. The report is better known as the Kennedy Report.

as evidenced by a report produced by the voluntary organisation, CARE (the Campaign for the Care of Deprived Children), which again noted the very small number of hostels and residential establishments for adolescents in Dublin (CARE, 1972).

Evidence of a youth homeless problem was provided in two further reports issued during the early 1970s. In the first, published by Simon Ireland, Whelan (1973) noted a lack of adequate provision for "unattached" youth in Dublin. A second report, this time from the Dublin Diocesan Committee, gave an account of homelessness in Dublin and provided a fuller picture of prevailing conditions. It noted that five hostels provided emergency accommodation for adolescent girls, except for those "in need of psychiatric treatment, or obviously members of the "drug scene" (Dublin Diocesan Welfare Committee, 1974: 7), and went on to identify four categories of young people who required services additional to those already in existence. They included: (sic) mildly mentally handicapped, girls on remand from the courts, girls who were "emotionally damaged" and adolescents sleeping rough.

While homeless children were increasingly visible on the streets of Dublin by the mid-1970s, a distinction was made between settled children sleeping rough and Traveller children sleeping rough. On 16 February 1976, An Coisde Cuspoiri Cioteann (The General Purposes Standing Committee of Dublin City Council) requested that a report be prepared on the problem of children who were begging or sleeping rough. Presented in the same year, the report distinguished between Traveller and non-Traveller children and argued that the number sleeping rough on any one night was "likely to be measured in tens rather than hundreds" (Clare and Byrne, 1976: 6). The authors observed that, whilst it was possible to identify a range of "causes" for children sleeping rough in Dublin, it was difficult to provide a consensus on this issue.

The report went on to state that "the children of travelling people who are sleeping rough must be treated separately because of their different background" (Clare and Byrne, 1976: 10). It noted that some 36 Traveller children were in urgent need of residential accommodation and attributed their homelessness to the alcoholism of their parents. As Helleiner (1998a: 310) argues in relation to the official understanding of Traveller children (and indeed settled children sleeping rough) during this period, "the labelling of Traveller children focused upon individual and family-related deficits rather than any structural (or cultural) causes of Traveller children's divergence from the model of 'proper children'". It is of note that, from the early 1980s onwards, the distinction between Traveller children and homeless children virtually disappears and reference is made only to the generic category "homeless children".

By the early 1970s, the large-scale institutionalisation of children was no longer an option with the demise of the Industrial School system. Emerging, perhaps for the first time in over 100 years, however inchoately expressed, was a growing visible presence of children sleeping rough on the streets of Dublin. Nonetheless, Fr. Peter McVerry, SJ, who commenced working with homeless children in the mid-1970s, recollected the absence of official recognition of homeless children and young people at this time (McVerry, 2003: 21):

> In the mid-1970s, there was no such social category as "homeless children". There were a small number of children who didn't live at home, but they tended to live with their granny on the next street, or with their married sister who lived a few doors away, or with the neighbour whose house they constantly visited anyway.

Task Force on Child Care Services

In 1974, the Minister for Health at that time, Brendan Corish, established a Task Force on Child Care Services.[6] A primary purpose of this Task Force was to "make recommendations on the extension of services for deprived children and children at risk". (Task Force on Child Care Services, 1980: 1). The Final Report of the Task Force was published in 1980 but, prior to this, the Task

---

[6] Ciaran McCullagh (1992: 3) has sardonically commented that "The title of the committee – a Task Force – suggests an image of urgency and incisiveness that the committee's deliberations did its best to overturn".

Force issued an interim report to address what they viewed as "glaring gaps" in existing services (Task Force on Child Care Services – Interim Report, 1975: 6). In relation to homeless children, this report argued that additional hostel accommodation was required. It further recommended that the Eastern Health Board (EHB) be given overall responsibility for the provision of this accommodation and, if this accommodation were to be provided by a voluntary agency, that the EHB accept financial responsibility for the agreed running costs.

The fate of the recommendations contained in the Interim Report of the Task Force can be gauged by the parsimonious approach adopted by the Department of Finance, which argued that:

> ... agreement to publication is not to be taken as a commitment to the recommendations or the views contained in it [it] is nevertheless concerned that publication of the report at this stage could lead to anticipations that the recommendations would be implemented at an early stage. The Minister for Finance also wishes to remind the Government that in the prevailing financial and economic conditions no extra money can be provided for in 1976 or for some time to come to implement any of the Report's recommendations unless such money is made available as a result of genuine reductions in other Government expenditures: that no matter what humanitarian reasons may require improvements in health and social services, they cannot be met without extra resources and such resources are not available.[7]

HOPE Hostel and the Eastern Health Board

In the same year as An Coisde Cuspoiri Cioteann requested a report on children sleeping rough, a new lay voluntary organisation, HOPE, was established to attempt to meet the needs of these children, particularly boys, who were not accessing appropriate

---

[7] National Archives, Department of An Taoiseach, Children: General File. Memorandum for the Government, Interim Report of the Task Force on Child Care Services, 10 October 1975.

emergency accommodation (Harvey and Menton, 1989). Having conducted a relatively crude assessment of the extent of home-lessness amongst young people in Dublin, the founders of HOPE estimated that there were at least 60 under-18s sleeping rough in Dublin each night, with most in the 13–15 age group (Coghlan et al., 1976).

In March 1977 HOPE established a hostel which was to pro-vide accommodation for 12 children. In its first full year of opera-tion, 59 children (58 boys and one girl) stayed in the hostel, with the average length of stay being four weeks. Of those, 53 per cent were aged between 16 and 18 years and a further 39 per cent were aged between 12 and 15. Although the majority of children were from Dublin, a fifth were from other parts of Ireland and just over 10 per cent were classified as Travellers. Fifty-two of the children who stayed in the hostel had left by the end of the first year of op-eration, with exactly half having returned home. Thirteen per cent went into statutory care and one died shortly after leaving. In ad-dition to the provision of the hostel, HOPE also provided a streetwork service which commenced formally in June 1977 with the appointment of three full-time street workers. However, this service terminated in December 1977 but it was recommended that a comprehensive research project be undertaken to explore the issue of "unattached youth" in Dublin.

What followed was a report entitled "Out in the Cold: A Report of Unattached Youth in Dublin in the Winter of 1978-79", the first detailed study of "homeless children" in Ireland rather than a de-scription of the existing services for such children. The research took place in both Dublin's city-centre and in the deprived subur-ban area of Fairfields (Finglas) and estimated that there were some-where in the region of 128 young people sleeping rough in Dublin. The majority (92 per cent) were male with one-quarter of all chil-dren sleeping rough described as "itinerants" (i.e. Travellers). The age range was 13-18 years, with the exception of some "itinerant" children who were younger, and some "older" young people who had been sleeping rough for years. The research identified a further 290 young people in Dublin's city-centre who may not have been sleeping rough but who had various degrees of unattachment. In the Fairfields area, the researchers met 125 young people (70 boys, and 55 girls) who they described as "usually barred from using the existing youth facilities" (HOPE, 1979: 20). Of these, 26 had been, or were "on gur", i.e. sleeping rough for periods.

Youth Homelessness in Dublin by the Early 1980s

Any attempt to ascertain the extent of youth homelessness in Dublin by the early 1980s is hampered by the absence of reliable data. HOPE was the only agency that regularly published information on the number of young people utilising their services and various parliamentary questions on the extent of youth homelessness suggest a perception that the number of homeless young people was not large.[8]

In one of the few available academic accounts of homelessness in Dublin at this time, Kearns (1984: 218), based on fieldwork conducted in 1982, estimated that there were 1,200 homeless persons in the capital city and that homelessness had, therefore, "become a highly distinguishable feature of Dublin's urban ecology". This report did not, however, mention homeless children specifically. Although many voluntary agencies were highlighting the emerging problem of youth homelessness, the issue remained somewhat blurred in official thinking. Indeed, the Final Report of the Task Force on Child Care Services (1980) did not contain any specific reference to homeless children. In general, youth homelessness was commonly assumed to be a manifestation of very specific unmet needs among a very small number of children and/or portrayed as an "itinerant" issue. However, this interpretation was to radically change by the mid-1980s.

---

[8] For example: The Minister for Health in 1979, Charles Haughey stated: "It is not possible to give a precise figure of the number of children under the age of 18 years who have no permanent accommodation. However, I am aware that there is a problem with regard to a small number of children living rough, usually in large urban centres. Many of these young people, because of difficult family circumstances, do not live at home". (Dáil Debates, Vol. 315, 4 July 1979).

Homeless Children – "A Disturbing Fact"

In 1984 the National Youth Policy Committee (1984: 156)[9] noted an apparent change in the composition of the homeless population and identified the problem of homelessness among the young:

> We have received very compelling evidence of the need to deal specifically with the problem of homelessness among young people. The homeless class of people were earlier seen as consisting mainly of men over 40, but there is now a new class of young homeless person – boys and girls. We are anxious that this disturbing fact should be borne in mind by the Government.

Significantly, the report noted that responsibility for the young homeless appeared to be divided between the Health Boards and Local Authorities and that there was no clear statutory responsibility for the provision of such services. It acknowledged that legislation alone would not solve the problem and recommended that the Government appoint a committee "to provide resources to alleviate the very real suffering which exists at present" (National Youth Policy Committee, 1984: 160). In December of the same year, the statutory Ad-hoc Committee on the Homeless (1984: 29) similarly acknowledged a "growing problem of homeless children" and also considered that their needs would be best met "by health boards or through the subvention of voluntary bodies".

The views outlined in these two statutory reports were echoed in two national reports on the extent of youth homelessness, conducted in the mid-1980s by voluntary agencies. The first of these was a national survey of youth homelessness in Ireland conducted by The National Campaign for the Homeless (1985). The survey

---

[9] This was a Government-appointed Committee established in September 1983 under the Chairmanship of the Honourable Mr. Justice Declan Costello. The committee was charged with the key task of preparing recommendations for a national youth policy.

included individuals aged between 10 and 30 years and the re-sults indicated that over 800 young people were known to social workers, Gardaí and other professionals to have experienced homeless over the previous year. Echoing the recommendations of the statutory reports noted above, it proposed that "the Health Board take the leading role in providing accommodation for all homeless people aged 16 to 40" (National Campaign for the Homeless, 1985: 15). A second survey, conducted by an *ad-hoc* group of voluntary agencies and social workers in 1986, found that 328 individuals (244 males and 84 females) under the age of 25 were being provided with accommodation by the responding agencies in the period January 1984 to January 1985. Around this time, a number of Dublin-based research projects also highlighted the problem of youth homelessness. For example, Kennedy (1985) encountered 14 young women between the ages of 13 and 19 re-siding in the two short-term hostels for homeless girls. The most common reason for their leaving home for the first time related to violence at various levels within their domestic settings.

Clear acknowledgement by the government of the problem of youth homelessness, and an apparent willingness to tackle the situation, came in 1985 in the form of a National Youth Policy en-titled, *In Partnership with Youth* (Government of Ireland, 1985). Broadly incorporating the recommendations of the Final Report of the National Youth Policy Committee, it contained the clearest articulation to date that youth homelessness was viewed by the State as an area distinct from adult homelessness and requiring specific attention (Government of Ireland, 1985, 34-35), when it stated that:

> The Government accept that it is the responsibility of the Health Boards to provide for long-term and short-stay ac-commodation for homeless young people incapable of in-dependent living and in need of special care.

The National Youth Policy further noted that new legislation was in preparation that would address many of the unmet needs of homeless children (The Children (Care and Protection) Bill, 1985

which eventually emerged as the *Child Care Act, 1991*), that homelessness should not in itself constitute an offence,[10] and that small-
scale residential provision was inherently more appropriate than
large-scale institutional care in meeting the needs of homeless
children.

The Closure of HOPE Hostel

In light of the various commitments contained in the National
Youth Policy, it was somewhat surprising that on 4 April 1986,
less than four months after its publication, the council of HOPE
closed its hostel, just 10 years after it had been established. This
occurred largely, though not solely, because of the inadequacy of
statutory funding from the EHB.[11] Despite assurances from the
Minister that the EHB social work staff would be able to meet the
needs of those children who had utilised the HOPE hostel, in June
1986, a report on youth homelessness compiled by the Dublin
Simon Community outreach team observed an increase in the incidence of youth homelessness during the two previous months.
The report argued that "[t]o us it is striking that these incidents of
young people homeless in this age group arose in the period after
the closure of HOPE hostel in April 1986" (Clear and Flanagan,
1986: 5). In November of that year, the Minister for Health, Barry
Desmond, established a Taskforce to investigate the setting up of
a hostel to replace HOPE. Reporting to the Minister in just over
three weeks, the Taskforce recommended the establishment of a
new hostel to be managed by the Catholic Social Service Conference. The hostel, which opened in December 1986, was funded by

[10] Under Section 28 of the *Vagrancy Act, 1824*, it was an offence to be "wandering
abroad ... not having any visible means of subsistence, and not giving a good
account of himself or herself". The *Housing Act, 1988* in effect decriminalized
homelessness by deleting this section of the *Vagrancy Act*.

[11] HOPE had insisted that they required £110,000 to run the service, but only
£65,000 was forthcoming from the EHB. The Minister for Health at the time,
Barry Desmond, caustically noted that HOPE "seem to be quite incapable of
managing their financial affairs, so much so that they accumulated a debt of
£90,000, £50,000 of which was due to the Revenue Commissioners in respect of
PRSI" (Dáil Debates, Vol. 365, 15 April).

the EHB to the sum of £250,000, some £185,000 higher than the amount offered to HOPE, albeit to cater for a greater number of children (Duggan, 1989).

In the year before the closure of the Hope Hostel, nine residential projects were identified that provided accommodation for homeless and deprived children in the greater Dublin Region. Two were established specifically for children from the Travelling Community (Trudder House and Derralossary House). Information on these hostels is contained in Table 1.1.

Table 1.1: Hostels for Homeless Children in 1985

Name of Hostel	Health Board Funding in 1985 (£)	Average Number of Occupants	Number of Staff	Organisation
HOPE, Dublin 7	68,000	6–8	6	HOPE
Los Angeles, Dublin 8	125,661	20	12	Los Angeles Society
Don Bosco, Dublin 9	99,278	10	7	Salesian Fathers
Tabor House, Dublin 1	79,744	6	4	Tabor Society
St Vincent de Paul, Dublin 1	45,000	6	5	St Vincent de Paul Society
Sherrard House, Dublin 1	22,500	10	5	Homeless Girls Society
St Annes, Dublin 1	9,600	6	4	Sisters of Our Lady of Charity
Trudder House, Co Wicklow	142,800	20	12	Dublin Committee for Travelling People
Derralossary House, Co Wicklow	105,600	9	7	Dublin Committee for Travelling People

Source: Dáil Éireann – Vol 369, Col. 1458, 5 November 1986.

International Year of Shelter for the Homeless

In March 1987, to mark the International Year of Shelter for the Homeless, a conference entitled "Streetwise" was organised by Focus Point[12] and UNICEF to highlight the situation of young homeless people both in Ireland and internationally. Summarizing the situation in Ireland, Kennedy (1987) noted that no accurate assessment of the extent of homelessness amongst the young existed. Fragmentary evidence was available, which suggested it was a growing problem, attributable in part to changes in the nature and provision of residential care. Somewhat ironically, it was at this time (15 January to 15 April, 1987) that the most detailed and sophisticated survey of youth homelessness in Dublin was taking place, conducted by social workers in the EHB (Eastern Health Board, 1987).[13]

The survey, which involved the distribution of a questionnaire to agencies and individuals having some involvement with potentially homeless children, obtained full information on 386 young people. Of these, the majority (63.5 per cent) were male and over half had a previous care experience. Just under 10 per cent were sleeping rough, with the majority residing with friends, in hostels or other residential care settings, or at home. Family relationship difficulties were identified as leading factors contributing to homelessness. Following the conduct of this survey, the EHB agreed to deploy five outreach workers in the areas identified as having the highest number of young people who were homeless (Ballymun, North Inner City, South Inner City, Tallaght and Ballyfermot/Clondalkin).

---

[12] Focus Point was established in 1985 in order to provide a range of innovative services to homeless households and operates today under the rubric of Focus Ireland.

[13] This research defined homeless youth as those under the age of 18 who were: (1) sleeping rough permanently or intermittently; (2) not living with a parent or guardian and unable to cope on their own; (3) in temporary hostel or child care accommodation because of a lack of a suitable home; (4) in emergency accommodation; (5) drifting frequently from one form of accommodation to another.

In late 1988, the social workers based in the above mentioned five areas identified as having the highest number of homeless youth, in collaboration with Focus Point, aimed to ascertain the number of young people who were actually "out-of-home" over an eight-week period. Contact was made with 88 young people and detailed information was obtained for 77 cases. This research project highlighted the fluidity of young people's movements during the eight-week period, with young people moving from hostels to "dossing" with friends to going home, emigrating and so on (Focus Point/EHB Homeless Social Work Teams, 1989). Nearly 40 per cent of those contacted had previously been in care. At the time of the research, there were only two emergency units for girls under 18 years (Sherrard House and St. Anne's) with 10 emergency beds between them and one for boys (Percy Place, with 10 emergency beds). In addition, a small number of places existed in the form of longer-term accommodation for out-of-home young people.

At this time, the EHB, the statutory agency with responsibility for those under 18 years and homeless, acknowledged the limitation of the available services. The Manager of the Community Care Services of the Board noted that the EHB's social workers continuously faced the problem of arranging placements for this group (Donohue, 1988).

Youth Homelessness in the 1990s

Thus, by the early 1990s, mounting evidence of a significant youth homeless problem had emerged (O'Donnell, 1990; 1992), and this was accompanied by evidence of a lack of suitable accommodation for children and young people once they became homeless, particularly but not exclusively, in Dublin.[14] According to Carlson (1990: 72-73):

Accommodation for homeless children is particularly scarce. These children are often more accurately described

---

[14] See Dillon *et al.*, (1990), and Dillon (1993) for evidence of youth homelessness in Counties Louth and Clare, respectively.

as unsettled, rootless or out-of-home. They may live with a relative for a few weeks, a friend for a few days, a hostel for a week, and onto the streets to repeat the restless cycle. The picture is of constant movement and a gradual drift into crime, substance abuse and even prostitution as a way of surviving on the streets.

The problem became particularly acute in the early 1990s, partly as a consequence of the passing of the *Child Care Act, 1991,* which gave Health Boards responsibility for children up to the age of 18. Research conducted in the EHB region in 1993 found 427 new cases of youth homelessness and some 40 per cent of the homeless children encountered had previously been in residential care (Eastern Health Board, 1994).

The Child Care Act, 1991 and Youth Homelessness

Despite the accumulating evidence of the existence of youth homelessness, it was not until the passing of the *Child Care Act, 1991* that specific statutory provision for homeless children in Ireland was legislated for. Before the enactment of this legislation, Health Boards had responsibility for children *only* up to the age of 16 (under the provisions of the *Children Act, 1908*) while other statutory bodies had responsibility once the young person became 18. There was therefore a gap in services for 16- and 17-year-olds. The Act remedied this situation by defining a child as someone up to the age of 18 and placed a clear obligation on the health boards, *via* Section 5 of the Act, to provide accommodation for homeless children (see O'Sullivan, 1995a and b for further details). However, considerable differences quickly emerged between the Health Boards, in particular the EHB, and voluntary agencies over the interpretation and implementation of the section, culminating in a series of High Court actions designed to obtain clarification. To fully appreciate this development, a brief excursion through the various Dáil Debates is necessary to comprehend the intent of Section 5 of the Act.

Section 5 of the *Child Care Act* was introduced at the special committee stage of deliberations on the Child Care Bill on the 12th of December 1989 as amendment No. 27. The amendment read as follows:

> Where it appears to a health board that a child in its area is homeless, the board shall enquire into the child's circumstances, and if the board is satisfied that
>
> (i) there is no accommodation available to him which he can reasonably occupy, and
>
> (ii) he is unable to provide or arrange accommodation for himself,
>
> then, unless the child is received into the care of the board under the provisions of this Act, the board shall take such steps as are reasonable to make available accommodation for him.

The introduction of this section was welcomed by the majority of the special committee. However, Brendan Howlin, TD questioned the rationale for the amendment and suggested that it was creating a new category of homeless young people:

> For this category, uniquely, all the health boards have to do is take such steps as are reasonable to make accommodation available for them (Special Committee Debates Child Care Bill, 1988, Col. 98-99, 12 December 1989).

The Minister, Noel Tracey TD, replied that the section was being introduced:

> ... to give the health boards an option to deal with adolescents as distinct from infants or older children. We are talking about the strong 15-year-olds and children up to 18 years of age. I expect that ... this provision will in the main be used to cater for older children, perhaps for 15-year-olds and upwards, who need bed and breakfast accommodation as distinct from a more permanent form of accommodation. (Special Committee Debates Child Care Bill, 1988, Col. 101, 12 December 1989).

This comment was much criticised by those working with the young homeless and it is worth noting that, in introducing the Bill to the Seanad, the Minister was far more circumspect in his description of the aims of the section. He stated that:

> Section 5 is an entirely new provision which was inserted at the special committee. It aims to deal with the problem of children and young people sleeping rough on the streets of our cities and towns. It requires a Health Board to provide accommodation for homeless children who have no accommodation they can reasonably occupy (Seanad Debates, 1991, Col. 493).

However, due to pressure from members of the Seanad, the Government introduced an amendment to Section 5. The purpose of this amendment was to substitute an entire new section for the original Section 5 of the Bill. The essential change was the deletion of the precondition of paragraph (ii) of the original draft, that a Health Board must be satisfied that a homeless child is unable to provide accommodation for himself. Thus, the final version of the section, which became Section 5 of the *Child Care Act, 1991*, read as follows:

> Where it appears to a Health Board that a child in its area is homeless, the Board shall enquire into the child's circumstances, and if the Board is satisfied that there is no accommodation available to him which he can reasonably occupy, then, unless the child is received into the care of the Board under the provisions of this Act, the Board shall take such steps as are reasonable to make available suitable accommodation for him.[15]

However, within a short period of time, considerable difficulties were encountered in the operationalisation of the Section by the Health Boards, particularly the EHB, with the absence of a range

---

[15] Section 5 of the *Child Care Act, 1991* was operationalised in November 1992.

of suitable accommodation generating considerable dilemmas for the newly formed Crisis Intervention (Out of Hours) Service.

The Development of a Statutory Response to Youth Homelessness and the Crisis Intervention (Out of Hours) Service

As noted above, from the time youth homelessness emerged as a specific issue of concern, the majority of services developed to meet the needs of such children were provided by non-profit or voluntary agencies. Until 1987, the EHB's direct involvement with homeless young people was limited, although many services could, in theory, have been provided under the terms of the *Health Act, 1970*, which established the regional health boards. Despite this, no specific powers or responsibilities fell to the State with regard to homeless children. The State considered that its duties to homeless young people were, by and large, adequately discharged by the provision of discretionary funding to voluntary agencies that ran hostels for homeless young people. However, from the mid-1980s, a number of social workers were deployed by the EHB to work specifically with homeless children. Statutory involvement in the provision of services for homeless children was further extended when, in March 1992, the EHB established an Out of Hours Service for homeless children and young people. The Out of Hours service was set up to provide children and young people (under the age of 18) *in crisis* with the necessary services when all other services were closed. It also aimed to prevent young people from becoming "encultured" to street life (Kelleher et al., 2000). The Out of Hours Service is a social work, rather than a specific accommodation, service but much of its remit relates to "out of home" young people. By the mid-1990s, there were 50 emergency beds available to homeless children as shown in Table 1.2.

Table 1.2: Emergency Beds Available to Accommodate Homeless Children in Dublin in 1996

Residential Centres	Management	Number of Beds
Parkview House, North Circular Road	Eastern Health Board	14
Sherrard House, Sherrard Street	Homeless Girls Society	14
Crosscare Residential Project, Eccles Street	Crosscare	14
Off the Streets Project, Stanhope Street	Focus Point	8
Total		50

Source: Dáil Debates, Vol. 463, Col. 78, 1996.

Despite the development of these services, considerable difficulties existed in relation to the implementation of Section 5 of the Act. In particular, there were insufficient facilities for homeless children and, as a consequence, many health boards were becoming increasingly reliant on Bed and Breakfast (B&B) accommodation in attempting to meet their needs. For example, in the EHB region, the number of homeless children placed in B&Bs doubled from 39 in 1991 to 76 in 1993.[16] On 1 January 1996, social workers were given instructions by their trade union and, subsequently, the EHB, not to place homeless children in B&Bs because of the inherent unsuitability of such accommodation. However, within a short period, the use of B&Bs resumed due to the absence of alternative placement options, albeit on a less frequent basis, and with the service of a nurse provided. The debate about the adequacy of the provision of B&B accommodation to homeless children ultimately ended up in the High Court.

Homeless Children and the Courts

Although the use of B&B accommodation, particularly for unaccompanied children under 18, was to decline, the issue prompted

---

[16] Ironically, one of the B&Bs utilised by the EHB was located at the site of the HOPE hostel that closed in 1986.

the use of the Courts, particularly the High Court, to explore the operationalisation of Section 5.[17] The key issue was by what criteria the provision in the Act stipulating that Health Boards "take such steps as are reasonable" be evaluated and what constituted "suitable accommodation" for homeless children (see Ward, 1995, Durcan, 1997 and Whyte, 2002 for further details). The first substantial challenge to the use of B&B accommodation for homeless children came in 1994. In the case of *P.S. v. The Eastern Health Board*, it was argued that the EHB had failed to provide for the welfare of the applicant under Section 3 of the Act and to make available suitable accommodation for him under Section 5 of the Act. The applicant, who was 14 years of age at the time, had a history of multiple care placements from a young age and had been discharged from a residential home and spent 35 consecutive nights sleeping rough before the EHB had agreed to intervene and provide him with accommodation. By the time the case reached the High Court, the applicant had been placed in a health board premises along with another child and a number of security staff. The EHB made the point that, under the *Child Care Act 1991*, they had no powers of civil detention and, if the applicant would not co-operate, they were limited in the service they could provide.

In a series of further High Court actions, the Courts clearly identified a gap in Irish child care legislation in that, unlike many other EU states, health boards were adjudged not to have powers of civil detainment. The judgments resulting from these actions led to the establishment of a small number of, euphemistically entitled, High Support and Special Care Units for children by the Department of Health, in conjunction with the health boards. However, the number of children before the High Court contin-

---

[17] Prior to the implementation of Section 5, Gilligan (1992) argued that the measure could only be effective if adequate funding was provided and if coherent directions were given to the health boards by the Minister for Health. In a critique of the operationalisation of Section 5, it was also argued that it excluded homeless children from mainstream child welfare services and effectively positioned them within a secondary child welfare system that provided minimal levels of support and accommodation and not care and protection (O'Sullivan, 1996a, 1998).

ued to grow and, in July 1998, Justice Kelly issued an order to force the Minister for Health to provide sufficient accommodation for the children appearing before him in order to vindicate their constitutional rights. By 2005, three special care units were established with an approved bed capacity of 30, in addition to 13 high support units with an approved bed capacity of 93. In 2005, 49 children were placed in Special Care Units, down 6 on the numbers so placed in 2004.

Report of the Forum on Youth Homelessness

As demonstrated, the 1990s were broadly characterised by, firstly, the EHB gradually coming to terms with their new legislative obligations towards homeless children and, secondly, explicit recognition of youth homelessness as a suburban issue, and not simply a city centre matter (Focus Ireland, 1995; Perris, 1999). In response to the flurry of often-reactive responses to youth homelessness during the 1990s, a Forum on Youth Homelessness, chaired by Miriam Hederman O'Brien, was established in February 1999 with the objective of strategically addressing deficits in service provision and ensuring that "the services on offer are effective and responsive to the needs of young homeless people" (Forum on Youth Homelessness, 2000: 5).[18] The Forum identified several fundamental weaknesses in the system of services targeting homeless children, including: poor co-ordination between current services, scarcity and inaccuracy of information on homeless young people and their needs, the mismatch between service provision and the needs of young homeless people, the inappropriate organization of emergency services and the general dearth of suitable accommodation. Its key recommendations focused on the co-ordination of services, access to services, care and accommodation issues, substance abuse, medical care, education/training and the needs of special groups (including travellers, refugees and asylum

---

[18] The Forum members comprised a range of individuals from both voluntary and statutory agencies working with, or having responsibility in some way for, services for homeless young people.

seekers). It also recommended a new administrative structure to deliver services to homeless young people.

A further initiative in 2000, the Report of the Review Group on Crisis Intervention Services for Children (Northern Area Health Board, 2000), identified a need for services and interventions to address the needs of newly homeless young people. It specifically highlighted the need for the Crisis Intervention Service "[t]o identify and intervene with children newly homeless in the city-centre in a focused coordinated process, to achieve return to their local areas as early as possible" (NAHB, 2000: 21), and went on to recommend the establishment of different levels of assessment of young people and the provision of accommodation to meet varying needs.

Table 1.3 provides a breakdown of the six units in Dublin city assigned to young people who are homeless. Between them, there are 52 beds and all are located in, or adjacent to, the city-centre of Dublin. Each varies with respect to their intake policies and support services. Some units, for example, will not take in young people with a history of drug abuse or violence, whilst others cater for "older" or "younger" adolescents. They also vary in their specified length of stay. At the time of writing, all were obliged to reserve an agreed number of beds for emergency purposes for use by the Out of Hours Service at all times. Such units offer support programmes which are linked directly to the needs of its clientele (Homeless Agency, 2004b).

When young people reach the age of 18 years, health boards no longer have a legal obligation to intervene or to provide services. This means that, on reaching the age of 18, young people must use adult services. This sudden change in classification, from "young person" to "adult" means that several key sources of support are often abruptly withdrawn from the young person on reaching the age of eighteen. The Forum on Youth Homelessness (2000: 18) drew attention to the unsatisfactory nature of this situation, pointing out that "people do not become completely transformed on the morning of a particular birthday"[19].

---

[19] "Caretakers" (managed by Focus Ireland) is the only hostel in Dublin city that caters for the needs of young people between the age of 16 and 21 years. It is a

Table 1.3: Residential Units Catering for Homeless Young People under 18 in Dublin*

Residential Unit	Managed By	Total Beds	Out of Hours Beds	Length of Stay	Age	Gender
St Jude's**	Dublin North East, HSE	6	0	Emergency/ short term	12–15	Male and Female
Parkview**	Dublin North East, HSE	8	0	Emergency/ short term	15–17	Male and Female
Le Froy/ Nightlight	Salvation Army	8	8	Emergency	12–18	Male and Female
Off the Streets	Focus Ireland	6	0	Short term	16–18	Male and Female
Sherrard House	Homeless Girls Soc.	10	2	Emergency/ short term	12–17	Girls only
Eccles Street	CrossCare	9	2	Emergency/ short term	12–17	Male only

* Based on information collated at the time of data collection in late 2004. Some of the figures (e.g. number of available beds) may have altered during the intervening period.

** St. Jude's and Parkview cater exclusively for the newly homeless.

Into the Twenty-first Century

The turbulence of the 1990s, which centred largely on clarifying responsibility for the provision of services for homeless children, gradually eased and, by the beginning of the twenty-first century, a new set of concerns emerged. These concerns focused on efforts to prevent homelessness from occurring rather than reacting to it; the achievement of greater inter-agency collaboration; and the recognition that homelessness was symptomatic, not simply of the absence of accommodation, but of deficits in other services and supports as well. These principles are embodied in a trilogy of

---

nine-bed hostel designed to specifically target young people who are using drugs and are currently living out-of-home.

strategies published at the beginning of the twenty-first century which continue to shape current policy and responses to homelessness.

Homelessness Strategies

In 2000, *Homelessness: An Integrated Strategy* (Department of Environment and Local Government, 2000) was published with the aim of developing effective and co-ordinated responses to homelessness. The terms of reference for the cross-departmental team charged with preparing the strategy was, "to develop an integrated response to the many issues which affect homeless people including emergency, transitional and long-term responses as well as issues relating to health, education, employment and home-making" (Department of Environment and Local Government, 2000: 3). This strategy represents a change in government policy on homelessness – away from the provision of crisis responses – toward the development of a holistic and comprehensive approach to the issue. With this publication, the semblance of a coherent policy approach to the needs of homeless households has become apparent for the first time in the history of the Irish State. The strategy set out an inter-agency approach to tackling the problem of homelessness in a coordinated manner, recognizing that the solution to homelessness did not lie in the provision of housing or shelter alone, and that there was a need for a comprehensive approach involving health, care and welfare, education, training and support, as well as accommodation, to enable homeless people to re-integrate into society and to prevent others from becoming homeless.

In October 2001, a national *Youth Homelessness Strategy* (Department of Health and Children, 2001) was published, with the Health Service Executive (HSE)[20] having lead responsibility for its implementation. Thus, a framework for tackling youth homeless-

---

[20] In January 2005, the Health Service Executive replaced a complex structure of ten regional Health Boards, the Eastern Regional Health Authority and a number of other different agencies and organisations.

ness on a national level was established, although the *National Youth Policy* recommendations on youth homelessness some fifteen years earlier should be noted as a precursor. The stated goal of the Strategy is (Department of Health and Children, 2001: 9):

> to reduce and if possible eliminate youth homelessness through preventative strategies and where a child becomes homeless to ensure that he/she benefits from a comprehensive range of services aimed at re-integrating him/her into his/her community as quickly as possible.

Acknowledging the vision underlying *The National Children's Strategy* (Department of Health and Children, 2000), it also recognized the multi-dimensional nature of youth homelessness and the importance of co-coordinated inter-agency work in tackling the problem. In its discussion of the context and nature of youth homelessness, and in outlining action plans for the future, the Strategy drew heavily on the analysis and recommendations of the aforementioned report of the Forum on Youth Homelessness (2000). The *Youth Homelessness Strategy* set out twelve specific objectives which were extremely ambitious in their coverage of the following three areas:

- The prevention of youth homelessness

- The need for a prompt responsive child-focused service, and

- The importance of co-coordinated inter-agency work in tackling the problem.

While the Strategy was welcomed by many commentators, and by agencies working with homeless young people, scepticism was expressed about the ability of Health Boards to respond to and meet its objectives (e.g. McVerry, 2001; O'Sullivan, 2001b).

There has been some progress in developing strategies for young homeless people, including the publication of National Guidelines on Leaving Care and Aftercare, which have been approved by the Youth Homeless Strategy Monitoring Committee and have been circulated to all health boards. In 2002, the Board of the Eastern Regional Health Authority (formerly the Eastern Health Board) approved a strategic plan (ERHA, 2002), which aimed to tackle youth homelessness in a "practical and focused way" and to ensure "a comprehensive response" to the problem.

The final element of the trilogy of strategies to address homelessness in Ireland, the *Homeless Preventative Strategy* (Department of Environment and Local Government, 2002), was published in February 2002. This document addressed the issue of prevention in relation to certain target groups including adults and young offenders, people leaving mental health residential facilities, people leaving acute hospitals and young people leaving care.

Thus, the ambition of current government policy in relation to homelessness is "to ensure that responses to it are integrated with other policy and legislative agendas" (Homeless Agency, 2004a: 2). In January 2005, the Government commissioned Fitzpatrick Associates to review the implementation of both the Integrated and Preventative Homeless Strategies (Fitzpatrick Associates, 2006). This report noted a range of positive developments and deemed that a large number of the objectives had been significantly progressed. In moving the homeless strategies forward, it recommended that all agencies working in this area refocus their energies to make themselves "largely obsolete, which should, after all, be its overarching goal" (Fitzpatrick Associates, 2006: 128). Regrettably, no such review of the *Youth Homelessness Strategy* has been commissioned. However, the *National Action Plan for Social Inclusion 2007-2016* (Office for Social Inclusion, 2007: 35-36) contains a commitment that "the Office of the Minister for Children (OMC) will undertake a review of progress on the implementation of the *Youth Homelessness Strategy* and develop a new programme of action in 2007".

Conclusion

This chapter has attempted to present a historical account of the emergence of youth homelessness in Dublin from the mid-1960s and has outlined how homeless young people (variously defined) emerged as a distinct group within the broader homeless population. The range of young people, from teens to those in their early or mid-20s, described as homeless makes it difficult to quantify the extent of the phenomenon. What is clear, however, is that a discourse on "youth homelessness" – discernible from various reports and statements on homeless children and young people – emerged from the 1970s. Rather than viewing homelessness as comprising an undifferentiated mass, various agencies, in particular Non-Governmental Organisations (NGOs), attempted to distinguish particular sub-groups within the homeless population that required specific interventions. Young people were identified from the early 1970s as one such sub-group. However, the boundaries of "youth" were to remain fluid until the early 1990s, when the *Child Care Act, 1991* established by statute that homeless youth were those under the age of 18 years.

Youth homelessness became a problematic legal construct in the early 1990s with the implementation of Section 5 of the *Child Care Act, 1991*. The various High Court judgments on the responsibility of the State towards homeless children and young people, and the latter's ambiguous status within Health Boards, coupled with the administrative structure through which services to this group were to be delivered, account in part for the high profile accorded to these children during the 1990s. A crucial outcome of these debates during the late 1980s and 1990s was to push the Health Boards centre stage in terms of the provision of services for homeless children. While NGOs remain involved in the provision of services, statutory bodies are identified as having primary responsibility for homeless children. This is a significant shift from the position identified at the start of this chapter. It also, in part, explains the increasingly managerial approach to the homeless problem, which is now evident in the trilogy of Strategies designed to reduce and, ultimately, eliminate homelessness. Although some progress has been made in reducing the number of young homeless people, many of the fundamental weaknesses identified by the *Forum on Youth Homelessness* (2000) – poor co-ordination between services, the inability of locally based services to identify at an early stage young people who are at risk of becoming homeless, the inappropriate organization of emergency services and the general dearth of suitable accommodation (both emergency and long-term) for both under and over 18-year-olds – continue to characterize the system for addressing the needs of homeless young people today.

The next chapter examines the difficulties associated with defining and, consequently, measuring youth homelessness and it also reviews dominant explanations for youth homelessness.

Chapter 2

UNDERSTANDING AND RESEARCHING YOUTH HOMELESSNESS

Having traced the emergence of "homeless children" in Ireland from the late 1960s onwards, this chapter extends the discussion to include several issues that are relevant to understanding the youth homelessness phenomenon. It starts by exploring the contested causes of homelessness and the immense difficulties associated with defining homelessness, both in Ireland and internationally. While outlining the various risk factors and triggers that can propel individuals into homelessness, it also draws attention to the problem of uncritically assuming that all individuals who experience certain risks will automatically become homeless.

Definitions of homelessness determine, in large part, those who are counted as homeless and, consequently, influence estimates of its prevalence. This chapter presents data on the extent of youth homelessness from the early 1990s when a more systematic approach to the collection of data began to develop. However, much of the available data on which to base an assessment of trends has been collected by statutory agencies and some of the difficulties with the methodologies employed to enumerate the problem are highlighted. This chapter also explores what research from other jurisdictions, as well as the relatively limited primary research base in Ireland, tells us about the consequences of homelessness for young people. It concludes by arguing for a complex and dynamic definition of homelessness. By this we mean a definition that views homelessness not as a fixed state, but rather a fluid experience that varies by age, gender, location, ethnicity and so on. Above all, we view homelessness as "socially constructed" by a variety of different agencies. In light of this understanding, we discuss the conceptual and methodological merits of investigating youth homelessness using a qualitative "pathways approach" that privileges young homeless people's own accounts of their life stories and experiences.

Explaining, Defining and Measuring Homelessness

Explanations for the causes of homelessness are often divided into two broad categories: structural and individual (Neale, 1997a, 1997b; O'Flaherty, 2004; O'Sullivan, 1996b). Structural explanations locate the reasons for homelessness in social and economic structures and cite poverty, negative labour market forces, cuts and restrictions in social welfare payments and reductions or shortfalls in the supply of affordable housing as the leading causes. Individualistic accounts, on the other hand, focus on the personal characteristics and behaviour of homeless people and suggest that homelessness is the consequence of personal problems, such as mental illness and addiction. Neale (1997a) argues that the individual/structural dichotomy is overly simplistic and that a sharp distinction cannot be easily made between the two sets of factors or influences. The implication, of course, is that both sets of factors are important in causing homelessness and that the interactions between them are complex. In broad terms, government responses tend to favour more micro-level or individual explanations of homelessness, while NGOs tend towards structural accounts.

The methodological problems associated with estimating the prevalence of homelessness have been widely discussed and debated. Any systematic effort to count the homeless, or to describe and explain homelessness, must begin by attempting to define the problem in precise, operational terms (Fitzgerald et al., 2001). Moreover, quantification is linked to definitions of homelessness and frameworks for housing provision as much as to any technical approach to enumeration (Anderson, 2003). The main difficulty in measuring homelessness arises because it is difficult to agree on a definition of what constitutes homelessness. O'Connell (2003) makes the crucial point that, despite the huge volume of research into homelessness in both the US and the UK, quantification of homelessness remains elusive. Even more recent attempts to quantify the homeless in Ireland, based on the most sophisticated enumeration techniques to date, are not free from incongruities (O'Sullivan, 2006a, 2006b). The question of how best to measure homelessness is likely to be the subject of continued discussion and debate. In an early review of various studies that attempted to ascertain the extent of homelessness in the US, Applebaum (1990: 13) offered the following axiom which remains valid to this day: "Take all results with a grain of salt: the stronger the claims of the study, the more grains of salt."

There is no single, universally accepted definition of homelessness (Jacobs et al., 1999). This absence of consensus relates to two key issues. Firstly, as Schiff (2003: 505) argues, "struggles over definitions reflect differing agents' efforts and sentiments regarding what homelessness is and how it should be responded to". Secondly, homeless people are a diverse population with various life histories and experiences and researchers have employed a spectrum of definitions depending on the scope, nature and purpose of the study (Anderson and Christian, 2003; Third, 2000). The transience of the homeless population exacerbates the problem of providing a single, all-encompassing definition. Irrespective of age, people who lack secure accommodation change location, status and living arrangements and this makes it difficult to delineate their diverse and changeable living situations. As Cloke et al. (2003: 32) argue:

> Homeless people are not static categorisations, but moving becoming beings. Their homelessness, mobility and spatiality shifts over time, often charting complicated pathways into and out of different accommodation, different "resting places."

Similarly, according to Hall's (2003: 141) anthropological account of homeless young people in a town just outside of London, homelessness:

> ... is temporary, first and foremost, because homeless is something most young people would rather not be, and where they see their way clear to doing so they have put it behind them. Some take longer to do so than others, and have a harder time of it until they do so. Some stay on the scene, in visible difficulties – a conspicuous presence around the town, and known to authorities – for months at a time, homeless again and again. But only for so long, not forever.

The most obvious definition of homelessness, and one that dominates public perceptions, is "street homelessness" or "rooflessness", terms used to refer to those who are without shelter of any kind. This also constitutes the narrowest definition of homelessness (Fitzpatrick et al., 2000) and includes rough sleepers, newly arrived immigrants, victims of fires and floods and others who face the prospect of, or are currently, living on the street. However, it has been widely acknowledged that rough sleeping represents the experience of only a minority of homeless persons and is associated with particular groups in particular places, generally males in public spaces. Consequently, it may blinker us from acknowledging "other (less extreme) forms of homelessness occurring among 'other' groups and in 'other' places" (Cloke et al., 2001: 275). In addition, the association in the public mind with rough sleeping *as* homelessness can maintain a view of homelessness as individual deviance (Pleace, 2000), particularly in relation to young people (Carlen, 1996).

At the other end of the spectrum – and taking a wider view – is a definition that includes all those people who are in "inadequate accommodation" and those who are "at risk" of homelessness. In between the two extremities of highly visible and relatively concealed or "hidden" homelessness are people living in emergency and temporary accommodation such as night shelters, hostels and refuges, as well as people who have insecure or impermanent tenure (e.g. staying with friends or relatives, squatting). It is therefore useful to consider homelessness as a continuum, ranging from people at risk of homelessness to people who are temporarily or episodically without shelter, to individuals who are persistently homeless.

In recent years, the tendency has been for researchers to utilise definitions of homelessness that are more directly linked to the housing situations of persons. The European Observatory on Homelessness, which was established in 1991 by the European Federation of National Organisations Working with the Homeless (FEANTSA), has adopted a conceptual classification or definition of homelessness that includes four distinct housing situations: rooflessness, houselessness, living in insecure accommodation and living in inadequate accommodation (see Edgar and Meert, 2006 for the most recent elaboration of this schema). The idea of a continuum of homelessness is reflected in this fourfold working definition. As a further elaboration, operational definitions are provided for each of the four housing situations to ensure that each of the categories is mutually exclusive and unambiguous. The use of operational definitions should, it is argued, enable the measurement of different elements of homelessness in any European country.[1]

Defining Homelessness in Ireland

The problem of definition has received considerable attention in an Irish context. Commenting on the absence of a uniform definition when presenting available data on the extent of homelessness in 1990, Daly (1990: 19) pointed out that, "[i]n effect, each study

---

[1] The Review of the Homeless Strategy by Fitzpatrick Associates highlighted in the previous chapter recommended that "[t]he definition of homelessness should be revisited in order to produce a clearer, unambiguous understanding of what homelessness means for measurement and funding purposes. This should be used as the basis for a common information gathering system establishing the causes, extent and nature of homelessness and rolled out to all areas of the country" (2006: 135). In particular, the report debated the utility of the ETHOS definition of homelessness and concluded that the "adoption of this type of working definition would prove beneficial" (2006: 135).

appears to use a different definition and, while each definition has advantages, it should be borne in mind that a fully satisfactory and fairly standardised definition of homelessness has yet to be developed". The absence of a universally accepted definition of homelessness was also discussed by O'Sullivan (1996b) when he distinguished between "visible" and "hidden" homelessness and those persons who are "at risk" of homelessness. A legal definition of the term "homeless" is, of course, provided in Section 2 of the *Housing Act, 1988,* which includes: people living in temporary insecure accommodation, people living in emergency Bed and Breakfast accommodation and/or in hostels or health board accommodation because they have nowhere else available to them, rough sleepers and victims of family violence. However, as discussed later in this chapter, considerable inconsistency exists in relation to the operationalisation of this definition across different local authorities.

The aforementioned Forum on Youth Homelessness (2000: 17) recommended that agencies use the following definition of homelessness:

> Those who are sleeping on the streets or in other places not intended for night-time accommodation or not providing safe protection from the elements or those whose usual night-time residence is a public or private shelter, emergency lodging, B&B or such, providing protection from the elements but lacking the other characteristics of a home and/or intended only for a short stay.

The *Youth Homelessness Strategy* (Department of Health and Children, 2001: 11) subscribes to this definition but also makes the point that youth homelessness is different from adult homelessness:

> The key difference is that the vast majority of children under the age of 18 have a place of residence from which to operate; this may be their home, or an alternative form of accommodation supplied by a health board or a voluntary

agency. In essence, when a young person becomes home-less, it is because they can no longer operate from this base.

"Official" and "Unofficial" Definitions

While there are many "official" definitions of homelessness based on national legislation, relatively little is known about young people's own definitions of homelessness and only a small num-ber of studies have examined how those who are objectively homeless perceive their situation. In particular, the life stories and experiences of homeless young people are rarely a core considera-tion in how a consensus on appropriate definitions is reached. Hutson and Liddiard's (1994) Welsh study found that young homeless people often interpreted homelessness quite narrowly as sleeping rough and it was common for those staying with friends not to describe themselves as homeless. In Canada, Clarke and Cooper (2000) found that two out of five of the young people who met the inclusion criteria for their study of youth homeless-ness did not view themselves as homeless, even if they were sleeping in emergency shelters, parks or squats. Fitzpatrick (2000), on the other hand, found in her Scottish study that young people generally adopted a broader definition of homelessness as having "no permanent house". For many, traditional forms of accommo-dation for homeless people such as hostels or shared living ar-rangements did not come within the bounds of their definition. A common point of agreement between these studies is that young people emphasise the degree of security and permanency of ac-commodation more often than the actual physical conditions when they describe homelessness. It appears, therefore, that when young people attempt to define homelessness they focus on the meaning of "home" as not purely a housing-based concept, but one with significant emotional, social and psychological dimen-sions. In Ireland, one study has similarly highlighted the empha-sis that children and young people place on the meaning of "home". Halpenny et al.'s (2002: 32) research on children in fami-lies living in emergency accommodation found that adolescent children of homeless families discussed their homeless status in terms of not having "their own home". The young people interviewed for the purpose of this study also conveyed an awareness of the stigma associated with the word "homeless".

It appears that the very notion of a "home" presents a problem for the concept of homelessness in terms of reaching a definition that has cross-cultural applicability (Watson and Austerberry, 1986). Young people (and adults) attach a variety of meanings to the concept of "home" (Kellett and Moore, 2003; Novac et al., 1996). From a subjective standpoint, then, the question of definition may be largely irresolvable since homeless individuals are likely to frame their situations in very different ways (Hutson and Liddiard, 1994). Furthermore, all definitions are, to some extent, "theoretically and socially determined, subjective and arbitrary" (O'Sullivan, 1996b: 4). It is useful to bear these issues in mind when embarking upon a discussion of broader dimensions of youth homelessness.

Agency Definitions of Youth Homelessness

The lack of consensus on either the meaning of youth homelessness or the extent of the problem has not proven a deterrent "to numerous dogmatic, sometimes wildly imaginative statements, particularly about the size and scale of the problem" (Brandon et al., 1980:6). For example, a report on youth homelessness by the charity Barnardos in the late 1980s argued quite dramatically that: "Homelessness is sadly becoming a way of life for whole generations of young people" (O'Mahony, 1988: 31). Describing the problem of youth homelessness in London in the late 1970s, Brandon et al. (1980: 26) noted that:

> Much of the energy of the voluntary agencies is directed towards campaigning and fundraising. They compete with other social causes and even amongst themselves for influence and resources. To command attention, they often present an alarmist picture of the extent and dangerousness of homelessness. The problem is packaged in black-and-white terms to ensure easy public assimilation and to provoke unambivalent feelings of anxiety, pathos and guilt. Home-

less young people are often exclusively depicted as victims of circumstances, as naïve, deprived, disturbed and lonely youngsters, "at risk" in a hostile and uncaring environment. This results in a hostile and overly negative picture of their situation and one that understates their capacities for survival, self-help and self-direction.

They went on to discern five models of youth homelessness that are articulated by voluntary agencies working with the young homeless, namely:

- Individual culpability – this model views "homeless young people as individually culpable for their condition and behaviour. The homeless person has chosen to be homeless" (1980: 60).

- Political – in this model "the important factors are political, social and economic rather than personal. The emphasis is on the social context of actions rather than on the actor" (1980: 63).

- Spiritual/Religious – in this model, the homeless person "is a sinner to be saved through the love of the Lord Jesus Christ…. Homelessness is a symptom and index of the spiritual impoverishment of our society" (1980: 66).

- Pathological – in this model, "homeless people are seen as socially inadequate, maladjusted and psychologically disturbed. The problems are much broader and less tangible than lack of accommodation and there is a need for counselling, befriending and even psychiatric treatment" (1980: 68).

- Child – "this model plays on the notion of youth as being one remove from childhood. Terms like 'naïve', 'impulsive', 'adrift', 'at risk' and 'vulnerable' are used to convey childlike qualities" (1980: 74).

Liddiard and Hutson (1991) observe that many agencies providing services to the young homeless oscillate between a pathological and a normalising model of youth homelessness in their public presentation of the situation. In the normalising model, young homeless people are not presented to the public as different from their non-homeless peers; rather, homelessness is viewed as arising from the normal process of growing up and leaving home. On the other hand, the pathologising model argues that homeless young people have particular problems not generally found in the housed population. In addition to this external portrayal of homeless young people, agencies internally define clients as either high or low risk. Those deemed "high risk", whose problems are so severe or extreme, are provided with services by only a relatively small number of agencies. Largely, only "low risk" clients are seen as deserving of agency services. According to Liddiard and Hutson (1991), this movement between being deserving and undeserving is also affected by the fact that young people are physically growing older. The implication here is that as young people grow into adults – legally and socially – the services available to them change. This same issue is highlighted by Hall and Montgomery (2000: 13), who argue that:

> Where young people in difficult circumstances (the young homeless in Britain, for example) are seen as belonging to a third category – not yet adults but no longer children – public response to their situation can be less than sympathetic. Young people thus defined may be seen as troublesome rather than simply in trouble, at fault rather than at risk.

A further consistent theme in the presentation of youth homelessness by voluntary agencies is absolute belief in the validity of their mode of intervention with homeless people, the absolute correctness of their interpretation of the issue and the absolute importance of the existence of the agency without which homeless young people would be in an even greater predicament. As Brandon et al. (1980: 192) put it:

> The annual reports and campaign documents of the voluntary societies stress their own centrality in efforts to 'solve' homelessness. Apparently, without their work in counselling and residential provision, young people would drift wholesale into petty crime, prostitution and mental illness.

> That belief is not borne out by this study. Informal net-
> works, grapevines, squatting and sleeping rough play a
> much larger part, at least quantitatively, in the homeless
> experience of these young people.

To maintain this illusion and to avoid scrutiny of their *modus oper-
andi*, Rooney (1980: 921), in a study of Skid Row missions in the
US, observed that a number of strategies are employed by such
agencies. Above all, "systematic evaluation of results must be
avoided", while the managers of the agencies provide the interpretation of success in the programmes they operate. Rooney argues that while many of the programmes are "no more than
minimally effective for certain limited objectives", this objective
organisational failure demonstrates the ongoing need for such
services articulated through the subjective analysis offered by the
agency. Cloke et al. (2005) suggest that at least three distinct ethoi
are evident amongst the myriad of voluntary agencies that provide services to the homeless. One ethos provides services without a corresponding expectation that the receiver of the service
will change their behaviour or lifestyle, whilst the other two insist
on a conversion to a non-homeless status or at least non-
dependence on the service. These can be divided between an
evangelical faith-based ethos, where spiritual needs are priori-
tised, and an ethos that provides care in return for behavioural
change.

Such tactics are not, of course, the sole preserve of NGOs.
Statutory agencies share many similar strategies but rarely engage
in the campaigning strategies of the NGO sector in relation to
homelessness.

Despite the efforts of both the statutory and voluntary agencies, those who are homeless, particularly young homeless people,
are not necessarily passive recipients of agency-imposed categori-
sations. In many cases, they reject administrative attempts to
shape them into the mould determined appropriate by the myriad
of voluntary and statutory service providers. Carlen (1994: 25)
makes the following observation:

Within local hostel and temporary accommodation circuits deterrence and denial are almost inextricably intertwined. The complex exclusion policies of the various hostels and schemes inevitably lead to equally tortuous assessment, categorisation and referral systems which further impede the delivery of an efficient service to the clients. Given that so many potential residents have already suffered the coercive objectification involved in the assessment and classification procedures of housing authorities and the categorisation and referral paraphernalia of social services, it is not surprising that a substantial number reject the assessment agency before it rejects them.

However, by rejecting the "caring hand" of the homeless experts, homeless children may be subjected to a more overtly punitive regime, whereby those sanctions imposed by the State to regulate their behaviour become the police, courts, detention centres and prisons. Because they have illogically refused the entreaties of the homeless experts, they are viewed as voluntarily having placed themselves into the punitive realm and must accept the due consequences. These young homeless tend to end up sleeping out or sharing squats with groups of similarly situated young people, as Fitzpatrick and Jones (2005: 399) observe:

It may seem obvious to housed people that a hostel – any hostel – is better than being on the streets, but that view is not always shared by people with experience of homelessness. While many hostels provide a high-quality, safe and supportive place for homeless people, others remain intimidating and threatening environments, or at least are perceived as such by some homeless people.

Consequently, these homeless young people are forced into a grim and bleak lifestyle where the criminal justice, rather than the child welfare apparatus, becomes the dominant form of state intervention in their often-fractured lives. Yet, as Carlen (1996: 123) has highlighted in her research into youth homelessness in England:

The most striking feature of the relationship between youth homelessness and crime as suggested by the young homeless narrators in the research was that while a majority of them had been victims of crimes whose perpetrators would never be punished, whenever they themselves had been seen to deviate – from social mores, respectability, or the criminal law – they had received punishments of a magnitude out of all proportion to their initial wrongdoing.

Extent of Youth Homelessness in Ireland

This book focuses on the lives of single young homeless persons. It does not, therefore, explore the experiences of children who are homeless as part of a family unit (in the Irish context see, inter alia, Bell, 1989; Halpenny et al, 2001, 2002; Waldron et al, 2001).[2] As highlighted in the previous chapter, definitions and understandings of youth homelessness in Ireland have varied over time, particularly in respect of the age at which a person is defined as "young" rather than "adult", making it virtually impossible to trace meaningful national trends.

A number of agencies within the statutory and voluntary sector collect information and data on young people who are using their services – and are homeless or "at risk" of homelessness – who may or may not come to the attention of Health Boards. A major difficulty with available Irish data, however, is that health boards and local authority figures do not include young homeless people who make no contact with services. This is problematic since young people may be reluctant to get in touch with services, particularly during the initial stages of homelessness. In Ireland, the absence of a centralised system of information and data gathering common to all statutory and voluntary agencies providing services in this area further hampers the production of reliable estimates of the extent of youth homelessness. The absence of routinely collected data also makes it difficult to monitor trends over time. Other issues requiring attention include double counting,

---

[2] Appendix I provides an overview of the extent of adult homelessness (and child dependents) in Ireland.

lack of information on outcomes, seasonal patterns, repeat presentations and the extent of hidden homelessness.

Since the late 1990s, data collated by the Department of Health and Children from the regional health boards provide information on the number of children (of whom they are aware) who have left home as well as the reasons for their homelessness. The most recent data available suggest that, nationally, 495 children were identified as homeless (with 213 or 43 per cent in the ERHA area) in 2004. This figure is up slightly from the figure of 476 in 2003 (with 207 or 43 per cent in the ERHA area). A total of 774 children were identified as homeless in 1999 and 588 in 2000, suggesting that, not withstanding the slight increase in 2004, the medium-term trend is towards a decline in the number of children presenting as homeless to the HSE (Figure 2.1 and Table 2.1). Of those recorded as homeless in 2004, there were slightly more females (254) than males (241).

Figure 2.1: Extent of Youth Homelessness, 1998-2004 (National and ERHA)

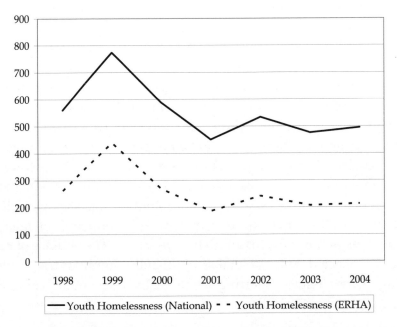

Source: Analysis of Child Care Interim Minimum Dataset, Various Years.

Table 2.1: Extent of Youth Homelessness (national and ERHA), 1998-2004

	1998	1999	2000	2001	2002	2003	2004
Males	281	398	289	218	240	218	241
Females	279	376	299	233	294	258	254
Total	**560**	**774**	**588**	**451**	**534**	**476**	**495**
Males ERHA	152	260	148	97	119	96	115
Females ERHA	110	179	120	89	123	111	98
Total	**262**	**439**	**268**	**186**	**242**	**207**	**213**
ERHA as % of all homeless male children	54.1	65.3	51.2	44.5	49.6	44.0	47.7
ERHA as % of all homeless female children	39.4	47.6	40.1	38.2	41.8	43.0	38.6
ERHA as % of all homeless children	46.7	56.7	45.6	41.2	45.3	43.5	43.0

Source: Child Care Interim Minimum dataset, various years.

As shown in Table 2.2, just over 63 per cent of all recorded homeless children in 2004 were aged 16 or 17. However, the equivalent figure for the ERHA was only 42 per cent. It would appear from the data that children under the age of 14 who are homeless are recorded predominantly in the ERHA area.

Table 2.2: Age of Children Known to be Homeless in 2002–2004

	Under 12	12 > 14	14 - 15	16 > 18	Total
2002	21	33	128	352	534
2003	14	35	128	299	476
2004	21	43	118	313	495
2002 ERHA	17	29	64	131	241
2003 ERHA	11	21	67	108	207
2004 ERHA	20	38	66	89	213
2002 ERHA as % of all homeless children	81.0	87.9	50.0	37.2	45.1
2003 ERHA as % of all homeless children	78.6	60.0	52.3	36.1	43.5
2004 ERHA as % of all homeless children	95.2	88.4	55.9	28.4	43.0

Source: Child Care Interim Minimum dataset, various years.

The Statistics sub-group of the Youth Homelessness Strategy Monitoring Committee (YHSMC), which is chaired by the Office of the
Minister for Children and is representative of the relevant stake-
holders, recommended the introduction of a new Youth Homelessness Contact form as a way of gathering more reliable and consistent statistics. The Department of Health and Children circulated the
form to the Health Boards in December 2003 for introduction on 1
January 2004. Therefore, in 2004, for the first time, in addition to
providing information on the number of homeless children recorded by the various health authorities, data were provided on
the number of contacts made by homeless children with both
statutory and HSE funded agencies providing services to homeless youth. Table 2.3 shows that the 495 individual children made
1,038 formal contacts with various service providers. Of the total
number of contacts, 70 per cent were made in the ERHA, suggesting that an eventual resolution of the young persons homelessness
was more prolonged in the ERHA than other areas. On average,
homeless children in the ERHA made 3.3 contacts with service
providers during 2004 compared to 1.1 contacts in the areas other
than the ERHA. Young homeless males in the ERHA had the
highest number of formal contacts with an average of nearly four
formal contacts during 2004.

Table 2.3: Youth Homeless Contacts in 2004 (number in brackets)

	Youth Homeless Contacts – Males	Youth Homeless Contacts – Females	Total
National	599 (241)	439 (254)	1,038 (495)
ERHA	455 (115)	260 (88)	715 (213)
ERHA as % of all home-less contacts made	76.0	59.2	68.9

Source: Child Care Interim Minimum dataset, various years.

In the ERHA, in over 70 per cent of formal contacts it was simply
noted that the young person had come to the attention of the Out
of Hours Service as shown in Table 2.4. Just over 10 per cent were
residing in temporary or emergency accommodation and some-

what surprisingly, no young person was sleeping on the street at the time of the contact.[3]

The reasons identified by the HSE for children becoming homeless in 2004 are outlined in Table 2.5. These categories have altered between 1998 and 2004 making it impossible to measure trends in the recording of the "principal reason" given for their homelessness. Moreover, the subjectivity involved in this form of categorisation and the multiple individuals involved in making such assessments renders interpreting medium-term trends particularly problematic.

Table 2.4: Youth Homeless Contacts by Former Health Board Area for 2004 by Current Sleeping Arrangement

	National	ERHA
Out-of -home and sleeping on streets	30	0
Out-of -home and sleeping in places not intended for night time accommodation	17	0
Out-of -home and sleeping in places not providing safe protection from the elements	9	0
Out-of-home and coming to the attention of the health board's out-of-hours service (currently relevant in the ERHA)	517	517
Out-of-home and sleeping in places, although providing protection from the elements, are intended for short stay only, e.g. emergency or temporary lodgings/accommodation provided by the health board or non-statutory organisation	167	82
Out-of-home and sleeping in places, although providing protection from the elements: The young person is not in a position to remain there	140	1
Out-of-home and sleeping in places, although providing protection from the elements: The health board would have concerns regarding the welfare of the young person if he/she remains in this accommodation	43	0
Total contacts	923	715

Note: The ERHA Northern Area returned 115 homeless contacts, but did not classify the contacts as per the categories above, thus information is only available for 923 contacts

Source: Child Care Interim Minimum dataset, various years.

---

[3] Half of those described as sleeping on the streets at the time of contact were located in the Southern Health Board.

Table 2.5: Youth Homeless Contacts by former Health Board Area for 2004 by the Principal Reason given by the Young Person for Needing Accommodation

	National	ERHA
Young person exposed to physical abuse	29	9
Young person exposed to emotional abuse	16	0
Young person exposed to sexual abuse	2	2
Young person neglected	64	50
Parent(s) unable to cope/parental illness	172	140
Family member abusing drugs/alcohol	111	104
Family dispute/breakdown	178	96
Young person abandoned by parents/care giver	12	8
Young person leaving/running away from care placement	22	7
Young person abusing drugs/alcohol	72	49
Pregnancy (young person)	5	2
Young person involved in crime	32	27
Other reason not listed above	323	221
Total Contacts	**1,038**	**715**

Source: Child Care Interim Minimum dataset, various years.

Within the ERHA area, as noted earlier, a dedicated Out of Hours Service was established in 1992, and data on the usage of this service provides another source of information on the extent of youth homelessness. As shown in Figure 2.2, the number of referrals to this service rose rapidly during the 1990s and hit a peak of over 4,500 referrals in 2000. Since then, the number of referrals has declined to 2,390 in 2006. These referrals include multiple referrals of the same homeless children, which in 2000 translated into just under 1,000 unique individuals seeking the Out of Hours Service. By 2006, the number of unique individuals had declined to 363. An immediate contradiction is evident between the contacts with the Out of Hours Service and the contacts recorded by the Department of Health and Children for 2004. The Department of Health and Children recorded 715 youth homeless contacts in 2004, but the Out of Hours service recorded 3,544 referrals. The explanation appears to be that not all initial referrals to the Out of Hours Service are recorded in the Youth Homeless Contact forms. Many of those young people who present to the Out of Hours are returned more or less immediately to their family or place of care. Only those young people who cannot return home are recorded in the Youth Homeless Contact Forms.

Figure 2.2: Referrals to the Out of Hours Service, 12-17 Year-olds Only, 1993-2006

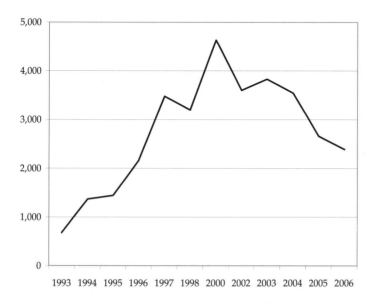

Source: Personal communication ERHA.
Note: data for 1999 and 2001 not available.

Table 2.6 indicates that a significant proportion of the total refer-rals to the Out of Hours Service are repeat referrals. A total of 48 and 46 cases of repeat referrals were recorded for 2003 and 2004, respectively. Repeat referral is presumably linked to a failure to find a suitable placement for the young people in question or to a subsequent breakdown in placements following initial contact with the Out of Hours Service.

Figure 2.3: Number of Individual 12 to 17 Year-olds Referred to the Out of Hours Service, 2000-2006

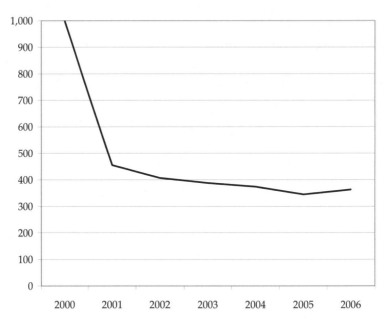

Source: Personal communication ERHA.

Table 2.6: Repeat Referrals to Out of Hours Service (12-17 year olds), 2003 and 2004

Number of Times Referred	2003	2004
20-30	9	13
30-50	20	13
50-100	8	13
100-150	10	6
150+	1	1

Source: Personal communication ERHA.

A further indication of the extent of youth homelessness in the greater Dublin region is the tri-annual survey of homelessness by the Homeless Agency. The data for the three surveys conducted to-date show a substantial decline in the number of single person households under the age of 20 from 210 in 1999 to 62 in 2005. Of the 185 rough sleepers identified in the 2005 assessment, 4 or 2 per cent were aged under 20, with a further 23 or 12 per cent between the ages of 21 and 25 (Wafer, 2006).

The data outlined above suggest that although considerable difficulties are evident in defining and enumerating the extent of youth homelessness in Ireland, it can nonetheless be inferred that while it increased during the 1990s, all indications are that it has declined in more recent years. However, the absence of reliable data thwarts any attempt to accurately trace and assess trends over time. Nonetheless, homeless young people clearly constitute a significant group within the overall homeless population. Youth homelessness in Ireland is primarily an urban phenomenon and Dublin city has consistently recorded the highest number of homeless young people nationally.

Risk Factors for Youth Homelessness

A broad range of factors are associated with homelessness among young people. Internationally, research has identified several risk factors for homelessness and available Irish research has high-lighted the role of many of these in bringing about homelessness. The most frequently cited risk factors for homelessness include:

- Family disputes and breakdown
- A care history
- Sexual or physical abuse in childhood or adolescence
- Offending behaviour and/or experience of prison
- Lack of social support networks
- Debts, especially rent or mortgage arrears
- Causing nuisance to neighbours
- Drug or alcohol misuse
- School exclusion and lack of qualifications
- Mental health problems
- Poor physical health.

It is important to note that not everyone who experiences these situations will become homeless. Rather, these factors work to make people more vulnerable to homelessness, particularly if they are experienced in combination. As well as being predictors of homelessness, many of these factors my result from, or be exacerbated by, homelessness. For example, alcohol and drug use frequently escalate following a period of homelessness.

A large number of homeless young people report problems with family members, including rows and serious conflict with parents, sometimes ending in violence (Craig et al., 1996; Fitzpatrick, 2000; Jones, 1995). Conflict with a step-parent or with a parent's new partner who joins the family is also commonly reported among young homeless people (Smith et al., 1998). Household friction can also be caused by young people's behaviour, including alcohol and drug use, school problems and criminal activity (Randall and Brown, 2001) and, in some cases, parents make threats of eviction in an attempt to control their children's behaviour (Smith et al., 1998). One study has observed that young women were more at risk of homelessness as a consequence of parental difficulties than were young men (Smith, 2005).

A large majority of young people experience homelessness for the first time having already been exposed to emotional trauma. A high degree of consensus has emerged in the US, UK, Canada and Australia that many homeless young people come from homes characterised by some level of physical, sexual, or emotional abuse and neglect compared to domiciled youth (Gaetz and O'Grady, 2002). Parental substance abuse is not uncommon among street youth (Ringwalt et al., 1998), and a history of physical, sexual and/or emotional abuse appears to be common (Kipke et al., 1997; van der Ploeg and Scholte, 1997). The link between youth homelessness and abuse is being increasingly realised, particularly as the extent of sexual abuse is becoming more widely recognised. Equally, however, it must be recognised that the connection between sexual and physical abuse and homelessness has many strands (Hutson and Liddiard, 1994). On the one hand, a young person may leave home because of an abusive situation while, in other cases, the disclosure and discovery of abuse can lead to family breakdown and to the child or young person being taken into care. Violence against girls and young women appears to play a significant role in the dynamics of their homelessness. While many homeless young people have histories of family instability, conflict and abuse, more young women than young men have experienced sexual and physical abuse within their families (Novac et al., 2002).

"Triggers" for Youth Homelessness

In addition to risk factors, research has focused, particularly in more recent years, on investigating and identifying specific events or "turning points" that can trigger homelessness. The identification of "triggers" is important since crisis points frequently prompt young people to leave home. At the same time, it is important to acknowledge that the events that affect young people immediately prior to becoming homeless are not always the sole or main causes of their homelessness. To be of value in a policy context, therefore, research needs to examine broader contributory factors and processes as well as the immediate precipitators of homelessness. The following "triggers" for youth homelessness have been identified in the literature:

- Leaving the parental home after arguments
- Leaving care
- Leaving prison
- An increase in alcohol or drug misuse
- Eviction from rented accommodation
- Family breakdown.

Unlike risk factors, "triggers" lead directly to homelessness (Crane, 1997). This means that many young people leave home for the first time in a crisis and with limited or no access to alternative accommodation. This can frequently be caused by a serious dispute, although the argument itself is, in most cases, the culmination of issues and problems that have been ongoing for a considerable period. Leaving care and leaving prison are other commonly reported "triggers" as many young people who have lived in institutional settings for considerable periods do not have close family contact and, following the withdrawal of institutional support, find themselves unable to cope with the financial and emotional demands of independent living. Finally, although many young people with drug or alcohol problems continue to live in the family home, a sudden or sharp increase in substance use can lead to a crisis that results in homelessness. While a considerable amount is known about the characteristics of young homeless people in an Irish context, knowledge and understanding of risk and trigger factors for homelessness is relatively poor.

It must be remembered that, although the causal factors and processes related to becoming and remaining homeless are complex and only partially understood in Ireland and elsewhere, poverty – and, in some cases, extreme poverty – is the factor that unites homeless young people (Anderson and Christian, 2003). Perhaps the most obvious manifestation of homeless young people's social exclusion and marginalisation is their inability to access and maintain safe, affordable housing because of their youth, their inexperience and, most importantly, their poverty.

Children in Substitute Care

One of the difficulties in assessing the strength of either risk factors or triggers is the lack of precision often associated with measuring and defining the variables under scrutiny. The issue of leaving care in Ireland can usefully illustrate this point. A reasonably consistent research finding relating to children leaving care is their heightened risk of becoming homeless compared to children brought up in their family of origin. Care leavers have to attempt the transition to independence at a much younger age than other young people who tend not to leave home until later. These problems are exacerbated by their lower level of educational attainment and fewer career options. As Stein (2006: 273) notes, children in care:

Are more likely than young people who have not been in care to have poorer educational qualifications, lower levels of participation in post-16 education, be young parents, be homeless, and have higher levels of unemployment, offending behaviour and mental health problems.

While Stein argues that this statement is true in a general sense, those leaving care can be sub-categorised as young people who have successfully "moved on" from their care placement; those who are "survivors" of the care system and those who are "victims" of the system. The latter two groups were likely to have had disrupted care placements and instability in their care history which increase their likelihood of post-care homelessness. In particular, the "victims" were those who have "the most damaging pre-care family experiences and, in the main, care was unable to compensate them, or to help them overcome their past difficulties". As a consequence, "after leaving care they were likely to be unemployed, become homeless and have great difficulties in maintaining their accommodation" (Stein, 2006: 277).

Irish research has consistently identified a history of institutional care as a key route into homelessness for young people. Three examples at different points in time and in different locations all highlight this point. Keane and Crowley's (1990) study of youth homelessness in Limerick found that 29 per cent of those young people who were out-of-home had previously been in care. Similarly, Perris (1999) found that twenty-one of the thirty-five homeless young people (60 per cent) interviewed in Clondalkin, a suburb of Dublin, reported a history of State care. Finally, Kelleher et al.'s (2000) national study of young people leaving care in Ireland found that 33 per cent of the young people leaving health board care had experienced homelessness within six months of leaving, with 66 per cent having experienced homelessness within two years of leaving their care settings. So close is the association between children in care and homeless children that it is claimed that, not only do the two groups have similarities but, they are "often the same individuals at different points in their out-of-home careers" (Houghton et al., 2001: 81).

Kelleher et al. (2000), in the most detailed study of young people leaving State care in Ireland, surveyed young people leaving
special schools for young offenders, those leaving care in three
health board regions (with over half from various residential
placements) and young people residing in two Dublin probation
hostels during 1996 and 1997. The young people were surveyed
six months after leaving care and again after a two-year interval.
Among those young people tracked following a time-lapse of two
years, 68 per cent of the health board population and 33 per cent
of the special school population had experienced homelessness
(see also Kelleher and Kelleher, 1998).

The strikingly high number of homeless children who report a
prior history of substitute care, particularly residential care, is not
altogether surprising in light of research conducted in 1991 on the
organisation of residential care in the Republic of Ireland. This
research showed that over 16 per cent of homes surveyed had no
formal aftercare system. There also appeared to be a degree of
confusion over who should be responsible for the administration
of an aftercare service (McCarthy, 1991).

In one of the largest international studies to date, Park et al.
(2004) estimated that, of the nearly 12,000 young adults who exited
the child welfare system in New York between 1988 and 1992, some
19 per cent had experienced a stay in a New York public shelter for
the homeless over the 10 year period following exit. Among those
young adults who experienced an out-of-home placement, 22 per
cent had experienced a shelter stay compared to 11 per cent who
had experienced non-placement child welfare services.[4]

Despite these apparently unambiguous findings, caution is
nonetheless advised in interpreting the results. As Park et al. (2004:
288) argue, "the extant studies with findings on childhood out-of-
home placement contain such methodological weaknesses as small
numbers of subjects and reliance on retrospective self-reports,
which can be faulty over a long period of time". The various stud-

[4] These figures may be underestimates as the study did not include privately
operated shelters, which provide up to 20 per cent of all shelter beds in New
York.

ies of youth homelessness in Ireland share many of the methodological problems noted by Park et al. (2004). Table 2.7 summarises the findings of numerous Irish studies that have examined different dimensions of homelessness, and which included some information on the care history of the homeless persons they interviewed/surveyed. It demonstrates that the percentage of those reporting a history of State care varies enormously, ranging from 4 to 68 per cent, as does the nomenclature utilised across the studies. It appears, therefore, that the number of homeless people who report a care history can vary significantly depending on the sample selected for study and the way in which "care history" is defined.

Table 2.7 Youth Homelessness and Non-familial Care History in Ireland

Title	Year	Age Group	%	Nomenclature
Dublin Simon Community	1978	Adults	12%	Institution for children or adolescents
Care and Accommodation for Young People at Risk or Homeless in Dublin	1986	14-25	10%	Discharged from prison/residential care or special school
Homeless Young People	1987	Under 18	51%	Residential care/special school/assessment unit/foster care/detention/adoption
A Study of the Work Skills, Experience and Preferences of Simon Community Residents	1988	Adults	9%	Raised in children's home
A National Survey of Young People Out of Home in Ireland	1988	Under 18	5%	Discharged from care without secure accommodation
Forgotten Children – Research on Young People who are Homeless in Dublin	1989	Under 18	40%	Young people previously in long term care
On My Own: Report on Youth Homelessness in Limerick City	1990	Under 18	29%	In residential care with a Health Board or Department of Justice
A Survey of Youth Homelessness in Co. Clare	1992	Under 18	17%	Young person who has been in care

Referral and Settlement in the Simon Community	1992	Adults	9%	Residential care
Youth Homelessness in the Eastern Health Board Area	1993	Under 18	40%	Residential care
Here There and Nowhere: A Study of Youth Homeless-ness in Tallaght	1995	Under 25	13%	Foster and residential care
Left Out on Their Own	1998	Under 18	68%	Had experienced homelessness two years after leaving health board care
Left Out on Their Own	1998	Under 18	33%	Had experienced homelessness two years after leaving spe-cial school care
Homelessness and Mental Health	1998	Adults	4%	Institutional care and foster care
Youth Homelessness in Clondalkin: A Community Perspective	1999	14-24	60%	Previously in care or institutional settings
Young Men on the Margins	2004	18-30	15%	Raised in care

The Homeless Experience

While much research attention has focused on measuring the extent of homelessness and on determining risk and trigger factors for homelessness, others have sought to examine the *nature* of the homeless experience. Many of these studies have used qualitative and ethnographic research methods that privilege individual accounts, thereby allowing homeless people's "voices" or stories to be heard. One of the main benefits of this approach is that it permits a perspective that is grounded in the views and experiences of homeless people, thereby offering the opportunity to bring to light the explanations of this highly marginalised population for their situations. These can, in turn, influence both public perceptions of, and policy debates on, homelessness (Fitzpatrick et al., 2000).

In Ireland, a number of qualitative studies have examined various dimensions of homelessness, whether among women (Kennedy, 1985), adult male hostel dwellers (O'Sullivan, 1993), children in homeless families (Halpenny et al., 2002), drug users (Lawless, 2003), or marginalised young men (Cleary et al., 2004). Similarly, research in the UK has focused on the experiences of particular groups of homeless people such as ethnic minorities (Davies et al., 1996), women (Dibblin, 1991; Jones, 1999; Watson and Austerberry, 1986) and young people (Carlen, 1996; Craig et al., 1996; Fitzpatrick, 2000; Jones, 1993, 1995). This extensive literature has contributed to a more rounded understanding of the nature of homelessness and has highlighted the heterogeneity of the homeless experience. What emerges most strongly from research conducted in Ireland and elsewhere is the marginalisation, alienation and exposure to risk that homelessness brings about. The most severely homeless young people who sleep rough are forced to live their lives under a very public gaze where they wear "a distinctive badge of otherness and exclusion" (Carlen, 1996: 83). Irrespective of age, homelessness is a demeaning experience and, for young people, it is a status that compromises their safety and well-being, as well as their prospects of growing up to be well-adjusted adults.

Residential Dislocation and Entry to Street "Scenes"

One of the most obvious ramifications of being homeless and young is the absence of a stable home and the shelter, security and protection that it affords. Homeless children and young people's low level of guardianship limits their ability to protect themselves or to be protected from the harm that potentially awaits them on the streets. Hostel life can be a daunting and frightening experience for young people. Verbal and even physical attacks are not uncommon among hostel dwellers and many young people understandably have fears about other residents and about the macho culture that tends to prevail within these settings (Carlen, 1996). The most common form of accommodation for such young people, the private rented sector, can be precarious, with poor quality accommodation and eviction a common experience (Hall, 2003; Lister, 2004, 2006). The absence of trusted adults and peers is a further source of stress, as young people face the task of establishing new relationships in a social world that is often fast-paced, unfamiliar and unpredictable. Once homeless for a period, young people's peer networks often become concentrated amongst other homeless people in a similar position to themselves (Fitzpatrick, 2000) and the friendships they establish in these contexts are often fleeting and unreliable (van der Ploeg, 1989). While homeless friends can identify with each other's experience, more often than not, street youth stress the exploitative nature of these friendships (Fitzpatrick, 2000). At the same time, as the only friendships available to them, many become deeply embedded within street-based social networks within a relatively short period of becoming homeless.

For rough sleepers and those young people accessing emergency hostel accommodation, one of the biggest challenges is finding ways to make the day pass. The very public lives of homeless young people are frequently played out in social spaces that bring them into contact with strangers, potential offenders, and other homeless people with serious substance abuse and mental health problems (Gaetz, 2004). A distinctive feature of homeless youth lifestyles – and, indeed, a manifestation of their social exclusion and economic marginalisation – is the range of money-making strategies they engage in at different times and for different reasons. While recent research demonstrates that most homeless youth are not avoiding work and that most do, in fact, want regular jobs (Gaetz and O'Grady, 2002), the vast majority face very significant barriers to obtaining and maintaining employment. As a consequence, large numbers are pushed into the "economy" of street life simply to survive. A good example is the priority of securing enough money to purchase everyday goods such as clothing, food or drugs, which may result in young people resorting to any or all of the following subsistence strategies: begging, theft, "copping" (delivering) drugs and selling drugs. According to one Dublin-based study (Eastern Health Board, 1997), homeless young people are vulnerable to involvement in an array of high-risk "occupations", including sex work.

There has been relatively little detailed investigation of the subsistence strategies of homeless youth in an Irish context. However, one study of older homeless men found their five main sources of income to be begging, unemployment assistance, smuggling, casual employment and theft (O'Sullivan, 1993). In an ethnographic account of begging in Dublin, Howley (2000) found that, while the majority of those begging were homeless, they were predominantly rough sleepers rather than shelter users. The various illegal or quasi-legal subsistence activities that homeless people engage in are the direct consequence of their very limited employment options, inadequate supports and their need to meet immediate survival needs (Gaetz and O'Grady, 2002; Lankenau et al., 2005). These same strategies also carry significant risks and dangers and they often increase the likelihood of negative interaction with the police and subsequent arrest and incarceration.

Social, Psychological and Health Dimensions of Youth Homelessness

Residential instability and the conditions that precipitate it almost always have a negative impact on the physical and psychological well-being of children and young people. Whatever the genesis of their homelessness, most are ill-prepared to manage the social and economic tasks associated with maintaining health and well-being. Internationally, homeless youth have been demonstrated to be at risk from a broad spectrum of health problems, ranging from malnutrition to drug addiction (Clatts et al., 1998; Clatts and Davies, 1999; Dachner and Tarasuk, 2002; Greene and Ringwalt, 1996; McCarthy and Hagan, 1992). Likewise, Irish research has documented a plethora of health problems among the homeless. Feeney et al.'s (2000) large survey of hostel-dwelling men in Dublin found that they had generally unhealthy lifestyles and the health-risk behaviours noted included smoking, drinking and lack of exercise. In a study of street drinkers, Costello and Howley (1999) documented a range of health problems including chest infections, ulcers, liver damage, stomach problems and headache, brought on by heavy drinking and exposure to the elements. Physical health problems were also reported by Smith et al., (2001) in their survey of 100 homeless women which found that most suffered from at least one chronic physical condition, the most common being hepatitis C. A recent study of 72 homeless men and women living in hostels, B&Bs, night shelters or sleeping rough found high vulnerability to poor diet and inadequate nutrition across the sample (Hickey and Downey, 2003).

Related to the extremely negative backgrounds common to many homeless young people and the subsequent stresses they face on becoming homeless, is a high incidence of mental disorders (Stephens, 2002; Whitbeck et al., 2000). In a cross-country comparative review of homeless populations, Martens (2001) found high rates of mental illness such as depression, schizophrenia, psychotic and personality disorders. Studies in Ireland (Feeney et al., 2000; McKeown, 1999; Smith et al, 2001) reveal different rates of mental health problems among homeless adults, with the children of homeless families having a higher likelihood of developing mental illness than their housed peers (O'Brien et al., 1999). Not withstanding these findings, we do well to bear in mind the warning issued by Snow et al. (1988: 195) "that assessing mental illness among the homeless is a highly precarious undertaking".

Although it is claimed that the majority of homeless youth suffer profound feelings of alienation and isolation (Forum on Youth Homelessness, 2000), much less is known about the mental health of young homeless people in an Irish context. Internationally, depression has been found to feature strongly among the mental health problems of homeless young people (MacLean et al., 1999; Whitbeck et al., 1999). Ayerst's (1999) comparative analysis of homeless and housed youth found that homeless young people were more likely to experience high levels of stress related to feelings of depression, and they used destructive coping strategies, including acts of self-harm (cutting, head banging and burning) and/or alcohol and drugs.

Drug Use and Drug Problems

Heavy drinking and alcoholism have long-since been documented among the adult homeless in Ireland and elsewhere (e.g. Archard, 1979; Collins and McKeown, 1992). However, drug use and drug addiction now feature prominently as significant problems among this group. Recent research in Ireland reveals a strong link between homelessness and drug use (Cleary et al., 2004; Cox and Lawless, 1999; Crawley and Daly, 2004; Feeney et al., 2000; Houghton and Hickey, 2000; Lawless, 2003; Smith et al., 2001), a finding which is consistent with research conducted throughout Europe (Avramov, 1998; Flemen, 1997; Fountain and Howes, 2002; Klee and Reid, 1998; Neale, 2001; Wincup et al., 2003), in the United States (Clatts et al., 1998; Greene et al., 1997) and Australia (Mallet et al., 2003).

Although a considerable number of Irish studies have examined drug use among the homeless, differences in the individuals targeted for research purposes (some focusing, for example, on a particular "group" of drug users such as women, others investigating drug use and homelessness within a specific local area and, yet others, examining the experience of homelessness among the clients of a single drug treatment centre or intervention), coupled with inconsistencies in the research methodologies utilised across the various studies, make it difficult to draw clear-cut conclusions about the precise nature of the relationship between drug use and homelessness. Nonetheless, it appears that drug use and drug problems are very prevalent among young homeless people. While many homeless drug users attribute their lack of housing to their drug use (Cox and Lawless, 1999), equally, the state of homelessness exacerbates drug consumption levels and has also been implicated in "risky" drug-taking practices and the transition to injecting drug use (Crawley and Daly, 2004). Homeless young people may find that drugs and alcohol offer an easy escape route from the harsh realities of daily life (Avramov, 1998). Klee and Reid's (1998) London-based research revealed how young homeless people used drugs, particularly opiates, as a form of self-medication to cope with the stress of a homeless lifestyle.

However, despite striking similarities in the risk factors for homelessness and addiction, the relationship between drug use and homelessness is extremely complex (Hutson and Liddiard, 1994; Neale, 2001; Fitzpatrick et al., 2000). This complexity creates what Neale (2001) describes as a "double jeopardy", making young people more susceptible to risk behaviour and ill-health. A recent New York study of homeless young men has shown that few of the men had used drugs prior to their becoming homeless; rather drug use emerged as a central behavioural adaptation to the state of homelessness and, once initiated, drug use had the potential to become a critical factor in determining subsequent risk trajectory outcomes for these homeless young men (Clatts et al., 2005).

Injecting drug users who are homeless are particularly at risk because they are forced to inject in some of the most dangerous settings, including outdoor locations where conditions are unsanitary and unfavourable to safe injecting practices (Fitzgerald et al., 2004). One Irish study has documented high levels of injecting risk behaviour, including the sharing of needles and other injecting paraphernalia, among homeless drug users (Cox and Lawless, 1999). It is also significant that, among street-based samples of homeless youth, recent illness experiences are frequently related to drug use such as abscesses from intravenous drug use (Ensign and Bell, 2004). Finally, for drug users living within the constraints of a homeless lifestyle, the continued demands of their drug consumption is a daily priority. If users are to avoid the sickness associated with withdrawal, they must have enough money to secure a supply of drugs. For young people who find themselves in this situation, the supposed deterrent effect of criminal sanction is frequently reduced by an over-riding focus on their immediate situation.

Survival Strategies

As documented earlier, young homeless people use a range of "survival" strategies and many of these involve criminal activity. Living on the streets or without stable accommodation contributes to youth crime, arrest and committal to prison (Hagan and McCarthy, 1992, 1997). For example, in a sample of 400 homeless young people in a Canadian city, Baron (2007) found that, while some engaged in little or no criminal activities, a significant number were high-rate offenders. McCarthy and Hagan (1992) identified lack of secure shelter and length of time on the street as the most consistent predictors of criminal activity and incarceration among homeless young people. This research was conducted in Toronto and Vancouver and concluded that "Toronto's social welfare model of providing access to overnight shelters and social services reduced exposure to criminal opportunities, whereas Vancouver's crime control model and absence of assistance made it more common" (Hagan and McCarthy, 2005: 196).

Analysis of the progression routes of homeless persons through the courts in Dublin demonstrates that of the 9,794 individuals who passed through the District or Circuit Court over a six week period in 2003, only 159 or 1.6 per cent were identified as homeless (and this was a rather broad definition, including as it did 17 individuals in transitional housing). Of the 159 homeless cases, 12 per cent were aged between 16 and 19 years (Seymour and Costello, 2005: 28-29). The same study found that in relation to the accommodation status of young people prior to detention in one of three children detention schools in Dublin, only one was homeless. On the other hand, while the experience of homelessness can potentially contribute to imprisonment through engagement in survivalist crimes such as shoplifting, begging and larceny, the experience of imprisonment is equally likely to lead to homelessness (Hickey, 2002). Thus, it appears that experience of prison and the criminal justice system can itself increase a person's chances of becoming (or remaining) homeless. Not only does offending make it more likely that a person will become homeless, but homelessness makes it more likely that people will re-offend (Gowan, 2002; Randall and Brown, 1999) and the likelihood of reincarceration is intensified for those who have a history of homelessness prior to initial incarceration (Metraux and Culhane, 2004).

While many homeless young people report a history of offending, the research evidence also indicates that they are highly vulnerable to victimisation, including verbal and physical abuse, robbery, sexual harassment and violence (Baron, 2003; Gaetz, 2004). Lee and Schreck (2005: 1074), in their representative sample of 2,401 homeless adults in the United States, found that "homeless people are victimised disproportionately often, both in an absolute sense and compared to their domiciled counterparts". Fear of crime is, in fact, a significant part of the experience of homelessness for many people and homeless young women are particularly vulnerable to violence and exploitation on the street (Hatty et al., 1996). Once on the street, young people's heavy dependence on other homeless youth, and their reluctance to form trusting relationships with adults, makes them doubly vulnerable since they generally rely on a narrow set of social supports to help them to deal with the consequences of victimisation (Gaetz, 2004).

The tendency for homeless young people to adopt a range of unconventional subsistence strategies is related to the extreme difficulty they are likely to experience in securing legitimate employment. Homeless men and women typically report school problems and early school leaving (Smith et al., 2001) and a history of conflict with teachers is also common among homeless youth (Novac et al., 1996). Irish studies have consistently noted school problems, ranging from poor attendance and underachievement, to early school leaving among homeless people of all ages (Focus Ireland, 1995; Perris, 1999; Smith et al., 2001). Cleary et al.'s (2004) study of homeless young men found that the vast majority left school at an early age and most also reported difficult school experiences which impacted on their attendance and ultimately contributed to their early departure from school. Homeless young people's lack of educational qualifications means that many are unable to compete in the labour market. Moreover, without a stable place to live, it is exceptionally difficult to seek employment and maintain it since many basic requirements such as clean clothes cannot be taken for granted. This "no home, no job" cycle for homelessness has long been recognised (Fitzpatrick et al., 2000).

For young people who become homeless, social exclusion is experienced across several domains: in terms of access to shelter and housing, employment and health. In most cases, this process of social exclusion begins before street youth become homeless but it intensifies through their experience of living on the streets or in insecure and unsafe settings (Gaetz, 2004). As an outcome of their homelessness, young people are typically pushed into circumstances and places that impair their ability to adequately ensure their safety and security. In this sense, the trajectory of social exclusion is cumulative in nature, making it difficult to escape since their constant exposure to risk compromises their health, safety and opportunity.

Service Access and Service Utilisation Practices

Although the health status of homeless youth is far poorer than their housed peers (Commander et al., 2002), many may not access, or are not reached by, the programmes and interventions intended for them. According to the Forum on Youth Homelessness (2000), less than half of the young people under eighteen years who were classified as homeless in 1999 used statutory emergency accommodation. Similarly, research conducted by Perris (1999) in Clondalkin found that 40 per cent of the homeless youth identified had no contact with any service, while 20 per cent had contact with some service but not with those designated for people who are homeless.

Homeless young people have greater problems with access to health care than do their non-homeless peers due to a more profound lack of payment source, greater anxiety over confidentiality, and more confusion over their ability to consent for care (De Rosa et al., 1999; Ensign and Gittelsohn, 1998; Geber, 1997). Young homeless people may also view the services available to them as hostile and dangerous places (Randall and Brown, 1996). Fitzpatrick (2000), for example, identified a considerable number of young people who would not avail of services in the city-centre of

London because they felt that venturing outside their own neighbourhood was unsafe. Other research has found that some homeless youth perceive greater levels of support and security on the street than in the services designed to meet their needs (Clatts et al., 1995). Young men and women may have different approaches and strategies when it comes to help-seeking behaviour. For example, Smith et al.'s (1996) UK-based research demonstrated that homeless young women approached agencies at earlier stages in their homeless careers than young men. Consistent to some extent with this finding, Fitzpatrick (2000) found young women more willing than young men to approach formal agencies when they did find themselves homeless. In a UK study, Dibbin (1991) found that young women were less likely to sleep rough than their male counterparts because they feared the dangers involved. At the same time, this group is among the most hidden and unrecognised of all homeless people and, in Ireland, homeless women tend to be less visible to the public eye and to opt for alternatives to hostel accommodation, such as "dossing, squatting or staying with friends" (Kennedy, 1985: 173).

Youth Homelessness: Towards a Dynamic Interpretation

As documented earlier in this chapter, the sterile debate between those who champion structural causes of homelessness over individualist causes and *vice-versa* has been replaced with a more nuanced appreciation of the complexity of the interaction of a host of factors in the causation of homelessness. This is not to suggest that a consensus exists on the causes of homelessness in Ireland or, indeed, the meaning of homelessness. As the Homeless Agency (2005: 16-17) has argued:

> Different agencies use different definitions of homelessness and collect different information in different ways. This makes it impossible to collate information, to make comparisons across services or sectors or to assess the impact of interventions. A similar situation applies in the area of research. Homelessness – and the people who are homeless – is constantly being researched by different agencies, with no

central planning or coordination, collation of findings or quality control.

Nonetheless, with a few notable exceptions, homelessness is increasingly understood as a complex, differentiated and multi-causal phenomena. For example, Williams and Cheal (2001: 250), based on research utilising the capture-recapture model of estimating homelessness, pose the question, "Is there any such thing as homelessness?", by which they mean:

> Both outcome states and antecedent conditions were so heterogeneous that, in the first case, the "homeless" population, however one defined it, could not always be isolated from a more general population and, in the second case, the pathways into the diverse range of housing situations we characterised (for the purposes of these studies) as homelessness were extraordinarily diverse.[5]

Drawing on this analysis, Pleace (2005: 5) argues for a complex definition and suggests that any meaningful notion of homelessness needs to be disaggregated "into meaningful and verifiable groups of people with shared pathways into and through homelessness". Such an approach would seek to identify distinct sub-populations within the overall homeless population rather than examining homelessness as a self-contained category. The category "homeless" is further divided by gender, age, location, response, and so on. A persuasive argument can therefore be made that the pathways and responses to homelessness amongst, for example, young homeless females in rural Ireland might well be very different to those of adult homeless males in Dublin. Just as homelessness amongst young people warrants investigation using the conceptual and methodological tools appropriate to that group, so too does the experience of homelessness, for example, among women (Edgar and Doherty, 2001; O'Sullivan and Hig-

---

[5] Early feminist analyses of homelessness also suggested that "the concept of homelessness is not a useful one, and should be rethought or abandoned" (Watson, 1984: 70).

gins, 2001), those who are older (Warnes and Crane, 2006) and/or living in rural areas (Milbourne and Cloke, 2006), those at the cusp of adulthood (Tyler and Johnson, 2006), and those who are members of minority ethnic groups (Netto, 2006).

In relation to homelessness in rural areas, Thrane et al. (2006) observe in their US study that young people from urban areas are more likely to leave home at an early age as a result of familial abuse than their rural counterparts. This, they speculate, is a consequence of the lack of appropriate services in rural areas. This same argument applies equally to policy responses. In the case of Australia, Beer et al. (2006: 244) argue that "[p]olicies that deal with youth homelessness generally may not be appropriate or feasible to rural settings". In understanding "visible" or street homeless women, May et al. (2007: 135) argue that, even within this relatively small sub-category of homeless persons, "the experience of street homelessness is different for different women". This strongly suggests that, even within what appears to be a relatively self-contained category, caution needs to be exercised in making generalisations. Researchers need to focus on age-specific homeless populations and on what are termed "homeless-emerging adults" (18 to 25 years of age), as they may differ "from homeless adolescents and homeless adults" (Tyler and Johnson, 2006: 153). Warnes and Crane (2006: 417) observe that, after living for years in conventional housing and having maintained familial and employment obligations, individuals can become homeless in later life due to a complex range of circumstances, thus suggesting very different pathways into homelessness than for those who are younger.

The *complexity perspective* suggested by Pleace (2005) is also informed by the view that explanations of homelessness cannot be directly inferred from the individual characteristics of homeless persons. In other words, for every homeless person with risk factors such as a care history, family breakdown, physical or sexual abuse, offending behaviour, lack of social support networks, and so on, there is a further unquantifiable, but nonetheless large number, who have some, if not all, of these characteristics, who are *not* homeless. Fitzpatrick, in a recent review of the literature on the causes of homelessness similarly argues that, "[t]he disparate causal factors thought to be associated with homelessness ... are often presented in an undifferentiated list, with neither their relationship to each other nor to the wider explanatory frameworks rigorously investigated" (2005: 1). For Fitzpatrick (2005: 4), the distinction between individual and structural causes of homelessness that dominated debates from the early 1980s as the number of homeless persons apparently grew, dissipated and was replaced with a new orthodoxy which stated that:

> Structural factors create the conditions within which homelessness will occur; and people with personal problems are more vulnerable to these adverse social and economic trends than others; therefore the high concentration of people with personal problems in the homeless population can be explained by their susceptibility to macro-structural forces, rather than necessitating an individual explanation of homelessness.

Although giving ascendancy to structural causes of homelessness, this new orthodoxy recognised the significance of personal factors and attempted to integrate these causes within a structural framework. However, Fitzpatrick (2005: 5) argues that the "new orthodoxy" does not adequately deal with the issue of causation and poses the question, "[w]hat is it about these structural and individual 'factors' that generate homelessness?". A review of positivist, interpretivist, feminist and structuration accounts of homelessness leads her to conclude that all of these accounts suffer from fundamental weaknesses. Fitzpatrick argues instead for a "Critical Realist" approach to understanding homelessness. Whilst acknowledging that achieving a coherent understanding of what is meant by "homelessness", and that differentiating between, for example, those living in Bed and Breakfast-type accommodation and those living in hostels and sleeping rough, will provide better explanations of homelessness, she nonetheless argues for a common methodology for theorising the causes of homelessness.

The causal mechanisms that can generate homelessness exist at four levels, but significantly, no hierarchy is assumed between them. These are:

> *Economic structures* – social class interacts with other stratifi-cation processes and welfare policies to generate poverty and to determine poor individuals 'and households' (non-) access to material resources such as housing, income, employment and household goods.
>
> *Housing structures* – inadequate housing supply and a deterioration in affordability can squeeze out those on lower incomes; tenure and allocation policies, coupled with the collective impacts of private choices, can lead to residential segregation and spatial concentration of the least advantaged groups.
>
> *Patriarchal and interpersonal structures* – can lead to the emergence of domestic violence, child neglect or abuse, weak social support, relationship breakdown, etc.
>
> *Individual attributes* – personal resilience can be undermined by mental health problems, substance misuse, lack of self-esteem and/or confidence (Fitzpatrick, 2005: 13)

A Pathways Approach to Youth Homelessness

Furthering our knowledge of the phenomenon of youth homelessness is necessary if policy prescriptions are to be well targeted and effective. Based on the review of literature above, we make a case for an approach to researching youth homelessness which focuses specifically on *pathways* into and through homelessness.[6] This conceptual framework views homelessness as a dynamic experience and as part of a process that can change, sometimes quite dramatically, over time (Anderson and Tulloch, 2000). Conceptualising youth homelessness as a process assumes

---

[6] The fundamental building block of the pathways approach is social constructionism (Clapham, 2002; 2003). Social constructionism is based on the tenet that social life is constructed by people through interaction and that it is through interaction that individuals define themselves and the world they inhabit.

that homelessness is not a fixed "state" but rather a fluid and evolving "status" that is continually subject to change (Mayock, 2007). It has the advantage of viewing homelessness in holistic terms, seeing it not simply as an isolated event but as one part of the multi-faceted lives of young people. More broadly, an emphasis on the dynamics of homelessness relates to the developing interest in longitudinal research throughout social policy, particularly in relation to a focus on changing disadvantaged people's "trajectories" (Fitzpatrick et al., 2000). The term "homeless career" – highlighting how people can move through a range of housing circumstances as part of an overall homeless experience – has been used to describe this process.[7] Wallace (1968: 97) provided one of the first accounts of a typical homeless trajectory.

> Recruitment into the skid row way of life may be divided into four phases with component community and social psychological characteristics. The incipient phase involves the dislocation from the basic social network of society accompanied by a sense of rootlessness. Exposure to skid row subculture follows, accompanied by isolation and desocialisation. The third phase – regular participation in skid row institutions – witnesses the beginnings of submergence into skid row subculture. The final phase in the natural history of the skid rower is marked by his integration into the skid row community, and by his acculturation.

There are only a relatively small number of studies that have examined young people's "journeys" through homelessness in an explicit and systematic way. In a similar way to Wallace (1968), Hutson and Liddiard (1994) argued, on foot of their study of homeless young people in Wales, that homelessness needs to be viewed and understood as a progressively problematic "down-

---

[7] Social scientists use the term "career" to refer to the transitional stages involved in the development of any form of biographical identity (Goffman, 1961; Becker, 1963; Snow and Anderson, 1993). A "career" is not a pre-determined treadmill of events, but a process characterised by contingency.

ward spiral" consisting of three phases: "early", "middle" and "late". Most of the young people in this study left home in an unplanned way and tended to stay with relatives or friends for a short period of time. Following this, some appeared to resolve their home-based difficulties and either returned to their family or moved into private rented accommodation. Others, however, moved into the "middle phase" of homelessness and lived in youth residential projects, used squats and, as time progressed, the use of adult hostels was more common. Among those who subsequently moved into the "late phase" of homelessness, many were viewed as too problematic to be accommodated in youth residential projects and were either sleeping rough or staying in adult hostels. Few of these young people were employed and many were heavily involved in criminal and drug lifestyles.

Similarly, Chamberlain and MacKenzie's (1994) Australian study identified three temporal categories of homelessness among the young people they studied: "short-term", "long-term" and "chronic". This research drew attention to wide variation in young people's homeless "careers", with some exiting following a relatively short period and others remaining homeless for far longer periods of time. The study also highlighted the increasingly complex needs of the young people who progressed through the three stages, with the chronically homeless presenting the most challenging needs due to their progressive participation in, and attachment to, a "homeless subculture".

Craig et al.'s (1996) London-based study was one of the first to attempt to track a cohort of young homeless people over a specific time period. The research initially included a sample of homeless young people as well as a comparative sample of domiciled youth and attempts were made to re-establish contact with both sub-samples following a time-lapse of one year. At the time of follow-up, only just over a third of the homeless young people with whom contact was re-established had achieved a "stable" (defined as remaining in an independent tenancy, shared accommodation, long-stay hostel or returned to the parental home for at least six months) or "fairly stable housing" throughout the follow-up year. Some 28 per cent had not achieved stable housing and were experiencing continued short stays in various accommodations and one fifth were still sleeping rough and using night shelters. Those young people who had achieved stable housing were more likely to be female, from black/minority ethnic groups and have educational qualifications. Additionally, those homeless for less than two years at first interview were more likely to achieve stable outcomes than those with longer homeless histories. Based on a broader sample of 315 young people, including both homeless youth and those perceived to be "at risk" for homelessness in the counties of Surrey, Hampshire and the Isle of Wight, Stockley et al. (1993) presented a more positive picture of young people's "movements" based on a one year follow-up of 72 of the young people. Their research revealed a trend from less adequate to more stable forms of accommodation and concluded that "some are likely to go through a period of accommodation instability making use of more marginal types of accommodation, before moving into more permanent or more adequate accommodation" (Stockley et al., 1993: 17).

Finally, Fitzpatrick's (2000) Glasgow-based qualitative study set out to build on previous research using a pathways framework and aimed to examine distinct processes and patterns of experience among homeless young people. This research described six homeless pathways taken by young people in an urban context which can be summarised as follows:

- Local youth homelessness: Mainly resulting from structural poverty leading to family friction, alternating between moving around friends' and relatives' houses and sleeping rough locally, with a strong attachment to the local area.

- Using "official" city homeless network: Typically young men who have had very difficult childhoods (e.g. involving physical and/or sexual abuse, the death of a parent, destructive step-relationships, residential care). They have little or no contact with their families, little attachment to any local area, and their social networks may revolve around hostel residents. Many have serious personal problems, including mental ill health and substance abuse.

- City centre homelessness: Young people who have moved
  immediately to the city centre on becoming homeless. They
  may already know people homeless in the city centre, or fear
  family or others in their home neighbourhood. Their homelessness is linked to severe family problems in childhood and
  they have complex needs. They typically alternated between
  rough sleeping for extended periods in the city centre, hostel,
  and prison or drug rehabilitation units.

The pathways identified by Fitzpatrick were not completely separate and some young people moved from one pathway to another
at different stages in their homeless career. This research uncov-
ered a sharp distinction between city-centre and local area homelessness. Few of the young people from the local area pathway
moved into patterns of homelessness which involved sleeping
rough in the city-centre.

One of the major strengths of Fitzpatrick's work is the focus on
the experiences and perspectives of the young people themselves
as they construct their own situation. The findings of this and
other studies of homeless young people that emphasise processes
and trajectories through homelessness (Hutson and Liddiard,
1994; Stockley et al., 1993) suggest that there is a general drift towards institutional accommodation as young people's homelessness lengthens, with adult hostels usually featuring later in young
people's homeless careers.

While research to date in an Irish context has not focused explicitly on tracking young people's homeless "careers", a number
of studies have drawn attention to the different routes that people
may take both into and through homelessness. For example, Halpenny et al.'s (2002) study of homeless families living in emergency accommodation reported a number of factors that led families into homelessness including: community difficulties, overcrowding in the family home, family conflict, violence from a partner and unaffordable housing. Cleary et al.'s (2004) Dublin-based
qualitative study of 20 men aged between 18 and 30 years characterised the path from home to homelessness as one of trauma and

loss. At a young age, most of the men had experienced a range of negative events and difficulties including death, family separation, reconstituted families, domestic violence, parental mental illness and addiction and care placements. The duration of their home-lessness varied from between three months and 15 years, with re-curring episodes of homelessness featuring in many of their life stories. Although this study did not document pathways through homelessness, per se, it did nonetheless convey a clear sense of the men's lives, their coping strategies and their experiences of home-lessness over time. It also drew attention to several barriers to their movement out of homelessness including social isolation, financial problems, low educational attainment and the practical difficulties of finding and maintaining a home.

As highlighted above, early interpretations of a homeless "ca-reer" suggested a progressive deterioration into skid row (Wal-lace, 1968). Contemporaneously, this might be construed as a lin-ear trajectory towards chronic homelessness. However, more re-cent research, as highlighted earlier in the chapter, suggests that homelessness is best understood as episodic, characterised by residential instability, rather than as an inevitable or ever-declining quality of accommodation.[8] For example, in their meta-analysis of research into homelessness, primarily in the US during the 1980s, Shlay and Rossi (1992: 141) found that:

> the average time spent homeless was just under two years; all but two studies reported that the average time spent homeless was greater than 14 months. At the same time, these studies reported that the majority of their samples were homeless for less than six months.

---

[8] Snow and Anderson (1993: 277) note that "there seem to be five possible career trajectories for the homeless. Some have only brief careers on the streets. Others sink into a pattern of episodic homelessness. A third career entails permanent embeddedness in a liminal plateau typically in an institutional niche outside conventional society. A fourth career leads to chronic, unrelieved homelessness. And a final possibility involves permanent, or at least relatively long-term, extri-cation from street life and return to conventional society after years, or perhaps even a decade or more, of homelessness."

Comparing homeless youths between the age of 12 and 20 years in Los Angles and Melbourne, Milburn et al. (2007) found that the majority returned home for extended periods of time within two years of first becoming homeless. Based on qualitative research in England, May (2000: 615) similarly argues that, "for the majority of single homeless people the experience of homelessness is neither singular nor long term but episodic, with each homeless episode interspersed with often extended periods in their own accommodation and with no increase in either the frequency or duration of homeless episodes over time".

Similarly, in relation to exiting homelessness, Wong and Piliavin (1997) argue that females are more likely to exit homelessness than males and that this is not linked to personal deficits; rather, institutional resources are a more significant predictor of exit. Dworsky and Piliavin (2000) note that not all exits from homelessness are equal and that the nature of the exit will have a strong bearing on whether or not the individual returns to homelessness. In particular, they argue that the most important factor in not returning to homelessness appears to be access to a private residence[9] rather than agency-managed transitional housing or informal arrangements such as staying with family or friends.

Conclusion

Youth homelessness self-evidently often starts at a very early age. Research conducted in Ireland and elsewhere reports that many adults first experience homelessness during their early to mid-teenage years. There is also evidence that youth homelessness can result in episodic and/or extended patterns of homelessness. Research on youth and adult homelessness in Ireland provides some information about *who* becomes homeless and about *how* homelessness is experienced. However, much less is known about the processes involved in young people's "journeys" through home-

---

[9] By this they mean private residences that individuals considered their own and for which they paid all or a substantial part of the housing costs, rather than, for example, social service agency run transitional housing.

lessness or about the factors and processes that lead to more enduring or chronic states of homelessness.

In their review of social science research on homelessness, Shlay and Rossi (1992) argue that research needs is to go beyond the typical "counting and characteristics" type of study to develop empirically-supported research and theory about transitions into and out of homelessness. More recently, Anderson and Christian (2003) and Clapham (2003) have argued for the importance of longitudinal analyses of homelessness. As a number of authors have noted, cross-sectional or single point-in-time research strategies can generate misleading information about the nature of homelessness, because such methodologies will over-represent the characteristics of persons with longer episodes of homelessness.

In this chapter we have argued for a pathways approach to homelessness which seeks to map out and explain patterns (and changes) in the experience of homelessness over time. This approach does not assume a progressive decline from being poorly housed to temporary accommodation to street homelessness and, instead, recognises that individuals can move into and out of homelessness at different stages in their life-cycle. Thus, the notion that individuals can move between being homeless, poorly housed and adequately or well housed is a key starting point for a complex and dynamic analysis of pathways into and through homelessness (Anderson and Tulloch, 2000). Methodologically, this involves generating biographical information on the life histories of homeless individuals *via* qualitative interviews and analysing these data in relation to the broader social and economic environments that structure their lifeworlds. Thus, the approach seeks implicitly to overcome the stale dichotomy between structuralist versus individualistic approaches to homelessness. It recognises, for example, that those with a care history as children, or those young people who consume illicit drugs, may be vulnerable to homelessness but, equally, not all individuals with these experiences become homeless and, if they do, they many not become entrapped in homelessness. It also recognises that agencies, either voluntary or statutory, with a claim on assisting the homeless are not necessarily neutral in their interactions with the homeless and that, instead, the experience of homelessness is strongly mediated by the nature of the interaction between the individual and various agencies. In some cases, the interaction may amplify and perpetuate the homeless experience while, in others, it may resolve it, either temporarily or more permanently.

This study attempts to take on some of the formidable challenges of researching homelessness in the hope of advancing a nuanced understanding of young people's homeless pathways within the theoretical and methodological framework outlined in this chapter. The following chapter describes the methods used to elicit a qualitative account of the lives and experiences of homeless young people in Dublin city.

Chapter 3

RESEARCH METHODOLOGY

The term "homeless" conveys a single experience of lacking a home. Yet, one might lack a home in numerous ways and for numerous reasons: through eviction or incarceration or because of abusive home conditions, for example. The homeless experience is itself diverse and is almost always subject to change: for some young people homelessness can be fleeting, temporary or episodic while, for others, it is a more protracted experience punctuated by periods of temporary accommodation. Other youth remain homeless for prolonged periods of time and face overwhelming obstacles in their efforts to leave street life. Whatever the living situation of a homeless young person at a given point in time, their circumstances may alter significantly as they move into and out of various forms of insecure accommodation or, alternatively, return to their family home for short or extended periods.

Conceptualizing youth homelessness as a *process* rejects the notion of a single or homogenous homeless experience. It also assumes that homelessness is not a fixed state and that it can alter significantly over time. As outlined in the previous chapter, this study set out to investigate homelessness using a pathways approach with the core aim of generating an in-depth understanding of youth homelessness from the perspective of young people.[1]

---

[1] This chapter outlines methodological issues of access, recruitment and sampling relevant to Phase I of a longitudinal study of youth homelessness. At the time of writing, follow-up interviews had been conducted with a large number of the participants initially recruited into the study. The findings of Phase II of the study are not presented in this book.

The study was designed to examine young people's past and current life experiences and to identify the routes they take into and through homelessness.

Research Strategy

The choice of methodology was influenced directly by one of the primary objectives of the study, which was to access detailed knowledge about the experience of homelessness based on the accounts of young people who are homeless, that is, living on the street, in hostels or in other unstable living situations. The research aims were pursued within a *life history* framework (described in detail later). Criteria for inclusion in the study were:

1. Being homeless or in insecure accommodation

2. Being between 12-22 years, and

3. Living in the Dublin metropolitan area for the past six months.

The study adhered to the definition of young homeless people advanced by the Forum on Youth Homelessness (2000: 17) and the *Youth Homelessness Strategy* (Department of Health and Children, 2001: 11):

> Those who are sleeping on the streets or in other places not intended for night-time accommodation or not providing safe protection from the elements or those whose usual night-time residence is a public or private shelter, emergency lodging, B and B or such, providing protection from the elements but lacking the other characteristics of a home and/or intended for only a short stay.

In keeping with the clarification offered by the Forum on Youth Homelessness (2000: 187) in relation to this definition, the research targeted "young people who look for accommodation from the Eastern Regional Health Authority Out of Hours Service" as well as "those in insecure accommodation with relatives or friends regarded as inappropriate".

There are a number of points that merit clarification in relation to the age range (12-22 years) targeted for participation in this research. The World Health Organization uses the word "adolescent" for ages 10 to 19 and the term "young people" to cover ages 10 to 24 years. In Ireland, statutory authorities have differing obligations depending on whether the person for whom they are making provision is an adult or a child. Under the Child Care Act, 1991, "child" applies up to the age of 18 years. Accordingly, statutory child care agencies responsible for the provision of services and care to homeless youth do not have a legal obligation to provide services to them once they reach the age of 18. It is widely acknowledged that this 18-year "cut off" point leads to problems and difficulties because of the sudden withdrawal of services from young people, leaving those who remain homeless on reaching their 18th birthday with no option but to use adult services. In recognition of this and other difficulties related to the 18-year "cut-off" point, the Forum on Youth Homelessness (2000) defined their age parameters as 12-20 years. For the purpose of this research, the upper age limit for eligibility for participation was set at 22 years. The use of this extended age range for the sampling and selection of research participants has a number of advantages. First, the retrospective accounts of "older" youth are important since they can potentially yield insight into how the homeless experience evolves and changes over time. Secondly and importantly in terms of gaining insight into the process of youth homelessness, it is desirable to have participants who vary in age and life experience. The inclusion of young people up to the age of 22 years permits an analysis of the dynamics of youth homelessness and of the development of youth homeless "careers".

Data Collection Strategy and Methods

Community Assessment Process

The study began with a "Community Assessment Process" (Clatts et al., 2002), a phase designed to inform service providers about the study and to facilitate entrée to field settings. This initial stage was essentially a period of engagement with professionals involved both directly and indirectly in the provision of services for homeless youth. Providing critical information about the structure of the homeless youth "community", it served as a stepping stone to gaining access to potential participants. In terms of the sampling strategy, this period of immersion in the field enabled the identification of various "sub-groups" of homeless youth that could potentially enable the study of diversity. Thus, opportunities for interaction with homeless youth were created and the process of rapport-building with prospective respondents could begin.

All of this was achieved through a mix of informal discussions with service providers and semi-structured interviews with "key informants" who are frontline workers with regular, direct contact with homeless young people (e.g. outreach workers, heath services staff, drug treatment providers, counsellors, social workers, child care workers and so on). The key areas addressed in the interviews included: the perceived extent of the homeless youth problem, the needs (both immediate and long-term) of homeless youth, the adequacy of current service provision, difficulties associated with service delivery, gaps in service provision, and so on.

The study's adult informants provided vital information regarding where, when and how young people might be targeted for participation. While many of the community assessment interactions and interviews took place prior to initiating the formal data collection process (i.e. the conduct of life history interviews with homeless young people), others were conducted throughout the course of fieldwork. This meant that the recruitment strategy was responsive to information gleaned through ongoing interaction and communication with the study's adult informants. Contact was established with almost 40 service providers during the course of the community assessment process and formal semi-structured interviews were conducted with 18 key informants across a range of organizations and agencies that deal directly with young homeless people.

Baseline Life History Interviews

A growing body of research has documented the developmental features of biographical narration evidenced in children's growing capacities to tell stories about their lives and their own development (Habermas and Bluck, 2000). This study used the life history interview as the core method of data collection. The method rests on the collection and analysis of stories that speak to turning point moments in people's lives. Life history interviewing thus has an individual life as its unit of investigation: through the telling of a life story, the individual constructs a picture that is anchored within a distinct society, culture or set of experiences. This telling or recounting of a string of events permits the identification of the unfolding history of people's experiences and encourages respondents' interpretation of a chronology of events that are personally significant (Denzin, 1989).

Life history interviewing helps to disentangle multiple meanings of a single term. Research subjects themselves may use the term "homeless", but the term can indicate vastly different conditions, situations and understandings. By placing emphasis on subjective experience and meanings, life history accounts allow a window into people's adoption of terminology such as "homelessness" and an opportunity to grasp respondents' understanding of their situations. In terms of the current study, the inclusion of life history questions provided the scope to listen to young people's accounts, not of "homelessness", but of "a life" in which homelessness transpires.

Perhaps the most significant value of life history interviewing is that it authorizes the young person to speak for him or herself. In life history interviewing, "the powerful" (i.e. the researcher) has less control over how the interaction and potential universe of responses are shaped, thereby affording a high degree of autonomy to interviewees. This is important, not only because of the stigma of homelessness, but also because young homeless people are vulnerable to exploitation within a range of settings and contexts. Finally, since the life history interview affords a high degree of autonomy to research respondents, it is particularly effective in capturing aspects of both social structure and human agency in accounts of young people in transition (Hubbard, 2000).

All of the interviews commenced with an invitation to young people to tell their "life story". Several key topic areas were then prompted during interview. Young people were asked to describe their family history, their experiences of "growing up", including their early family environment and childhood experiences, engagement with school, and any key events or milestones during childhood and adolescence. Questions also focused on the young person's social world, including the important people in his/her life (e.g. family members, peers, friends, romantic or sexual partner), their economic situation and current "hang-outs". A great deal of attention focused on the events and circumstances leading to each young person's initial homeless experience as well as the chronology of events and experiences subsequent to their leaving home or care for the first time. Later sections of the interview included questions on young people's alcohol and drug use, their health-related behaviour, level of contact with youth and/or homeless services, coping strategies and their perceptions of current needs.

The schedule was designed to allow for flexibility in structure and content and to facilitate the exploration of experiences and issues raised by respondents. The interview itself was deliberately informal in style, reflecting the perspective that talk generated in an interview context is jointly constructed (Gubrium and Holstein, 2002). If a young person raised issues not included on the schedule, interviewers pursued these topics and allowed the respondent to elaborate. Interviews were conducted in a variety of settings, including coffee shops and outdoors, but most frequently at a hostel or other form of emergency or short-term accommodation. They ranged in duration from 40 to 100 minutes, with the majority lasting for between 60 and 90 minutes. All respondents received a gift token from a high street store of their choice to the value of €20 as a token of appreciation for their time and effort.

At the time of conducting life history interviews, socio-demographic information was also collected from each research participant using a pre-coded questionnaire. The information sought included: age, gender, school history, past and current living situation, school and employment history. Data were also recorded on each young person's alcohol (regularity, amount, type of beverages etc.) and drug use (lifetime, past year, past month and past week use) history.

Access and Recruitment

From the outset, it was important to access appropriate recruitment sites and to enlist the co-operation of a range of professionals with responsibility for the provision of services to homeless young people. The process of gaining access was initiated in conjunction with the "community assessment" when the possibility of using specific interventions as recruitment sites was discussed with service providers. Managers and frontline workers (child care staff, unit managers, social workers, and so on) were anxious to facilitate the study and, in general, went to great lengths to make their services available for the purpose of recruitment. Despite this, the process of engaging study participants was a protracted one in many cases and usually necessitated several steps. In the case of each recruitment site, interviewers met initially with the manager and staff of the unit/intervention to discuss procedural and ethical issues and to explain the interviewing process. Having gained permission to use individual settings as recruitment sites, site visits were then arranged and the process of meeting with young people commenced. Permission was initially sought from eight statutory and voluntary agencies to use their premises for recruitment. However, as time progressed, the range of recruitment settings was extended to include additional hostels, residential settings, night shelters and drop-in centres as well as several street-based settings. The non-agency settings used in this research included a number of street corners and other locations used for begging or sleeping. Over the course of the recruitment effort, contact was established with in excess of 25 homeless services and agencies.

A combination of the sensitive nature of the topic under investigation and the vulnerability of the target population meant that building rapport prior to the conduct of formal interviews with young people was crucial and demanded a heavy investment of time. People may deny their homelessness (O'Sullivan, 1993) or make no public reference to the fact that they are users of hostels. For this reason, the term "homeless" was not used when introducing the study to young people; instead, it was explained that the study focused on young people who live "out of home" or "away from home". In this way, the imposition of status and meaning was avoided and each young person was allowed to define and frame their situation as they perceived it. Great care was taken to ensure that young people did not feel obliged or pressured to participate in the study and interviews were rarely conducted on the day of first contact with young people (although contacts made in street-based settings were an exception).

Homeless people, by definition a highly mobile group, are difficult to identify and contact for research purposes (Third, 2000). The problem of transience, that is, the temporary and fleeting nature of their social milieu, hampered efforts to make contact and establish rapport. This problem of transience has been noted previously by researchers seeking to recruit street samples of drug users (Dunlap et al., 1990; Lewis et al., 1992). It was also difficult, at times, to make meaningful contact with young people within some recruitment sites (particularly within emergency hostels) due to the unpredictability of their daily lives. Within other settings, space was an issue and the availability of a room for the purpose of conducting an interview was not a given by any means. Finally, there were times when young people were too drug or alcohol intoxicated to participate in the interview and, when this situation arose, the interview was postponed. The recruitment process took longer than anticipated and extended over a five-month period (September 2004-January 2005). Many of the difficulties associated with access and recruitment reflect the inherent instability of these young people's lives and the chaotic nature of the everyday worlds of a large number.

Sampling, Targeting and Selecting Research Participants

This study did not aim to generate a representative sample of young people whose experiences are generalisable to the entire homeless youth population; instead, the aim was to recruit a cohort of young people with a diverse and illustrative range of experiences of homelessness. The study targeted young people in the Dublin metropolitan district which, as outlined in the previous chapter, has recorded the highest number of homeless youth countrywide.

Young homeless people are often treated as a homogeneous group when, in reality, they have a wide range of experiences which they may articulate in a variety of ways (Hutson and Liddiard, 1994). This research aimed to capture a variable set of pathways into and through homelessness. A purposive sampling strategy (Patton, 1990) was used initially to select young people for participation. This iterative process (developing new approaches as the study progresses, in the light of information gleaned along the way) allowed the selection criteria to evolve as data collection and early analysis proceeded. During later months of the fieldwork process, purposive sampling was combined with "targeted" sampling techniques (Watters and Biernacki, 1989) to assist the achievement of variability. This technique of "targeting" particular individuals or groups for participation was informed by information gleaned from the community assessment process and by the interviewing process itself.

The recruitment strategy aimed to achieve diversity across key variables including age, gender and geographical location, and also sought variability in relation to respondents' current and past living arrangements. In other words, it was recognized that while homelessness may be a transitional status for some, it can be a more enduring or chronic condition for other youth. Whilst it was anticipated that many young people might be recruited from services based in the city-centre of Dublin, the study also targeted young people from suburban localities (e.g. Tallaght, Clondalkin, Blanchardstown) previously identified as having a homeless youth population (Focus Ireland, 1995; Perris, 1999).

Ethical Issues and Challenges

Homeless young people are an especially vulnerable group because of their age, socio-economic disadvantage and stigmatized status (Ensign, 2003). All participating young people received a detailed explanation of the purpose of the research as well as a full account of what precisely their participation involved in terms of a commitment of time and the nature and content of the interview. Assurances of confidentiality were given, including the assurance that their name would not be mentioned in any written dissemination of the research findings. However, all participants were also informed at the outset of the interview that if they disclosed information indicating they were at risk or in danger, it was the obligation of the researcher to inform an appropriate individual.

The voluntary and informed consent of each young person was obtained prior to their participation in the research. Young people over the age of 18 were in a position to give consent independently but this was clearly not the case for young people under the age of 18. Where possible, parental consent was sought but in a small number of cases this consent was not obtained.[2] In all instances, careful consideration was given to the young person's circumstances and welfare and the decision *not* to seek parental consent was taken only on the grounds that seeking such consent could potentially compromise the individual's safety (Rew et al., 2000). It is widely recognised that there are circumstances when the requirement of parental consent may not be in a young person's best interest, particularly when the research involves the participation of high-risk and multiple-problem youth

---

[2] According to Ensign (2003), the requirement for obtaining parental/custodian written consent may be waived in the case of some homeless youth because the requirement is unworkable and could potentially jeopardize their safety and well-being. A number of the young people interviewed for the purpose of this study had little or no contact with home or with their parents. Others had left home because of extremely difficult experiences, including violence and abuse. The question of parental consent for young people's participation in research is clearly important and is one which, among other issues, highlights the tension inherent in balancing the rights of adolescents and their parents (Brooks-Gunn and Rotheram-Borus, 1994). It is claimed that, by the age of 14, most adolescents are as capable as adults of making competent decisions about participation in research (Levine, 1995; Petersen and Leffert, 1995).

populations (Brooks-Gunn and Rotheram-Borus, 1994; Ensign, 2003; Meade and Slesnick, 2002). In cases where parental consent was not obtained, consent was given instead by the young person's social worker and arranged in co-operation with the manager of the setting where the young person resided.

Data Generation and Analysis

Analysis for this study was iterative and inductive (Ezzy, 2000). During the course of fieldwork, interviewers met on a regular basis to discuss emerging impressions, themes and disparities. Early interviews were transcribed, read and discussed as close as possible to the conduct of interviews, some minor adjustments being made to the interview schedule during the early weeks of data collection.

Verbatim transcripts of all 40 baseline life history interviews were prepared.

Analysis commenced with a close reading of several transcribed interviews for key themes enabling the development of a preliminary coding scheme. While some of these themes had been identified during the planning and design phase of the study, new (and often unanticipated) themes emerged both from the fieldwork experience and the interviewing process. Pattern coding (Krippendorf, 1980) facilitated the analysis of configurations of factors such as gender, age, family circumstances, geographical area of residence, and so on, enabling the identification of sequences of events such as those related to the first experience of homelessness. All interviews were coded manually in accordance with 15 separate coding categories, generated with close consideration of the study aims. However, categories were also identified on an iterative basis as revealed by the data, thereby incorporating issues and themes arising directly from the young people's life stories (Fetterman, 1989). The final stage of the process of making sense of the data centred on the clarification and integration of concepts and themes, a stage at which all of the research evidence was confronted, not just the "bits" that "fit" the analysis (Dey, 1993). Accounting for negative instances, that is, data that contradict emergent or dominant ideas and views was a core strategy used to explain evidence that both challenged and extended existing themes and arguments (Becker, 1970; 1998; Seale, 1999).

Generating a perspective on youth homelessness that reflects their experiences, views and interpretations was a primary aim of the analytic task. Constructed around young people's narratives, the findings allow a range of conceptual themes to emerge from similarities and differences in their stories. All of the quoted excerpts from full interview transcripts that are presented are as close as possible to participants' spoken words. In some cases, however, minor editing was required to make accounts more comprehensible to the reader. Each study participant was assigned a pseudonym, which is used consistently throughout the presentation of findings. In addition, all identifiers (birthplace, names of friends, family members, social workers and other professionals) have been removed from quoted excerpts as a further measure to preserve the anonymity of young people.

Conclusion

In summary, this study was designed to examine youth homelessness in Dublin using the life history interview as the core method of data collection. Efforts were made to recruit young people with a diverse and illustrative range of experiences. This was achieved through contact with professionals involved directly in the provision of services for homeless youth as well as street-based recruitment strategies. Using a pathways approach, the study aimed to gain an "insider" perspective on the homeless experience and to document young people's "journeys" into and through homelessness.

Chapter 4

BECOMING HOMELESS

This chapter examines young people's lives prior to their first experience of homelessness and documents the key pathways associated with their becoming homeless. It is important to stress at the outset that the identification of routes "into" homelessness is an enormously complex area of analysis. For example, young people differed in their ability to articulate the sequences of events leading to their homelessness. Additionally, the early age of first homeless experiences – between 12 and 14 years for a large number – points to home and family situations as key contexts for understanding how and why young people become homeless. For the vast majority, family and personal experiences prior to their homelessness were painful and some found it difficult to talk about this period of their lives in great detail. As a consequence, accounts of family life varied in terms of their level of specificity, particularly in relation to family dynamics and relationships which are, in any case, extremely personal and sensitive domains of experience. Finally, the data informing this analysis were collected from young people at only one point in time and are retrospective rather than based on contemporaneous observation and interviewing. It is important to bear these limitations in mind when approaching this analysis of pathways "into" homelessness.

The chapter begins by describing the study's sample, including the age of first homelessness, the duration of their homelessness and their living situations at the time of interview. This is followed by a discussion of some broad features of the *process of be-*

coming homeless. A detailed analysis of the dominant pathways to homelessness followed by young people is then presented.

The Study's Sample

A total of 40 young people – 23 young men and 17 young women – were interviewed for the purpose of the study. Of these, 35 were born in Ireland, two in Nigeria and the remaining three in Romania, South Africa and Bosnia, respectively (none of these young people entered Ireland as unaccompanied minors).[1] All of the young people who participated in the study were between the ages of 14 and 22 years. The average age for the total sample was 17.5 years, with young women slightly younger on average (16.5 years) than the young men (18.3 years) at the time of interview. Table 4.1 provides a more detailed breakdown of the age and gender of the study's participants.

Table 4.1: Age and Gender of Study Participants (N=40)

AGE	MALE	FEMALE	ALL
12-14 years	—	2	2
15-17 years	9	11	20
18-21 years	12	3	15
22 years	2	1	3

Half of the young people interviewed were between the ages of 15 and 17 years and a further fifteen were between 18 and 21 years. Only two young people (both young women) were 14 years or younger. This may reflect positively on preventive strategies targeting homeless or other categories of "at risk" youth. Alternatively, it may simply highlight a tendency for homelessness to remain "hidden" during the early stages and/or for young people

---

[1] This analysis does not permit an exploration of factors or circumstances that are specific to homelessness among those young people who were not born in Ireland. This is due largely to the diversity of their circumstances and experiences. Follow-up data on these young people may permit an analysis of issues specific to their homeless pathways.

not to present to services for some time subsequent to becoming homeless. Significant in this regard is that several of the study's young people spent a period of time – ranging from a few weeks to one year – moving between the street and the homes of friends or relatives before making contact with agencies or services (this issue is explored in greater detail in Chapter 5). All of the young people had been living in the Dublin metropolitan district for at least six months prior to interview. Of the 35 Irish youth in the sample, 29 had lived in suburban areas of Dublin city as children. The remaining six young people grew up in an inner-city Dublin locality or in an area adjacent to Dublin's city centre.

Age of First Homelessness

During interview, efforts were made to ascertain the age at which young people first experienced homelessness. Nine of the young men and 10 young women (almost half of the total sample) reported that their first out of home experience occurred at or under 14 years of age. An additional nine young men and three young women found themselves in a situation where they had to seek alternative accommodation to home (i.e. to the family home, the home of a relative or a care setting) at the age of 15 years. For the remainder, first homeless experiences occurred between the ages of 16 and 18 years. These figures suggest that the period of highest risk for homelessness among the group was the early to mid-teenage years.

Duration of Homelessness

The duration of young people's homelessness (Table 4.2) varied enormously, ranging from a few months to nine years.

Ten were homeless for less than one year and a further eight for a period of between one and two years. Of those remaining, 11 had been homeless for up to four years and seven for up to six years. Four young people (three of them young men) had been homeless for over six years. Young men had spent longer, on average, without stable accommodation, with 16 reporting homeless histories of three years or more compared to 6 of the participating young women.

Table 4.2: Duration of Homelessness by Gender

	Young Men (n=23)	Young Women (n=17)	All (n=40)
Under 1 year	5	5	10
1-2 years	2	6	8
3-4 years	8	3	11
5-6 years	5	2	7
6-7 years	2	1	3
> 8 years	1	0	1

Care Histories

Sixteen of the 40 young people reported a history of State care. These histories varied in terms of type and duration. Foster care was the most commonly reported placement type followed by a combination of foster and residential care placements. Three young people who did not have a history of foster or residential care as children had spent time in a special school for young offenders during their teenage years. Table 4.3 presents a breakdown of these placement types by gender.

Table 4.3: Care Placement(s) by Gender

	Young Men	Young Women	All
Foster Care Only	2	5	7
Foster and Residential Care	3	2	5
Residential Care Only	1	0	1
Special School for Young Offenders Only*	3	0	3
Total	9	7	16

*An additional three young men with a history of foster and/or residential care also spent time in one or more of the country's special schools for young offenders.

Three young people (two young men and one young woman) stated that they were taken into care as young children, at the age of 4 years or younger. A further six (four young men and two young women) were placed in care between the ages of 5 and 12 years. The remaining seven young people – including those who attended a special school for young offenders but did not have a history of either foster or residential care – had their first experience of the care system during their teenage years.

Current Living Situations

The living situations of the study's young people at the time of conducting interviews are presented on Table 4.4.

Table 4.4: Current Living Situation (N=40)

Accommodation Type	Young Men (N=23)	Young Women (N=17)	All (N=40)
Emergency/short-term residential care setting or "hostel"*	12	13	25
Longer-term residential setting or "hostel"	2	0	2
Adult hostel	2	1	3
Between "hostel" and home	1	0	1
Prison	3	0	3
Street	2	0	2
Supported/transitional housing	1	1	2
Home	0	2	2

* This broad "category" includes the Out of Hours emergency and short-term residential care settings for young people under the age of 18 years as well as a number of short-term settings for homeless youth up to the age of 21 years. See below for an explanation for the use of the term "hostel".

Before discussing the living situations presented in Table 4.4, it is important to comment on the terminology used throughout this text in reference to the accommodation types accessed by the study's young people. All of the living locations for young people under the age of 18 (including emergency or short-term accommodation) are residential care settings which are subject to Social Service Inspectorate rules and regulations. However, young people consistently referred to these residential settings as "hostels". This use of the term "hostel" by young people is significant and appears to reflect their experience of (and sensitivity to) the highly transient and frequently chaotic nature of these living situations (see later sections and Chapter 5 for further detail). In keeping with the language used by the study's respondents, this text frequently applies the term "hostel" when discussing young people's experiences of living in emergency, short or long-term residential care settings that target "out of home" youth in Dublin.[2]

Table 4.4 indicates that young people's living situations at the time of interview varied and they differed by gender. Thus, young women were far more likely than young men to have been placed in short-term accommodation on becoming, or within a relatively short time of becoming, homeless. They were also less likely to have slept rough or to have used adult hostels. Among the 23 young men interviewed, twelve had an emergency or short-term hostel placement at the time of interview, three were in prison, two were living in adult hostels, two were sleeping rough and one alternated between home and a hostel. A further two of the young men had long-term hostel placements and one lived in a transitional housing unit. Thirteen of the study's young women resided in emergency or short-term hostel accommodation; one was staying in an adult hostel and one in a transitional housing unit. A further two young women had recently moved home after a period of homelessness.[3] None of the study's young women were sleeping on the street or incarcerated at the time of interview.

[2] It is important, nonetheless, to distinguish between "hostels" or residential care settings for young people under the age of 18 years and adult homeless hostels. Chapter 1 provides detailed information on current residential provision for young homeless people up to the age of 21 years.

[3] Although not currently homeless, these young women (both 17 years old) were admitted to the study on the grounds that they had experienced homelessness in the past six months. Both had recently returned home but their living situations were relatively unstable and conditional, to some extent, on their ability to succeed within the drug treatment setting where they had recently enrolled.

At the time of interview then, 25 young people were staying in either emergency or short-term accommodation. Although emergency beds in hostels are allocated for crisis intervention purposes with the general aim of finding a more stable placement for young people within four to six months, several of the study's young people had been using this form of accommodation for relatively lengthy periods. One young woman, for example, had been living in an emergency hostel for a period of one year and a further three were living in "short-term" care settings for between one and four years. This tendency for young people to remain in short-term accommodation for prolonged periods was particularly strong among the study's young women and highlights a blurring of boundaries between the provision of emergency and long-term placements for children and young people who experience homelessness. It further raises the question of whether emergency/crisis placements are appropriate settings for vulnerable young people in the medium to long term.

Becoming Homeless

Young people did not suddenly become homeless; rather the process can be traced to childhood which, for the vast majority, was characterised by difficult life experiences related to one or more of the following: parental illness or death, family conflict, parental drug or alcohol abuse, school difficulties, and/or experiences of violence or abuse. This section provides an overview of the dominant themes to emerge from young people's accounts of their early life experiences before proceeding to document the three pathways "into" homelessness to emerge from a detailed analysis of their life stories.

As children, the vast majority lived in poor neighbourhoods and many accounts of childhood memories referenced scenes of hardship linked to household instability, poverty and difficult life events. Personal bereavement and family illness were also commonly reported by young people. The death of a parent had a dramatic negative impact on those who lost a mother or father at a young age and several stated that they continued to struggle to come to terms with this loss. Five of the young men and two of the young women lost a parent during childhood and an additional two young people reported the death of a sibling in tragic circumstances. The death of a loved one is a critical life event for any child. Derek told how his problems began following his mother's death when he was thirteen years old.

> *My life was (pause) ... it was grand 'till me ma died, do you know what I mean. And after that it just went all down hill like, and then on to the drugs. Then after that I got into robbing cars and then in and out of prison. And I've been living rough on the street. — Derek (22)*

Other forms of reported childhood disruption centred on difficult family dynamics and relationships. Young people frequently reported crises with one or both parents, ranging from arguments or disputes to physical violence. Household disagreements varied in nature and severity and were related, in some cases, to young people's own behaviour (e.g. staying out late, drinking, drug-taking and/or getting into trouble with teachers or the police). Others arose from family instability or change: for example, some young people described deteriorating relationships with their parents linked to the presence of a stepparent (most often a stepfather). Where tensions existed between young people and a parent(s), they typically escalated during early adolescence.

At the more severe end of home-based crises, the experience of physical violence was reported. Seven of the young people reported an episode or prolonged period of physical abuse by a parent or caregiver (stepparent or aunt) and a further four witnessed violence against a family member (mother or siblings) in their homes during childhood. James attributed his homelessness to his fear of returning home because of the threat of physical violence.

> *I'm living on the streets. Why I can't go home is because I keep getting beat up an' all. Went to school about two year ago and I don't go to school any more. — James (18)*

An additional three young people (one young man and two young women) reported sexual abuse during childhood. The perpetrator of abuse was a family member in two cases and a stepfather in the third. When asked about growing up, Shane, who was a victim of sexual abuse, told how he never really had "a life" as a child.

> *Well my life was brutal like, you know. My father abused me. I'm gay, my mother will tell you that. He (father) raped me when I was younger so like, you know, I've had a brutal life, he beat me up. He's dead now you know but I've had a brutal life ... I didn't really have a life as a child, you know. — Shane (22)*

A total of eleven (seven young men and four young women) reported that a parent, and in three cases both parents, had an alcohol problem. In addition, five (four young men and one young woman) reported that one parent had a drug problem. Parental alcohol or drug problems therefore affected 40 per cent of the young people interviewed, with the negative impact of drug or alcohol abuse ranging from neglect, household friction and, in fewer cases, to domestic violence. The life stories of the majority of the young people, in fact, suggest multiple family problems which in turn triggered a variety of tensions and difficulties. Joe, who had been homeless since the age of 15, talked about a range of home-based problems.

> *I've a father that's going through a drink, alcohol problem, you know what I mean. I've a mother that's dying of cancer. I've a bleedin', I've a brother that's locked up, I've a sister that has two kids, she's only seventeen. It's a rough life, ya know what I mean. — Joe (19)*

The anxiety arising from these problems was immense for young people; it impacted seriously on their quality of life as children and placed an enormous strain on their relationships with their parent(s). Unsurprisingly, perhaps, in light of such adversity, schooling was seriously disrupted and many stopped attending at an early age. Eighteen of the study's young men (78 per cent) left school at or before the age of 15 and only two had completed any Junior Certificate examinations. Young women reported longer periods in education and, at the time of interview, eleven were attending school. They were also far more likely to have completed some examination subjects at Junior Certificate level. The school histories of the young people therefore suggest that young men were more disadvantaged than their female counterparts in terms of their educational status and achievements.

Schooling suffered for young people not only because of the instability of their living situations but, also, because many failed to cope with the demands of the school environment. For many, educational experiences were dominated by trouble with teachers as well as by suspensions or extended periods out of school following a move to a new locality. Practically all who left school at or before the age of 15 years had no formal educational qualifications. Of significance also is that three of the young people reported that they had learning difficulties as children. One was currently attending, and a further two had formerly attended, a school for children with special educational needs. Conor, who had been homeless since the age of 16 and now lived in emergency/crisis accommodation targeting 16-21 year olds, described his school history.

> [What about school then? When did you finish school?]

> I finished school when I was thirteen. First year I made it, I was in the special school from six to eleven because I got expelled out of my first school in first class so they put me there for kids with behavioural problems and disabilities, they can't learn or whatever. So I was there for a good few years. Didn't get much in there, you know. — Conor (19)

To summarise, the vast majority of the study's young people had suffered multiple forms of childhood adversity whether through economic hardship, neglect, inadequate or inconsistent care or abuse. Most had experienced high levels of stress as children linked to instability, tension or conflict within their homes. To a large extent, their childhoods were characterised by a series of struggles and disappointments that placed them at risk for a range of problems upon entering their teenage years.

Pathways "Into" Homelessness

As highlighted in Chapter 2, this research adopts a pathways approach to youth homelessness. This analysis of pathways or routes into homelessness focuses primarily on the identification of typologies of the events and circumstances preceding young people's first out of home experience. On this basis, three major pathways were identified from the biographical narratives of the forty young people interviewed.

While these pathways are discrete, there is considerable overlap between them and, as "categories", they are neither fixed nor impermeable. For example, practically all of the young people came from low-income backgrounds and a large majority experienced difficulties during childhood. As discussed, most reported disruptions and discontinuities of various kinds linked to home-based difficulties and many indicated that their relationships with parents or carers became progressively fraught during their teenage years. Additionally, practically all of the young people reported inconsistent schooling and there were many reports of early drug experimentation. It is important to bear these similarities in mind and to avoid the assumption that there is a simple "fit" between individual experiences of becoming homeless and the three pathways identified below.

Pathway 1: Care History

As noted earlier in the chapter, sixteen of the forty young people reported a history of State care. Of this group, seven had lived in foster care for either a short or long period, five had lived in a combination of foster and residential placements and one in a residential children's home. Of the thirteen who lived in foster or residential care, two had also spent time in one of the country's five special residential schools for young offenders. An additional three young people (all young men) who did not report a history of foster or residential care as children had spent time in a special school for young offenders during their early to mid-teenage years.

Although it is widely acknowledged in Ireland that a history of State care creates vulnerability to housing instability and homelessness during adolescence and in later life (see Chapters 1 and 2), relatively little is known about how young people frame the transition from care to homelessness. This leaves a gap in our understanding of how histories of care create vulnerability to homelessness.

Young people's life histories reveal quite diverse experiences of care. For example, among the nine respondents who reported a history of foster care, three had been in care since infancy or early childhood (under five years). The remaining six moved from home to a care setting in later childhood (between the age of eight and twelve years). The experience of living in care impacted on young people differently depending on the duration of their care histories and their understanding of how and why they were placed there. A number, for example, appeared not to know why they had been placed in care, while others were unsure about the timing of their first care placement: "I think I was four. My aunty told me that I was collected at the petrol station down the road from my nanny's house". Those young people who explained the circumstances surrounding their placement in care invariably made reference to family problems and a number recalled frequent moves from one living situation to another during early childhood. Melissa's account illustrates the kinds of home-based instabilities that typically preceded early care placements.

> I was born in (a city-centre) hospital and then I was living with me ma and me nanny in the flats up there in (city-centre street) 'till I was about, I was around four. And then I kept moving back and forth to my other nanny and granddad down in (area adjacent to city centre) and I always moved up and back down. And then I was living in me nannies and then I got taken into care from there. I don't know where I was first but I was in eight foster families altogether.

[So you started off living …?]

With my ma and my nanny, yeah. But there was loads of others there, my aunties and cousins living in the same flat and there was only two bedrooms.

[What's your first memory of living away from your family?]

I can just remember one of the foster families I was with, that's the only foster family I can remember. Like I was small, I don't even know why I moved from there (first foster home) but I was a bit wild. Me da an' all told me that I was very bold when I was small and I think that's the reason why I was taken out. —
Melissa (14)

Upon entering foster care, none of the young people found a stable home environment. Instead, they embarked on a cycle of movement between successive foster families, returning periodically, in some cases, to the family home or the home of a relative. Melissa ran away from several foster placements and, at the age of 10, lived with a member of her extended family for a period of two years.

Most of the families I was with were in (south Dublin suburban area) and (another south Dublin suburban area) and I liked a few of them. And there was one I liked in particular but I moved from there too because I kept running away. And then I moved to this house … it was like a foster family but I wasn't meant to be there long term, I was only meant to stay there say a few months. Then I got in contact with my aunty and after that I went to live with her. I was about 10 then. — Melissa (14)

For some, new placements or living arrangements brought further instability. Melissa went on to describe the period she spent living with her aunt:

When I was living with her (aunt) I always got locked out of the house, like she'd just give me money and tell me to go off for the day and, "don't come back 'till late". And she hit me once with a runner across the face and stuff, and I just, I hated it then and she

*was always drinking and stuff. She was always in the pub and I'd
be left out in the lashings of rain and stuff.*

*[So what comes to mind when you think of living with your
auntie?]*

*Just being left outside. It was good because, in a way you were al-
lowed to do what you want. But that's not like good at all, if
you're just given money and told to go off for the day you feel
that no one even minds you or anything …*

Constant changes in their living arrangements produced exceptional vulnerability in these young people as children, as did their
separation from their parent(s) and siblings. At the age of 13,
Melissa was placed with a new foster family and lived a considerable distance from Dublin city.

*I didn't get to see me family much when I was in foster homes up
here (in Dublin) but like it was worse when I was down there because I used to go to me nanny's every weekend and then I
couldn't. I saw my ma like every Christmas and I saw all me
aunties and cousins. That was just it, at Christmas only and I
never saw me da … I just kept running away (from foster care)
until they got the message.*

This foster placement was again unsuccessful and, at this juncture, Melissa presented herself voluntarily at a local Garda station
and requested alternative accommodation. She was subsequently
placed in emergency short-term "out of home" accommodation in
Dublin city and had been living in this setting for a period of four
months at the time of interview.

In general, the life stories of those young people who lived in
successive care settings described difficult family dynamics. Their
separation from their parent(s) and siblings was a major source of
distress. Fergal, who was placed in care at the age of 12, expressed
deep resentment towards the agencies of the State, which he held
responsible for his separation from his siblings.

> *I only agreed to go into care if I could be put with me family (sib-*
> *lings) and they said they would put us with a family, all together*
> *or in a home. Me like a dope, "Yeah, yeah", and got into the van.*
> *They brought me in to a bleedin', a place out in (south Dublin*
> *suburb). And when I sat down, "We need to talk to you … there*
> *wasn't a big enough family to take all your family, all your family*
> *are split up, they're all separated". I snapped, I did. I was only in*
> *the gaff two nights and I legged it (absconded). Dirty scum bags.*
> *Eastern Health board, social workers the lot. Think you're great;*
> *they're fucking making it worse. Scum bags. I don't like them. —*
> *Fergal (18)*

Placement breakdown was preceded in some cases by violations of household rules and, in others, by the young person abscond-ing from care. Most expressed dissatisfaction with their place-ments and typical accounts strongly suggest a perceived need to escape from these settings. Running away from care created prob-lems at all ages but, in particular, upon entering their teenage years. A number of young men became involved in offending be-haviour at an early age, triggering a period of consecutive place-ments in care institutions for young offenders. Ronan is one such young person:

> *Me ma got cancer and she died from it so we all got put into fos-*
> *ter families … that was it and I went through voluntary care*
> *homes, about twelve foster homes I went through, em, about eight*
> *years ago. Yeah, about twelve different houses. Then I was put in*
> *St. Michael's (remand and assessment unit) for six months when*
> *I was only twelve or something. — Ronan (17)*

A considerable number also started to engage in regular drinking and drug use during early adolescence and this period sometimes marked the onset of a drug "career" that would later exacerbate the challenge of finding a stable living situation.

> *Well I was in foster care since I was one, you know, since I was a*
> *kid. All four of us, there was me and my two brothers and my sis-*
> *ter got put in another foster care. I went to (suburban Dublin lo-*
> *cality) with me sister and me brothers went to (other suburban*

> *locality). So we were sort of together, you know what I mean, me*
> *with me sister and me other brothers together. And we used to go*
> *on access visits every month. But then when I was 13 I started*
> *hanging around with older lads and smoking hash, and just, just*
> *acting the ball. I left school, was robbin' on me foster parents, and*
> *it all just built up and they had to throw me out, you know. I un-*
> *derstand that they had to throw me out, 'cos there's their other*
> *kids as well, you know, that they're bringing in fostering like. So*
> *they had to throw me out. Yeah, I was 13, and I was homeless*
> *then ... — Paul (19)*

While placement breakdown was associated with a range of circumstances and motivations, few left on the spur of the moment.
Rather, they absconded or, in some cases, orchestrated their removal from care in response to a felt need to escape. In this sense,
their homelessness arose out of their inability to cope with un-
happiness and crisis in their lives.

To summarise, the childhoods of those young people who reported a history of State care were characterised by short or prolonged periods of separation from family and multiple care
placements, leading to a high level of disruption to their lives.
Successive care placements broke down for a range of complex
reasons. Most of the young people failed to integrate and a number appeared to reject the very notion of doing so. Relatively isolated and already socially marginalised through their poverty and
social disadvantage, young men, in particular, often looked for
alternative sources of support and several developed peer associations that exposed them to drug use and criminal activity. For
both young men and women, the anxiety arising from successive
failed placements, coupled with their lack of contact with a nur-
turing home environment, placed them at high risk of homelessness and a range of potentially damaging behaviour including
early alcohol and drug use.

Pathway 2: Household Instability and Family Conflict
As documented, many who reported a history of State care experienced some form of family instability during childhood or

early adolescence which led to their placement in care, either voluntarily or under a care order for their own protection. Many who did not report a history of State care also described family problems and, for a total of 22 of the young people interviewed, household instability and family conflict emerged as factors precipitating homelessness. The variety and number of family difficulties varied, ranging from one to multiple disruptions to family life and relationships. The aim here is to explore the family dynamics that worked to push young people out of home.

A considerable number of young people experienced a succession of moves from various housing locations and living situations as children, suggesting a high level of household instability. In some cases, this pattern of unstable housing – whether due to eviction or accidents (often a fire) in the home – overlapped with reports of family homelessness.

[So you moved a lot?]

Through me life, yeah.

[What was it like for you when you were moving?]

Bad enough. Like me ma'd be drunk some nights and like me step-da, the name callin' an' all that. And she'd pack the bags and runnin' down the road, she'd be drunk and roaring. I was only a kid, eight or nine like, gettin' dragged into a hostel. It was like that most of me young life, in hostels. Like, we'd be livin' in houses, yeah, but when me sisters moved out (of the family home) it just went mad, it did. — Colm (20)

For those who reported household instability of this kind, homelessness was often preceded by periods spent with other family members or friends. Lisa's story usefully illustrates the complex sequence of events that led to her presenting to a Garda station to access the Out of Hours Service for the first time at the age of fourteen.

We moved around a lot and we never lived in a house for more than three years. And then when I got older we would move every year. And we never had a choice, we just had to move. And then when I got to about 11 or 12 we (pause) … moved again. It was alright at home but it was hard.

[Can you tell me some more about moving?]

Yeah. It was first we lived somewhere around town and then we went to (North Dublin suburb) and (other North Dublin suburb), I think. And then we moved to Kildare and then to Dundalk and then Lusk and then Meath and then Donameade and then back into town … Dundalk was the longest place we ever lived; that was about three years. I was about 10 'till about 13. And we stayed in a family hostel when we moved from Dundalk and we were waiting for a house. We had to wait.[4] — Lisa (15)

Frequent and unexpected moves such as those recounted above proved highly disruptive. Lisa went on to explain the negative impact of moving house on her friendships.

[What would you say was the hardest thing about all the moving?]

Leaving your friends behind and getting on with your life and just starting up all over. After a while I just got sick of it. Like sometimes, when I was about 12, I did go out and look for friends but then one day I got fed up and then I bumped into this girl and just started talking and stuff and we became good friends.

[So you stopped trying to make friends?]

Yeah, I was sick of it.

Sometimes opting to stay with extended family members during these periods, she continues:

I would go down to my Auntie and down to my cousin and then I would stay with them. I didn't like going back to the hostel so I would stay with my cousins.

---

[4] All of the place names in this narrative have been altered.

Having lived for only a relatively short period with her aunt she was placed with a foster family. This care placement subsequently broke down due to the illness of her foster mother. Lisa described how her placement in emergency hostel accommodation came about:

> [*Did you go to the Out of Hours?*]
>
> *Yeah. I went to the guards ... waited then for about an hour and they brought me here (hostel).*
>
> [*So how did you find out about the Out of Hours?*]
>
> *My foster mum took me. She was sick, she got cancer. She waited with me for a while and then she had to go. So after that I waited on my own.*
>
> [*And did you consider contacting your mum or dad at that stage?*]
>
> *No. I did not want to have anything to do with them.*

Young people who experienced this kind of instability sometimes harboured strong resentment towards their parents. Lisa's relationship with both parents had deteriorated over several years and she attributed her move out of home to a particularly distressing argument with her father. At the time of interview, she had been living in emergency hostel accommodation for seven months and had had no contact with her parents since the time she left home.

> [*You have not seen your parents. Can I ask you what led to that?*]
>
> *It was just, we had a really bad fight one night and they said things and it was just from there on [...] It was not a normal fight. It was just very, just it was more like (pause) ... we said things that people do not say to each other in their whole life (pause) ... I can't forgive him (father). And I don't expect him to forgive me.*

There were several dimensions to the family problems recounted. In general, these difficulties had been ongoing for several years, even if a specific experience or event provided the "trigger" for the young person's move out of home. For young women, in particular, a pattern of living for periods with friends or members of their extended family sometimes followed. Amy's story further illustrates the tendency for young women to be cared for by family members or friends prior to their first experience of hostel life:

> *The reason like I'm here (in a hostel) like was because me ma was a drinker like and her and me da used to always be arguing like, they used to always be arguing. This night like me da was in the pub and me ma was like drinking and the house went on fire and after that like I was staying with friends. And then I moved in like with me cousin, and like it wasn't working out. Then I moved in with me ma's friend and that wasn't working out like either. And then I just moved here (hostel) like. — Amy (15)*

While the nature and sources of home-based difficulties varied, they worked – in various combinations and over varying lengths of time – to push young people out of their homes. Wayne, for example, described his first out of home experience:

> *I remember, I can remember as far back when I was about six, we moved from (suburban Dublin area) down to (another suburban area) and I went to school an' all and everything was grand. And then after me Junior Cert I left, you know what I mean. I left school and I became a tiler, a floor and wall tiler. And then when I was fifteen then like there was a bit of a row in the family and me mother and father split up so I went to live with me da and like it was workin' out for a while. But then like in 1999, like he hung himself. So I had to go and live in me ma's and I started usin' drugs then. And another death then came in the family in 2000 and I was strung out by then. And then like me ma, like I didn't get thrown out this time, I left ... I would have been sleepin' in cars, sleepin' here, there and everywhere or sleepin' in me uncle's garage, do you know what I mean. — Wayne (21)*

Conflict arising from the presence of a stepparent was reported by a number. Young people who entered into a reconstituted family generally described a tense or extremely difficult relationship with a parent's new partner (most frequently, a stepfather). Accounts of negative relationships with a step parent were more common among the study's young men, who almost always reported tremendous friction and conflict with their step fathers. For Brendan, running away was the solution to a home situation that became increasingly difficult.

> *He's (stepfather) gone now; she's (mum) not with him any more. He'd be the cause of all this shit now that's after happening to me like running out of the house, not staying in the house. I ran out of there because I didn't like him [...] It wasn't good at all, it wasn't. He used to be fighting with me ma and I'd get involved then. He'd batter me and he was a big bloke, you know what I mean. So I sort of said, "Fuck her if she wants to stay with him, fuck it, I'm not staying here". She'd always just stay with him so I used to just go into town, stay in the hostels and that [...] I think that the thing that messed me up was the violence at home that I kept running away from, that's what. — Brendan (17)*

Gavin was also physically assaulted by his stepfather and attributed his homelessness directly to his need to escape from a violent man who also drank heavily.

> *Well I'm on the streets about six, seven months. I used to get beatings at home and all by my stepfather and all. My real father is dead and, my mother, she's an alcoholic and she always drinks and all. And any time she gets drunk an' all and he gets drunk he always beats me up. And that's how I ended up being on the streets. Came into town and stayed on the streets, going into hostels, shit like that and all, you know what I mean. — Gavin (15)*

As previously stated, parental drinking frequently played a role in undermining the stability of young people's lives. Heavy drinking by a parent or stepparent created stress for all members of the household and invariably led to severe disruption to family life and relationships.

> *In 1999, during that year, my father lost his job and he became heavily dependent on alcohol. He used to take what he called days off ... his days off consisted of going down to the pub and getting very, very drunk at which stage I was taking care of my dad, taking care of my brother, making sure that after he got home he got fed. — Neil (20)*

Finally, a number of young people described inconsistent parenting and unfair treatment by a parent(s), including any or all of the following: conditional support and love, getting blamed wrongly, and unequal treatment of siblings by a parent or stepparent. In some cases, this behaviour was linked to heavy drinking on the part of a parent or carer. Lyndsey, who left home voluntarily at the age of 14 having endured physical abuse and punishment, described her home situation:

> *Even when I was younger like, if money went missing or something she'd be blaming the whole lot of us, she used to kill the whole lot of us. The last time money got taken, it was out of the banking machine. She couldn't blame me, no way could she blame it on me because I don't know how to use the bank machine ... But she picks on me. One day I was up making me lunch for school and she came in and just hit me. And me brother just turned around and said, "don't take that". John (brother) gives her a lot of cheek and stuff ... But she was drunk at the time. — Lyndsey (15)*

Lyndsey subsequently complained to her social worker and was placed in city-centre emergency accommodation. While young men who were victims of abuse within their homes tended to respond by leaving or running away, young women frequently made an official complaint to a social worker or teacher, as Jacinta's story further illustrates:

> *I was at school one day and the night before I took my dad's car keys and hid them and me ma came into the school and she said,*

"I'm bringing you home, your uncle is in the car". And I shouted
in front of all my class to her and said, "Listen, I'm fed up of you
always hitting me, I'm not going home with you". And then the
teacher came in and she told me ma to go home and I sat in the of-
fice for the rest of the day and social workers came in. — Jacinta
(16)

An absence of emotional support, coupled with neglect and/or
abuse and violence in some cases, dominated these stories. Following years of difficult, and sometimes traumatic, experiences
many felt that they had no option but to leave home on reaching
their teenage years.

Pathway 3: Negative Peer Associations and "Problem" Behaviour

Nine young people (five young men and four young women) described types or patterns of behaviour that led to tensions and
conflicts in their homes or care settings. For these young people,
the period spanning the early to mid-teenage years saw their progressive affiliation with social settings and groups that exposed
them to drinking, drug use and other "risky" activities. As time
progressed, their involvement in one or more aspects of such behaviour gave rise to problems at home and brought a number into
contact with the police. Since the precise origin of this conduct is
difficult to trace on the basis of retrospective accounts, the exploration of this third pathway focuses primarily on the explanations
young people advanced for their situations.

Some of these young people described their homelessness in
terms of past "mistakes". Luke, for example, who experienced
homelessness for the first time at the age of 15, attributed it to his
drug use and aggressive behaviour as a young teenager.

[Just in relation to the situation you're in now?]

How would I describe it?

[Yeah]

I'd say I've made a few mistakes in life. It's more or less the reason I'm living the way I am now. When I started off when I was younger, when I was twelve I started using deodorants, you know, sniffing deodorants and I got a bad temper and I just sort of got very aggressive and had problems at home. And I left (pause) … taking drugs, it never works. — Luke (18)

Luke was staying in emergency hostel accommodation at the time of interview. He left school at the age of 16 and had been "kicked out" of home on a number of occasions prior to making contact with the Out of Hours Service. During that time, he either slept rough or negotiated a night or more in the home of a friend:

… like I was kicked out of home twice and I got back in and I was kicked out then after that and I'm still out. But the first time I got kicked out I was sleeping rough. I got back home the next week then 'cause I was just gettin' into too much trouble. Ya see me ma found out through me uncle that I was sleepin' in a car so she took me back.

[What sort of trouble?]

Just like robbin', shopliftin'. But then I didn't get caught shopliftin' but like, you know, I was robbin' food out of the shops and just people seen me and they'd ring me ma.

[So you were sleeping rough, then you went back home and then you were sort of kicked out again then?]

Yeah, kicked out again but I had somewhere to go, I was sleepin' in me friend's house.

Allowed to return home initially, Luke was asked to leave a short time later and subsequently spent several months alternating between sleeping rough and staying with friends in his local area. This period saw him developing close associations with a network of peers who were involved in drug use and criminal activity. A number of other young men described a similar pattern of behaviour but, unlike Luke, they also referred to various tensions and problems within their own homes. This is how Seán talked about his family which consisted of mother, father and one sister:

Yeah, well my mother, father, a sister and myself. Eh, my father is an alcoholic and ... (pause) I never got much attention from me father because he was more interested in drinking and (pause)... he sort of mis- (pause), yeah he did mistreat me and my mother in ways, not sexually now but like just in being very ignorant and arrogant to her, you know. So I looked for attention in older lads which didn't work but they did have, eh, loads of girlfriends and loads of cars, loads of money and, you know, I wanted to be one of them. Like I would be coming home at 8 o'clock and 9 o'clock in the morning after being out all night and seeing people going to work saying, "Jesus aren't they the wasters like, going to work for what I am earning in a night like", you know that sort of way. I was about 14, 15 and I suppose I was looking up to an older crowd and getting a name for myself. And when I say a name for myself, it was sort of like, "Oh he is wild like, he is more wilder beyond his years; he is more tuned in than the average like 16 or 17 year old". — Seán (21)

Seeking the attention and affirmation not available to him at home, Seán quickly developed a reputation as a young man older and wiser than his years. By mid-adolescence he had experimented with a range of drugs.

And so I started, well the first drug I would have done would have been hash when I was 11 or 12, cannabis, smoking joints with me mates and, eh, going to school and at lunch time then going out and having joints and that. That was 'til about 14 or 15 and I started doing Es then, ecstasy. And then I started taking heroin about six (pause) ... six years ago.

Declan was also kicked out of home during his teenage years:

Like, I've being homeless since I was 14 years of age, you know, and have been in and out of different places. Yeah, kicked out of home, living in hostels. Now this hostel is where I am at the moment.

He went on to explain how his homelessness and other problems came about:

> *I used to live with me grandad when I was a kid. He died in 1996.*
> *After that, I don't really know, I just started getting into trouble.*
> *I left school. Like I never used to get into trouble, I never thought*
> *I would be in trouble, but however. I wouldn't blame it on anyone*
> *but, I would blame it, like the people I used to hang around with*
> *used to take drugs, smoking hash, drinking a lot and staying out.*
> *That's the real reason why I used to stay out, you know what I*
> *mean. That's why I started getting kicked out. — Declan (19)*

While identifying his grandfather's death as an event that triggered change in his life, he also described conflict between his parents. These home-based problems and difficulties appeared to push him further towards unconventional activities and, by mid-adolescence, he had grown accustomed to "staying out", partly due to dread and partly out of fear of returning home.

> *There was too much fighting going on in me house with me ma*
> *and da, they were too strict, fighting every single day. I couldn't*
> *handle it, do you know what I mean. Anytime they were fighting,*
> *either I get the blame or someone else gets the blame. Do you*
> *know what I mean? It couldn't be proper like, it couldn't, they*
> *couldn't like be nice to anyone. They were just fighting, fighting,*
> *fighting for the slightest stupid thing that ever happens, you*
> *know. So I got sick and tired of it so I started saying, "No". And*
> *then I was afraid to go home 'cos I knew what would have hap-*
> *pened. So I actually started staying out and I started getting used*
> *to it. I just got into the habit of staying out all the time, do you*
> *know what I mean. — Declan (19)*

Among the specific events or "triggers" reported by young people, the death or serious illness of a family member featured in their stories of life prior to becoming homeless. Julian told how the death of his mother turned his life around.

> *My life was, it was going grand 'til me ma died, do you know*
> *what I mean and after that it just went all downhill like and on to*

the drugs and then after that I went in to robbing cars, you know what I mean, and then in and out of prison, and I've been living rough on the street ... Like she was the head of the house like and when the head goes the neck goes, you know what I mean ... I was thirteen years of age. — Julian (22)

Although the focus so far has been on the "problem behaviour" of young men, a number of young women also identified their own behaviour during early adolescence as a factor leading to family tensions of various kinds and, later, to their first out-of-home experience. While young men were generally told to leave – usually expressed as, "I was thrown out" or "I was kicked out" – young women tended to leave voluntarily. Some did state that their parent(s) threatened to evict them from the family home, but this was not generally realized, and two of the young women described patterns of running away from home during their early teenage years. For a considerable number, a family death once again emerged as an event which appeared to "trigger" a downward spiral of events and behaviour. Sarah explained:

My granddad died when I was 15 and I was very close to me granddad ... I loved my granddad to bits like and he died of cancer. And when he died that's when I started kind of, you know kind of going, running away and rebelling against my parents. I had a great up-bringing, my mam and dad were always there for me, we got what we needed, you know, when we were growing up. So when he died I took it very hard and I started going out with me friends and drinking and then I met this bloke and we started hanging around (in an area) that would have been a lot rougher than where we were from. — Sarah (22)

Sarah quickly found herself in a relationship with a young man and, following a period of "hanging out" with friends in the city-centre, she "ran away" with her boyfriend.

I started doing drugs, I was hanging around in town. I started off with taking, you know, ecstasy and fucking coke, and I met this gang that were taking heroin so I decided to take heroin ... So I started going out with a bloke and, at the time, I had absolutely no idea that he was on heroin. I was very young and naïve at the time. So that relationship progressed and we kind of, we started being with each other and we decided like, "Ah fuck it", we thought, "We'll run away to England". He wasn't running away, he was a lot older, well I was 15, 16, he would have been 18, 19. So we said we'd go to England.

Having returned to Ireland following a difficult period with little money and no stable accommodation, she subsequently spent a number of months moving between home and temporary living situations (friends, squats). However, as her drug use escalated, she stopped returning home and alternated between the street and rented accommodation for several months. Her story of early drug involvement, coupled with early entry into a relationship with an older man, mirrored a small number of others. Emma also told about a combination of drugs and peers and a relationship she grew to depend on for a daily supply of heroin:

So then I was with a fella; he was making the money, do you know what I mean, to buy heroin like, and I was kind of depending on him all the time like. So I was with him all the time, know what I mean. And then I just started staying out like, he started making money at night time. And I didn't want to tell me family that I was on it (heroin) and so I started, you know, staying out on weekends and that. I'd stay out three nights a week, you know. And me ma would be wondering and you know stuff like this. But I'd be trying to make up excuses, trying not to tell her like what I was doing. But anyway, then me ma started getting serious about it like, and started, you know saying, "What are you doing?", kind of thing like. And one week I stayed out and then when I went home me ma says, "You're not going out again". But I needed heroin so I sort of ran out and when I got into town I said to me fella, "I'm not going home again, like fuck them now", you know. And then I just ended up being homeless. — Emma (17)

The stories of the young people who described a pathway "into" homelessness linked to their own "problem" behaviour almost always referenced events and home-based crises that created vulnerabilities in them as children. Most, for example, experienced a significant traumatic life event – frequently a death – and this was often accompanied with problems and conflict in the family home. Thus, although these young people talked at length about their own "bad" behaviour, there was also evidence of problems that impacted on them as children and on their ability to cope with daily life as teenagers. Their accounts point to an absence of structures and supports that might have acted to protect them from seeking attention from sources and people who led them further down a path of harmful and damaging behaviour.

Conclusion

As outlined in Chapter 2, the causes of homelessness are best understood in terms of the interaction of structural (macro-level) and individual (micro-level) factors. The young people interviewed for the purpose of this study are among the most marginalised in Irish society: they come from poor families and they grew up in poor neighbourhoods; their educational attainments are low and a large number experienced some form of housing instability as children. Poverty contributes to pathways into homelessness in a number of ways and increases the likelihood of overcrowding, household stress, friction and break-up. Although parents' economic status may not affect the age of leaving home (Jones, 1995), it does affect the reasons for doing so. Both economic and personal stresses on parents have a follow-on impact on all family members and may culminate in premature home-leaving.

The connotations of "leaving home" are of a young person making a conscious decision to embark on a relatively autonomous lifestyle as a young adult. However, for the young people in this study, leaving home was neither an active nor a positive life event. None left home because they were ready to do so and, almost without exception, they had difficult childhoods. These findings support those documented in previous research and demonstrate that young homeless people do not leave home voluntarily (Stockley et al., 1993; Fitzpatrick, 2000). Many of the young people interviewed perceived themselves to be unsafe or unwanted at home and the origins of the problems of a large number, including their homelessness, can be seen as a continuation of disruption and problems that commenced long before their first contact with homeless services. The high number with prior experiences of living in care settings is consistent with previous Irish and international research which has identified a care history as a risk factor for homelessness (Kelleher et al., 2000; Perris, 1999; Randall and Brown, 1999).

The vast majority of young people narrated a series of deprivations and losses regarding housing, caregivers and school. Although the sources and severity of home-based difficulties varied, family conflict emerged as a unifying theme across all of the pathways into homelessness. A large number also experienced a misuse of parental or carer power by some combination of emotional, physical or sexual abuse within their families and violence emerged as a factor in many accounts of leaving home. It was not the only factor, however: parental alcohol or drug abuse was also identified by young people as a source of stress within their homes. Caution must be exercised, nonetheless, in attributing "blame" for young people's homelessness to their homes, their parent(s) or caregivers. Young people, in fact, often indicated that their parents experienced financial hardship and that they were themselves socially isolated and/or victims of violence or emotional abuse.

Although each of the young people recounted a unique story, many of the stories told had the common theme of gradual or sudden dislocation. By the time young people found themselves out of home for the first time, their experiences of a number of key institutions, including the family, school, State care or detention, had been overwhelmingly negative. At a relatively early age, a large number were therefore living outside, or marginal to, the structures that play a critical role in preparing young people for the transition to adulthood.

Chapter 5

THE HOMELESS EXPERIENCE

This chapter presents a picture of what is a highly diverse "out of home" experience and starts the work of tracing young people's pathways through homelessness. It opens by examining their first nights out of home, documenting a number of early patterns and trajectories associated with the initial weeks and months of homelessness. Following this, their experiences of living in a range of accommodation types are examined in some detail. With dislocation emerging as a core theme permeating their accounts, the findings highlight the negative impact of the residential displacement associated with becoming homeless.

The First Night Out of Home

Young people's recollections of their first nights away from home almost always referenced feelings of anxiety, confusion and apprehension. These emotions were especially intense for rough sleepers, who invariably spoke of fear, physical discomfort and loneliness. Several also described a sense of powerlessness linked to feelings of rejection and social isolation. Paul was 13-years-old when he first left home and slept rough in his neighbourhood:

> *That night I slept in, you see, my house is there and then the neighbour's house was at the back of mine. And across from his house was a field and bushes. I stayed in there, I did. I was walking up the road, you know. First I was walking around for ages and I had the intention to sleep out but I was walking by a skip and found a mattress. So I just dragged that over and carpet an'*

*all, put that over me. I had a phone an' I was talking to (pause)
.... I had a girlfriend at the time. I was talking to her, was crying,
ya know, all night I was. And when I went back round to me gaff
(house) to get me clothes, I was bleedin' roaring crying. I couldn't
hack it, I couldn't (laugh). But I had to, yeah, it was bad it was,
bad knowing that like, that was it, "I'm fucked like", know what I
mean, so that was rough enough yeah. — Paul (19)*

Other accounts focused on the experience of presenting at a Garda
station. Some of these young people (although by no means all)
had had no previous contact with the Gardaí. Derek appeared to
have little understanding of what was happening when he first
presented at a Garda station at the age of 14:

*My mother brought me to the social worker ... and she said, "I
don't want him, he's not my son". And I felt very upset and I went
out looking for her and I couldn't find her. So they told me to hand
myself in as homeless and they would put me through the Out of
Hours. So I was waiting from 4 o'clock to 12 o'clock for someone to
come out (to the Garda station) and pick me up. And when someone came out, we were still in the Garda station because he (the social worker) had to make phone calls to see where I could go and
then they just found an emergency bed for me. — Derek (15)*

For those who had endured a particularly traumatic event prior to
leaving home for the first time, the experience was even more distressing:

*Me ma beat me up and I walked up the road to the Garda station.
I was shittin' it. I didn't know what was happening. Me nose was
broken and I had a black eye. — Rachel (15)*

Irrespective of when precisely they accessed hostel accommodation, first nights for young people in these settings were anxious
ones. As newcomers to the "scene", they entered into unknown
territory with no notion of what the future held. Most depictions
of the experience referenced fear and an overwhelming sense of
uncertainty. Neil, Roisín and Melissa all described how they felt:

I can honestly say it was probably one of the scariest nights I've had. I was in a new place with none of my friends, none of my family, I didn't know what was happening. And, as I say, the one thing I was mainly worried about was what the hell was going to happen because I don't like things I don't know ... When I moved into (city-centre hostel for under-18s) I had no clue what was going to happen to me, how long I was going to be there for, if I'd see my brother again at that stage because visitation rights hadn't been sorted out. And what was going to happen because I was just finishing off my Junior Cert. The only thing I knew was that I could find my way home, I knew my way home and if anything got too bad I would walk home and I would go to my friends house and I knew he would let me stay there. So I always had that at the back of my mind but I can honestly say I did not like not knowing anything. — Neil (20)

I was scared because of the things that I heard about hostels. I had heard stories, your shoes get robbed off your feet, that sort of stuff. — Roisín (16)

When I was here (hostel) for the first night like I was finding it hard because I didn't know where I was going to be living. — Melissa (14)

At the time of moving to a hostel for the first time most appeared to know little about the setting, much less what to expect. For some of the study's younger respondents, such as Lisa, this experience was relatively recent. Here is how she described her first impressions of the hostel where she was placed two months prior to interview:

No, I did not know anything like about this place here and I was never told about it or anything like that and I was just brought here (to the hostel).

[What can you remember about that?]

I was just scared. When I walked in the door and saw everything, it was, "Oh my God, get me out of here". — Lisa (15)

Other accounts focused on the need to defend oneself and one's belongings. Colm told about his first night in emergency accommodation following contact with the Out of Hours Service:

[Can you remember what your first night was like?]

Rough. 'Cos I was never, I never done heroin before that and when I went in there (hostel), there was junkies in the same room as me. I just didn't like it; they were slaggin' and tryin' to push me about but I didn't let them. I told them, "If you come near my stuff I'll punch the head off you". I had stuff there, money and stuff. — Colm (20)

Relief on leaving home was reported by a small number of young people. This sentiment was expressed variously, sometimes in anger, and was almost always symptomatic of the trauma they had experienced during the months and weeks prior to their leaving. The following account strongly suggests a need to escape from home situations that had become increasingly difficult:

[Did you feel upset?]

No. I didn't really care 'cos I didn't want to live with me ma's friend anymore. I don't know? I didn't even care. I was glad to get out of there anyway. — Amy (15)

Like Amy, a number of others felt the need to escape difficult home situations and they took the initiative in leaving by walking out or running away. For many who left in such circumstances, the event brought mixed feelings:

I just didn't know what was going on, you know. But the situation I was in, I was more happy to get out of it, you know what I mean. D'you know? So I was kind of a bit happy but wary, you know. — Christian (17)

Leaving home is a challenging transition for most young people and one which requires preparation and support. For the young people in this study, home-leaving often arose unexpectedly and was always a distressing experience. On becoming homeless, they stepped into an unfamiliar world over which they felt little control and where they had little or no immediate access to social or emotional support.

Early Homeless Pathways

Young people's situations and living circumstances during the days and weeks subsequent to their leaving home varied. These early trajectories through homelessness are important for a number of reasons. Firstly, they illustrate differences in *how* homelessness is experienced, even during the very early stages. They also reveal variation in young people's living situations and in their status as "officially" or "unofficially" homeless.[1] This section is concerned primarily with the *location* of young people's homelessness and the *accommodation* they accessed during the period subsequent to their leaving home. It must be remembered that the vast majority of the study's young people have long since moved out of this particular phase of homelessness, even if many continue to move back and forth between the same or similar living situations.

Sleeping Rough in the Local Area

Some young people spent the first days and weeks sleeping rough or staying with friends or relatives in their local area. Sleeping out meant sleeping in nearby fields or parks but, more often than not, young people sought out more sheltered or secluded settings – cars, buses, sheds or derelict buildings – where they set up home for several days or weeks. Young men were far more likely to sleep rough in their local area during these initial days or weeks and they frequently did so alone. Tony described the places where he slept after leaving home for the first time at the age of 15:

---

[1] "Unofficial" homelessness is a term used in reference to young person who have not accessed youth homeless services while those who are "officially" homeless are known to these services. Unofficially homeless young people move to the officially homeless category once they make contact with services targeting homeless youth.

Sleeping in the sheds, you know, it was like all in (the suburban area where he was born). Like a neighbour of ours sold sheds in his garden and I'd climb through the window of a shed and just make me bed. I had a sleeping bag and a quilt and a pillow and, me cousin, he'd throw me a few munchies (food) out of his gaff like to keep me going during the night and a few smokes and a bit of hash. I slept in cars as well, it was mad awkward, it was rough.
— *Tony, 22*

While some young people returned home intermittently, others stayed with relatives or friends for short periods. Eoin alternated between sleeping out and staying with friends for several months and, during this time, he also returned home periodically:

There was a field near my house and that was the first time I ever slept out. But any time I ever slept out I went back to my ma's house like after. And I would either get back in or I would get a change of clothes and go. And there was a garage around the corner from me ma's house and I stayed in there for about three months. I slept in the cars as well and in a friends place. I don't know? I was doing that for a few months. — *Eoin, 20*

It was unusual for young women to sleep rough in their local area but a considerable number did initially stay with members of their extended family or friends. In most cases, however, these arrangements were temporary and did not provide a stable or lasting living situation. Periods spent sleeping rough in the local community and/or alternating between friends and relatives who lived locally are essentially phases of *hidden* or *unofficial* homelessness. Some young people started on this pathway when they left home and quickly moved to other accommodation. Others, however, were unofficially homeless in their local area for very considerable periods before they came to the attention of authorities or were directed to city-centre services by friends, relatives or a social worker.

Out of Local Area to City-centre or Other Locations

On becoming homeless, yet others made their way to the city-centre where they slept rough for a period. At the time they left home or a care setting, these young people had little or no understanding of how to go about finding a safe place to stay. Practically all who reported this pattern of initially sleeping rough in the city-centre were male. Brendan described leaving his suburban home neighbourhood and sleeping rough for the first time in the city centre:

[Can you remember the first time you slept out?]

I remember, yeah, I was about twelve, twelve and a half. I ran away from me ma's into the city and just got known, got in with the wrong people. The first few weeks I wouldn't have stayed in hostels. I would have just been out like, breaking into apartments, sleepin' on landings and that. — Brendan (17)

Only one young woman slept rough in the city-centre during the weeks subsequent to leaving home but a number did report an immediate move out of their local area. Two, for example, spent the first period out of home in the company of a romantic partner: one running away with her boyfriend and living in England for a time and a second staying with her partner in a caravan for several weeks. Like others who initially followed a path of leaving their local neighbourhood, these young women were *unofficially* homeless for a considerable period of time. Neither resolved their home-based difficulties, although one did return home periodically. Both later moved to other forms of unstable accommodation (e.g. staying with friends) or alternated between hostels, rough sleeping and private rented sector accommodation.

Direct to City-centre: Out of Hours Service and Emergency Placements

A large number of young people made immediate contact with the Out of Hours Service and were then placed in emergency accommodation in or near the city-centre. While all of these young people entered into and, for the most part, remained in the *official* city network of homeless youth, their early out of home experiences differed. Those young people who took this initial path through the Out of Hours Service can be divided into two groups:

- The first comprises those who started on a path of using the Out of Hours Service repeatedly, moving back and forth between various city-centre hostels. Their movement out of hostels was frequently precipitated by trouble or rule-breaking of one kind or another which resulted in their exclusion from this accommodation for a period of days or weeks. Others moved out of the hostel "scene" for a period to return home or to travel abroad but re-established contact with the Out of Hours Service at a later stage. For a considerable number, this repeated use of emergency and crisis accommodation worked to enmesh or draw them into a street-based culture. By their mid- to late teenage years, many were heavily drug-involved and/or engaging in criminal activity to finance their everyday needs.

- The second group consists of those placed in an emergency hostel bed but, unlike the former group, they remained in this setting for a relatively lengthy period. Some continued to attend school or resumed their education. More young women than young men reported this path following their first out of home experience.

Direct to Short-term Hostel Placement

Finally, a small number of young people – almost always young women – were placed in an emergency Out of Hours bed by a social worker without first making contact with the Gardaí (which is the typical first step to using the Out of Hours Service). Those who followed this path initially were almost always younger (between the ages of 14 and 15 years) and their move out of home (or a foster or residential care setting) was usually precipitated by a crisis of one kind or another. Although placements in short-term hostels are seen as a temporary measure, a number remained in these settings for several months and, in fewer cases, for up to one year. Indeed, at the time of conducting interviews, a considerable number of the study's "newly" or "recently" homeless young people had been residing in the hostel where they were initially placed for a period of several months. During this time, some travelled to a school in their local neighbourhood while others resumed their education close to the hostel where they were placed.

The Early Days Out of Home

These early pathways highlight differences in young people's initial homeless "journeys" and they also draw attention to a period of *unofficial* homelessness that many young people experienced. Another key finding relates to young people's movement between home and other living situations during their early weeks out of home. Many who initially slept rough or stayed with relatives or friends in their neighbourhoods returned home intermittently, suggesting that there was a period during which parents (or carers) and young people tried to resolve their differences. This willingness on the part of young people to negotiate with parents or caregivers highlights their reluctance to leave their homes, however difficult their home situations may have been. Finally, entry into the *official* network of homeless youth signified a critical "break" from home, family and community for a large number.

Accommodation Accessed

All of the young people were asked about their experience and use of a range of accommodation types including the Out of Hours Service, emergency and short-term hostels, rough sleeping and squatting, staying with friends or relatives, the use of adult hostels and life in supported lodgings. As might be expected, there was enormous variation in the range of accommodation places used by young people. Some had lived in only one hostel since the time they left home or a care setting, while others had repeatedly used one or several of these living situations. In general, the longer the duration of homelessness, the more likely young people were to have used several or all of the accommodation types listed. Table 5.1 presents an overview of the range of accommodation types accessed by the study's young people since the time they left home.

Table 5.1: Types of Accommodation Accessed since First Becoming Homeless

Accommodation Type	Young Men (n=23)	Young Women (n=17)	All (n=40)
Emergency/short-term residential settings and hostels*	18	15	33
Out of Hours Service	18	10	28
Friends/family member	13	13	26
Rough sleeping	15	9	24
Squats	11	6	17
Adult hostel	10	3	13
Long-term hostel	5	---	5
Supported lodgings/transitional housing	4	1	5

*Includes those young people who used emergency and short-term hostel accommodation targeting under-eighteens *and* specialised crisis/short-term hostels for 16-21 year-olds.

As the table demonstrates, the Out of Hours Service and emergency/crisis hostels were the most commonly used services. A large number of young people had resided in one or more of the short-term hostels, with far fewer having accessed longer-term hostel accommodation. While almost two-thirds had spent periods with friends or a member of their extended family subsequent to becoming homeless, far more young women than young men were doing so at the time of the interview. Strong gender differences are also evident in experiences of sleeping rough and in the use of adult hostels and squats, with young women less likely to have used these sleeping places. Overall, one-third of the young people had slept in an adult hostel at some time and almost two-thirds had experience of rough sleeping. Of the five young men who had lived in a long-term under-18s residential setting, three subsequently returned to short-term hostel accommodation through repeated referrals to the Out of Hours Service. At the time of conducting interviews, only two young men had a long-term residential placement.

Young men were far more likely than young women to report a cycle of movement between two or more of the short-term residential settings (hostels) targeting youth under the age of 18. Of the 18 young men who reported the use of these hostels, eleven had stayed in at least two, while seven had resided in three or more of these emergency settings. In contrast, only four of the 15 young women had accessed two short-term accommodation places and a further two had resided in three or more of these settings.

Reasons for the gender differences in service utilisation noted above are complex. Firstly, young women's homelessness tended to remain "hidden" for longer. Several, for example, reported periods of living with family members, friends, or a romantic partner and some alternated between home and these living situations for a considerable period. In addition, three of the study's young women had never made contact with homeless services for young people under the age of 18. As teenagers, two had lived for a time with a romantic partner in a range of unstable living situations (B&Bs, staying with friends etc.) and had also spent periods squatting and sleeping rough. Both became heavily drug-involved and neither entered into the official homeless network until these relationships ended. A third young woman explained that at the time she started sleeping rough with her boyfriend, she was not aware of hostels for young people under the age of 18:

> [Was there a reason why you didn't stay in a hostel then?]
>
> I don't know? You see the hostels, I didn't really know about hostels. Well, I knew hostels yeah, but I always thought hostels were for old people, like not old people, but people over eighteen like. — Anna (17)

Young women's accounts also suggest that their parent(s) were reluctant to evict them and often allowed them to return home after occasions when they had run away or stayed out of home for a period of days or weeks. Attempts, in fact, by two of the young women to access accommodation through the Out of Hours Service had met with refusal of parental consent:

> *I tried to get into hostels an' all and they were telling me, "You have to get permission off your mother". And I was like, "But me ma won't tell ya that I'm homeless", which she wouldn't. She'd say, "She's not homeless, she can come home", do you know what I mean. — Emma (17)*

The accounts above draw attention to situations and responses (on the part of young women or their carers) that may prolong this period of hidden homelessness. In a small number of cases, young women's home-leaving was related to a romantic relationship. When parents expressed their disapproval of these relationships, the young women left home and subsequently spent a period living with their boyfriends either in unstable situations (e.g. staying with friends) or on the street. These periods of invisibility may carry significant risks and can work to enmesh young women in situations that compromise their safety and their ability to seek help.

Living Out of Home

For the study's young people, living out of home was a highly differentiated experience and one which, for a large number, was in a constant state of flux. The extent of young people's movement in and out of various accommodation types meant that many had a repertoire of living situations and experiences. Younger teenagers in the sample, and those who were "newly" or recently homeless, tended not to report a range of living situations or circumstances. Nonetheless, it must be remembered that even among those who had lived in only one hostel setting, there were many who had previously resided with extended family or family friends during the period preceding their first official out-of-home experience. The following broad typologies of accommodation places were identified based on a thematic analysis of the living situations reported by the study's young people.

*Table 5.2: Typology of Accommodation and Other Sleeping Places
Occupied by Young People as They Moved in and out of Homelessness*

Accommodation Category	Examples
Formal temporary accommodation for under-18s	Emergency, short- and medium-term residential placements for "out of home" young people under 18 years (referred to by young people as "hostels")
Informal temporary accommodation	With friends, relatives or "associates".
Rough sleeping	Locations include: the street, parks, cars, sheds, doorways and stairwells, bus shelters.
Adult hostels	Single-sex and mixed hostels for adults of all ages.
Criminal justice and other institutions	Juvenile detention centres, prisons, residential drug treatment centres.
Other	Squats (unfinished buildings, derelict buildings), caravan, tents, boats.

As stated, young people differed in terms of their relationship with the categories of accommodation described above. Some, for example, had not used adult hostels or spent time in detention or prison and young women reported fewer episodes of rough sleeping and more frequent periods living with friends. Despite these and other differences, there were nonetheless experiences that many of the young people shared. The remainder of this section examines young people's perspectives on some of the most frequently used accommodation types: the Out of Hours Service, emergency or short-term settings (hostels) for the under-18s, rough sleeping, squatting and adult hostels.

The Out of Hours Service

Twenty-eight young people had used the Out of Hours Service at some time. In keeping with official procedures, they went to a Garda station where they identified themselves as homeless and then waited for a social worker from the Out of Hours team to arrive. According to the young people, the wait at the Garda station extended over several hours and most had vivid memories of the event.

> *It was a bit (pause), a bit weird. I didn't know where it was like. I didn't know what was going to happen to me like. I thought they were going to send me to a boys' home or something. — Eoin (20)*

The terms "weird" or "strange" were used frequently to describe the experience of going to a Garda station to seek accommodation. This is not altogether surprising since law enforcement agencies are not generally perceived by young people as places where support is readily available at a personal level. Several, in fact, commented on the absurdity of having to take this course of action to avoid sleeping on the street. This perspective was particularly strong among young people who had prior contact with the Gardaí because of their criminal offences. Gerard's account highlights the incongruity of going to a Garda Station for help for those who had a prior history of "trouble" with the Gardaí.

> *[Can you remember going to a Garda station for the first time?]*

> *I was 13 (the first time). You had to go to a Garda station for 8.00 o'clock in the evening and you had to wait there for two to three hours and then you get took down to a hostel or other places like that. It's all weird like because of all the times you get arrested and you have trouble with them and now you have to go to them for a place for the night. — Gerard (16)*

A considerable number also claimed that the amount of time a young person spent waiting in a Garda station depended on whether he or she (or a family member) had previously been cautioned, charged or convicted of a crime. It was routinely asserted that those individuals who were known to the Gardaí invariably waited for longer for a social worker to arrive. This was seen by young people as an unauthorised punishment over which they had no control.

> *Yeah sitting in a Garda station just waiting for hours ... especially if the Garda knew you he wouldn't even ring the social worker for*

you. You would have to go in again and say it to them and, they'd say, "Ah we forgot", that's what they used to do. — Conor (19)

In general, young women reported more favourable treatment by the Gardaí. However, both young men and women commented on the indifference of some police officers:

Ah, it's horrible 'cos you're just sitting in the Garda station starving, just looking for the Out of Hours. You could be waiting up to 1.00 o'clock in the morning, 2.00 o'clock. And then you're just waiting there for them to come. So you go in and say, "Will you call the Out of Hours for me?", and he (the Garda) puts your name down in this book and he puts your parents' address and your date of birth. Some of them are nice and some of them are not. It's (pause) … 'cos they don't know. They think, "Ah, she's in here 'cos she's a little bitch or her ma threw her out". — Rachel (14)

It was frightening the first time because I didn't know where I was going, you know. It was, it was frightening … and the Garda was slagging me, like you know, "Why don't you go into town?" I was like, "Give me the bus fare and I'll go into town", ya know, "I mean, I'm really homeless". — Tony (22)

The Out of Hours Service was the first point of contact with services for the majority of young people. Many were in a distressed state when they first approached the Gardaí and it is significant in light of this that so many found the experience to be confusing, frightening or simply at odds with what is generally regarded as affirmative intervention.

Emergency and Short-term Settings (Hostels) for Young People under the Age of 18

Following contact with the Out of Hours Service young people were almost always placed in an emergency bed in one of the available residential settings (hostels) targeting homeless youth. These short-term hostels vary in policy and support services, some catering specifically for younger teenagers (aged 12-15 years), while others cater for older groups (15-17 years). The majority offer services to both sexes and a smaller number provide for young men or women only. Not all will admit young people who have alcohol or drug problems.

At the time of interview, nearly half of the study's young people were staying in one of the available short-term hostels. These hostels varied, not only in terms of their policies and admission criteria, but also in terms of their location (although all were located in, or adjacent to, the city-centre), the physical structure of the building, staffing arrangements, daily routines and household rules. While some operate a tight and quite rule-bound daily schedule of activities with specific expectations in terms of school attendance and participation in out-of-school activities (homework, chores etc.), others have a less structured daily routine which permits greater freedom of movement.

Young people spoke favourably about several aspects of hostel life. Living in a hostel meant that they did not have to make contact with the Out of Hours Service on a nightly basis and this was considered to be among the chief advantages of a short-term residential placement. In general, it was acknowledged that hostels provide a bed in a secure environment as well as regular meals, shower and laundry facilities. A large number also recognised and appreciated the efforts of staff to care for them, offer advice and make them feel "at home":

> *What I like about the hostel is that they bring you out, they bring you to the cinema twice a week. It's nice that we get brought here 'cos I know I'm off the streets. And like I can go to the staff, there'll always be someone there for me. — Roisín (16)*

Despite the services and facilities provided, many found it difficult to adapt to hostel life and there were many dimensions to the problems young people experienced in these settings. Among them, the issue of choice – or rather, the absence of alternatives – emerged as a key issue affecting young people's sense of security and identity:

> *There is one thing about staying in the hostels, you're in them. The bad thing about being in them, you're in them full stop and*

it's not your choice full stop whether you're in them or not. At 16 or 17, you can't get a flat really. I mean, so that's the bad thing about them really. It's the actual situation or else you're walking around the streets all night. — Brendan (17)

The transience of hostel life was raised repeatedly as an issue that affected their everyday lives, making daily life unpredictable and limiting their opportunities to form stable and meaningful friendships. It also impacted negatively on their enthusiasm for friendships, which they feared would be abruptly broken when people moved to other settings. Indeed, a number of young people indicated that relationship building was openly discouraged within the short-term setting where they lived. Rachel, who was 14 at the time of interview, had learned not to form personal attachments:

Everywhere you go you're told not to get attached to people. But ya do. Makes you cold hearted though. And obviously people are going to put their guard up. Like anybody could come in here and I don't know their history. They could be on gear (heroin) and I wouldn't know. They could be a thief and I don't know … You're better off just keeping yourself to yourself and people are making the mistake of getting attached to people. It's their mistake, 'cos basically either people are going to be horrible to you, untrustworthy, or else they wanna leave before you and they do leave and they don't come back and see ya. — Rachel (14)

The theme of transience was also strong when young people talked about their relationships with staff members. Many commented on the high turnover of staff and the constant presence of relief workers. While some had a "favourite" staff member – an adult who they felt they could talk to about issues and problems in their lives – very frequently, this person was not around when they needed them most. Added to this, hostels were portrayed as volatile environments where tensions often ran high. Indeed, for residents, daily life had an intensity that is uncharacteristic of most other living situations: people were admitted and others left, there were rules and regulations guiding practically every aspect of daily life and a diverse range of personalities and needs to be

catered for on an ongoing basis. Young people openly acknowledged their own frustrations and several told of situations when
they resorted to outbursts or temper tantrums as a problem-
solving or coping strategy. This, in turn, created problems for staff
and other residents and for themselves. In more extreme cases,
isolated incidents led to their exclusion – for days or weeks – from
the setting where they lived. Even if young people were not personally involved in such confrontations, most were regular observers of quarrels and disputes and these experiences were a
constant source of disruption. Others who were more accustomed
to chaos within previous living situations had grown to accept –
and indeed, to expect – some level of confusion and disorder.
Overall, respondents experienced a profound lack of control over
these environments and often commented on the lack of privacy,
which they usually related to the constant turnover of residents.

> *There's not enough privacy. Like at the minute now, it's okay,*
> *there's only three people in the hostel but when it's full there's no*
> *room, you know. You can't do nothing. And people coming in*
> *and out of here, peer pressure and all that. — Luke (18)*

Hostels, like other institutional settings, must operate according to
a strict set of rules and regulations in order to protect young people. In general, however, it was strongly felt that the need for personal space was not acknowledged. Several claimed that they
were constantly watched and monitored by hostel staff and did
not equate this surveillance with kindness or care:

> *It's like they don't get out of your face in here, they don't leave*
> *you alone they don't give you time by yourself, like they come and*
> *check on you every fifteen minutes if you're in your room. They*
> *don't leave you, they don't give you any peace at all, just con-*
> *stantly on your back … You don't have any privacy at all. It's*
> *supposed to be for your own good, they're supposed to be check-*
> *ing on you to make sure nothing is going on but it's making it*
> *worse. — Rachel (14)*

Unlike many other institutional settings for "at risk" youth, emergency care settings lack the authority to make their residents stay and several young people, in fact, exercised their right to leave. In some cases, leaving or running away – even for a short time – became a way of protesting the restrictiveness of certain household rules as in the following account:

> *[Have you considered running away recently?]*
>
> *There's a lot of times I'd consider that I'd run away. There was another stage there, instead of running away, I'd be gone for about a few hours but I'd just come back. I wouldn't actually run away because the police would come after me. — Jacinta (16)*

The timing of movements from short-term stays in hostels to more long-term placements was frequently a source of anxiety attested to in several accounts:

> *[What kinds of things do you worry about?]*
>
> *Trying to find out where you are going to be moved on to and things like that. Just things about the places that I am going to be moved on to and what is going to happen next. Where am I going and how long is it going to be and the stress. — Cathy (15)*

Delay or deferral of placements had come to be accepted by some:

> *I'm supposed to be gone in March, hat will be six months here but I know I'll be here more than March. — Melissa (15)*

Such accounts are symptomatic of a general lack of willingness to consult or adequately inform young people about decisions affecting them.

Above all else, there was a profound stigma attached to living in hostels. Young people often refused to disclose their living arrangements to their peers and many would not allow friends to visit them. As a result, they had to cope on a daily basis with the burden of concealing the reality of their living situations from their friends and class mates. Jacinta explained why people who live in hostels are viewed "differently":

Like people see you differently because you live in a hostel because they say, "Ah she doesn't live with her family and they always seem to have more sympathy for you ... I wouldn't class this place as for a family but some people, some of the girls here would class this place as their family and they wouldn't mind going around and saying, "Yeah listen, I live in a house with loads of girls", and all that. But I don't really, loads of people would class me different.

[And how do you think they see you as different?]

I think they feel sorry for you.

[What do you feel when people do that?]

Stupid. Just a really stupid person. It's just like another place but it's bigger with loads of young ones there. It's shit! — *Jacinta (16)*

For the most part, the residential settings referred to by young people as "hostels" are short-term, crisis-oriented facilities characterised by intense and highly transitory relationships. By and large, young people acknowledged the efforts of staff and appreciated the facilities and opportunities available to them in these settings. At the same time, most found transitory group living to be stressful and difficult. While emergency and short-term residential placements clearly play a critical role in catering for young people in crisis, equally, they are ill-equipped to cater for their longer-term needs. The inherent limitations of models of temporary crisis care – in terms of providing for long-term needs – are exposed by the frustration, dissatisfaction and disappointment expressed by the young residents who felt trapped "in the middle" with no real notion of what the future held.

Sleeping Rough and Squatting

Twenty-four young people (fifteen young men and nine young women) stated that they had slept rough at some time since becoming homeless, and of these, two (both young men) were sleeping rough at the time of interview. While a small number portrayed rough sleeping as a choice, it was more often a last resort arising out of one or more of the following situations: inability to secure an emergency hostel bed, non-availability of hostel beds, or fear of intimidation or bullying within particular residential settings. For some, rough sleeping was episodic and did not extend beyond two or three consecutive nights. Several others alternated between sleeping rough and staying in hostels for periods ranging from a few nights to two or more weeks. Although the duration of rough sleeping varied, approximately half of the young people had spent several consecutive weeks or months sleeping outdoors in the past.

Young women were far less likely than their male counterparts to have slept rough and, irrespective of age, they considered rough sleeping to be dangerous:

> *I think most women that sleep on the streets always stay with blokes, but for a woman to stay on the streets on her own, yeah, it would be very dangerous. — Sarah (21)*

> *There's nasty people going around out there, do you know what I mean. Like rapists, you know yourself, like people that do bad things. — Aoife (19)*

Of the nine young women who did have experience of rough sleeping, two had slept on the street on one occasion only. In general, rough sleeping was avoided by this group who feared for their physical safety and the safety of their personal belongings (jewellery, clothing, footwear and drugs). On occasions when they did sleep rough, they felt extremely vulnerable and most would only do so in the company of friends or a romantic partner. A young woman who, unusually, had considerable experience of sleeping rough, was Siobhán.

> *I was on the streets for a good while. I used to be afraid. I was frightened thinking when I was asleep someone was going to come up and, you know, someone's gonna do something like. I wouldn't even sleep like, you know. I cuddled into me mates and all. Then I just ended up getting used to it. — Siobhán (22)*

In general, young people depicted rough sleeping in extremely negative terms: it was dangerous and created vulnerability to illness, particularly during bad weather. The unpredictability of street life was also considered to be a major threat and created strong perceptions of danger and risk.

> *[Were you scared sleeping on the street?]*
>
> *Yeah. Scared of something happening. Like anyone coming up, you know what I mean, doing something to you. You wouldn't know like what would happen on the streets. No one knows. —* Declan (19)

Apart from the physical discomfort and personal risks associated with sleeping rough, the experience was dehumanising. Sleeping under the public gaze was embarrassing and evoked feelings of shame, rejection and distrust, particularly among those who had been homeless for some time. Siobhán and Julian explained:

> *[How would you describe sleeping on the street?]*
>
> *I didn't find it very nice. Like people are sayin', "Look at her like, that young one, she should be ashamed of herself", an' all. It's hard like. When you're on the gear you don't care like, you know what I mean, like you're just sayin', "I don't care what they're saying". But in your heart you do care like. —* Siobhán (22)
>
> *It wasn't nice. People walking by you that kind of know you or something like that, you know. And you're getting your head up in the mornings out of a duvet and people seeing you and knowing you, and know your family an' all. They're saying, "Jesus Christ, look at the young fella, he's bleedin' sleeping rough", and all that. You never think of anything like that, but that's what happens when you have nowhere to go. —* Julian (22)

Finally, sleeping on the streets resulted in exposure to aggressive behaviour and several of the study's rough sleepers had witnessed violent incidents:

*There's a lot of violence on the street, yeah. There's a lot of mug-
gings and robberies, a lot of violence, yeah. A lot of violence, a lot
of shootings, a lot of stabbings. But when you're homeless you
don't really care about anybody, you know what I mean. —
Declan (19)*

Squats had also been widely used by rough sleepers for short or
extended periods and a total of seventeen (eleven young men and
six young women) had inhabited such a shelter at some time.
Most used squats intermittently and it was rare for young people
to squat in one location for more than a few weeks. Almost always
portrayed as dirty and uncomfortable, young people nonetheless
recognised that these shelters provided respite from the rain and
cold, particularly during the winter months:

[What about squats then?]

*Just a place to go, it keeps you out of the rain, that's it. And some
of them are warm, some of them have broken windows and the
breeze is blowing in and it's rough. It scars you for life being
homeless, you know. Like I'm homeless now, seven years I'm
homeless and I'm used to it, you know. — Tony (22)*

The young people most likely to use squats were those who self-
identified as dependent drug users. As indoor settings, they provided secluded sites for injecting and the presence of other squat-
ters had the advantage of providing backup in the event of an accidental overdose. Squats were generally vacated or abandoned
within a relatively short period of time as young people frequently came to regard the building as too unsanitary or unsafe
for living purposes.

Adult Hostels

*[Have you been in a situation recently when you didn't know
how things were going to turn out?]*

*Yeah. I got kicked out of here (under-18s hostel), there a couple of
months ago. I thought I was going to be homeless when I was 18*

*d'you know what I mean. Because it was two months to me birth-
day or something, you know. I thought I was going to be left on
me own, you know what I mean, nowhere to live or anything and
I'd be in the over-18s hostels or something. I didn't want that. I
was angry as well. — Christian (17)*

[Do you worry about the future?]

*I worry that I'd have to go through the fucking adult hostels. I
know what they're like, I know most of the people in them but, I
know that's not going to happen. That just can't happen. –
Ronan (17)*

Christian and Ronan had been moving between numerous unstable living situations – hostels, squats, the street, the home of
friends or relatives – since their early teenage years and, at the
time of interview, both were approaching their eighteenth birth-
days. Both considered themselves to be well-versed in the impera-
tives of street life following years of experience of street scenes
which had, to varying degrees, come to structure their daily lives.
Equally, however, they had grown tired of "a life" dominated by
risk, uncertainty and trouble. For young people like Christian and
Ronan, the period approaching the transition to formal adulthood
was threatening and stressful. They were aware that their eligibility for admission to Out of Hours accommodation was drawing to
a close and that a whole range of services would not be available
to them once they reached the age of 18 years. Yet, life remained
unchanged and there was little prospect of their finding secure
housing.

Fear and loathing of adult hostel life was based, in some cases,
on stories and rumours and, in others, on first-hand experience of
staying in these settings. For many, the thought or reality of adult
hostel life constituted a significant crisis point, as Sarah's account
of her first night in an adult hostel demonstrates:

[Do you remember your first night in an adult hostel?]

*Yeah, I was fucking in bits, I was. I cried myself to sleep that
night, I was terrified.*

[Why were you afraid?]

I don't know? The life that was ahead of me I suppose. You know, choosing this life. The life I was choosing and afraid of what was to come. I felt there was no turning back, I don't know why? — Sarah (22)

Eighteen of the 40 young people interviewed were between the ages of 18 and 22 years and, of these, 12 had used an adult hostel at some time. Many had been regular clients of the Out of Hours Service as teenagers; they were familiar with the homeless street scene and knew most of the "players" – whether clients or service providers – following years of alternating between various accommodation types. Additionally, a large number reported histories of drug use and criminal activity. When questioned about their experience of services both prior and subsequent to their eighteenth birthday, all agreed that there were major differences:

[Is there a difference between the places you stay and the services you get before 18 and after 18?]

Is there what! I tell you it's rough, I never knew when I had to change. My 18th birthday, I went into an under-18's hostel on a Friday and they were meant to give you a weekend bed, right, so I went in. It was my birthday on the Saturday so they let me in until Monday but when I went back to get my bed they said they needed the bed and because I was 18 that I'd have to leave, so that was my birthday present. Went to an adult hostel and that wasn't the best place. It was some jump alright I tell you. The under-18's have it a lot easier than the likes of us. They're kids as well so they need it more than we would. But there's a lot of difference, there is. — Conor (19)

Like other young men in their late teens, Brendan, who was homeless at the age of 13, had moved from one city-centre accommodation to another over a five-year period:

[Have you stayed in many hostels?]

Yeah I've stayed in them loads of times yeah, loads ... (lists four different emergency under-18s hostel). The hostel I'm in at the minute, it's actually for over-18s. None of the rest of me friends now would be in there. The Out of Hours banned me. They said they didn't want me using the services so I had to go to another hostel. And that's, that's like another leap. Like the over-eighteens hostels, you know, it's more like everybody is like a fuckin' zombie in them, you know what I mean, they're out of their heads you know. — Brendan (17)

Adult hostels were consistently depicted as "rough" and young people talked constantly about the bleak physical state of the buildings. The presence of much older adults frequently led to fears that they would end up in a similar situation:

It is not a nice experience. It is sleeping in the dorms, with old fellas and young fellas and I would not advise it. — Eoin (20)

I stayed in (name of adult hostel) for only one night. I didn't like it 'cos it was mainly all older women and, me, like I was the youngest. Like they were all old enough to be me mother, you know what I mean. They'd be talking about like things that you wouldn't even want to be talking about like, what they done like and what they're at and all now like, you know what I mean. Like you do feel very odd like, you know, 'Jesus like I'm only a kid to all these like, why am I here? why did they not put me anywhere else?'. — Siobhán (22)

Perceived as hostile environments, many young people appeared genuinely shocked and frightened by the scenes they had witnessed in these settings. For some, like Paul, drug intoxication provided an effective coping mechanism:

See that hostel there (refers to city-centre adult hostel). Ah Jesus like, I wouldn't stay there myself. I have stayed there when I was strung out 'cos you don't give a fuck when you're on the gear. It was fuckin' (pause) ... they have five bunk beds going this way, five bunk beds goin' that way. That's like twenty people, ya know what I mean. And all bleedin' alcohos (alchoholics) an' all that shit. Really smelly place, they bang (inject) in their feet an' all, you know. Like I went in there and I had a few lines of gear or something, a few joints and then I'd just go to sleep. — Paul (19)

The move from under-18s services into the adult world of hostel life was traumatic for those young people who had already made this transition and a major source of anxiety for those whose eighteenth birthday was approaching. By the time many reached, or were close to, the age of 18 they had already spent several years moving between a range of unstable living situations. The realisation that they had to step into the adult equivalent was regarded as a major transition and appeared to symbolise the beginning of a new and daunting chapter of their lives.

Dislocation from Home Neighbourhood

Young people's homeless "journeys" are clearly complex and diverse. While for some, homelessness was a relatively recent event, others had spent months or years alternating between temporary living situations. Irrespective of the duration of their homelessness, this residential displacement brought about much hardship and the instability many subsequently experienced was strongly linked to the loss of social bonds, networks and familial supports. Social ties of all kinds were quickly severed when young people moved away from home, and few had maintained the connections and relationships that were once familiar and routine.

[Do you still hang around with your friends at home?]

Not really now, not now. Because I'm out of me house, ya know what I mean. It all changes when you're out of home. — Declan (19)

As demonstrated, young people moved into unfamiliar settings on leaving home where they had to deal with new, and sometimes threatening, situations and relationships. Although they shared these living spaces with people in similar situations, the relationships they forged in these contexts were often a source of further stress, alienation and risk. Many describe fleeting peer relationships and they struggled to find reliable friends. This is exemplified in their use of the terms "associates" and "acquaintances":

> *I did have good friends, but when I started on drugs I lost all me friends and got acquaintances instead of friends. You get more associates than friends when you're on drugs, you know, you can't trust anyone. — Sarah (21)*

The stigma of hostel life emerged strongly from many accounts, pointing to young people's limited access to a positive sense of identity, security and self-worth. Christian's anger is palpable in his account of what it feels like to be one of the "hostel people":

> *You see in hostels, people look down on the likes of all of us. This is the thing like, if you're from a hostel. This is all genuine, because I have friends that are not from here (hostel) and I know their ma's and all, and I'm telling you that this is genuine right, if any crime gets done or anything like that, "Oh it's the hostel people, it's the hostel people". But what they don't realize is that their kids are just as bad. It's just 'cos we're from here, people like to have someone to blame. And that has a big effect on the likes of all of us; makes you angry, d'you know. It used to make me go mad an' all, you know, and tell them to fuck off. But they like to talk and that does go through to ya (it hurts). Like they think you're dirty an' all, you know what I mean. But like I go around in better clothes than fuckin' half their own kids. And where did I get them? I didn't have to pay a penny for them, you know what I mean. I didn't rob it or anything, well sometimes I did, but, I still looked after myself better than all their kids. I tell you, I've more common sense than most of their kids as well. I'm telling ya. Like hostels are bad things, I know they are bad. I don't like them as such myself but when it comes to fucking getting intelligent toward the streets an' all, right, way beyond what their kids are used to. They are pampered. — Christian (17)*

As might be expected, the regularity of contact between young people and family members varied subsequent to their home-leaving, as did the nature and quality of their relationships with parent(s), carer(s) and siblings. At one end of the spectrum were young people who had regular weekly contact with a parent(s) and, at the other, a smaller number who reported little or no communication with family members for periods of weeks, months or even years. Some did not want contact with their parents and expressed strong views on this issue. It is perhaps significant that, among the study's young men, there were several reports of practically no contact with their fathers throughout their lives. Six stated that they had never or rarely spent time with their biological father.

Approximately 15 young people (eight young men and seven young women) had regular contact with one or both parents at the time of interview. Some of these visited their homes once weekly, others had regular visits from a parent(s) in the setting where they lived temporarily and a smaller number stayed in the family home on specific days and nights of the week. All who returned home for over-night stays had longer-term or more stable placements in a residential setting where the staff and management had worked with young people and their parents to facilitate home visits. Returning home for short periods appeared to work well for the young people who had this arrangement and a number felt that their relationship with their parent(s) had improved since the time they left home. Equally, several stated that they were not ready or prepared to move home permanently. This was certainly the case for Derek who spent most weekends with his family:

> [Would you like to stay at home for longer?]
>
> No, it's just too much for me when I go home. — Derek (15)

Like Derek, others (including several who returned home only intermittently) valued their family relationships but had no aspirations to moving home permanently. Indeed, a number felt that their improved relationship with parent(s) or carer(s) hinged on the relative distance between them:

Like I don't have to be around me ma all the time. I get on better with me ma when I'm here than when I'm living with her. There's a few good things about living in a hostel. — Finn (16)

Others described sporadic and conditional home visits. Gavin visited his mother only if he felt certain that his step-father would not be present:

I go out to see my mother sometimes. She was sick there last week, that's the reason why I went out. I would go out if she wants.

[And what about your step-dad? Is he still there?]

Yeah, but I wasn't talking to him. I didn't see him. I said to my mother, "If I'm going out to see you, I don't want him there". — Gavin (15)

In other cases, young people avoided contact with family members because they felt unable cope with the emotional consequences of such meetings. Brendan, who was incarcerated at the time of interview, sometimes refused family visits because the experience evoked bad memories:

I don't take visits off any of my family really. It just brings back bad memories of the past. — Brendan (17)

Brendan had become heavily involved in heroin use following a period of living out of home during his mid-teenage years and, like other drug-dependent youth, regretted the distress that his drug use had caused to family members. He wanted to make amends but simultaneously resented the chastisement and physical abuse he had endured as a child after his step-father moved into the family home. His conflicting views and emotions on family relationships – and how to resolve them – were common among the young people interviewed.

Despite the range of challenges associated with their home circumstances and relationships, a large number missed home and regretted how events had unfolded, irrespective of who they felt was responsible or to blame. Those who did communicate with family members almost always stated that contact was important to them, even if their meetings with parent(s) or carer(s) were intermittent, conditional or difficult:

> [Contact with your family, is it important to you?]

> Yeah, very important, without it I'd say I'd be bleedin' lost, probably dead, do you know what I mean. You get lonely without them, do you know what I mean like. People say "Ah, are you ringing your ma?", and all this. They say, "Ah, you're on the streets now, be a man". But I think those people are lonely for some reason. At the end of the day you want to turn to someone, you don't want to turn to someone on the streets that's just gonna keep noddin' his head, "Yeah, yeah, yeah", believing everything you say. Ring someone who you could bleedin' talk to. — Wayne (21)

Even if their relationships with parent(s) were fraught or tense, young people tried to maintain contact with their siblings. Many portrayed their relationships with siblings as warm and affectionate and several singled out one brother or sister who was special. Maintaining contact with siblings was not always easy, however, particularly for those who moved between living situations, and contact with siblings was sometimes sporadic among those who had been homeless for longer. A number worried about the siblings they had left behind. Brendan had left home because of the violent behaviour of his step-father and wondered if his brother and sister might have to endure this same treatment:

> [Do you ever worry about them (brother and sister)?]

> Yeah, like the thought of them being there with him (step-father) and seeing like him and what he and me ma were like, that it could be the same thing with him and his girlfriend, do you know what I mean. It does, it scares me a bit now like. — Brendan (17)

As with many other aspects of their lives and experiences, the quality of young people's relationships with family members varied and they were also subject to change over time. We have seen, for example, how relationships with parents improved for some young people following a period of living out of home. Indeed, levels of contact with family members were higher than might be expected given the range of difficulties young people had experienced in their homes as children (see Chapter 4). This finding strongly suggests that at least a proportion of young homeless people are motivated to resolve family conflict. While communication with parents or carers was a source of ongoing stress for a number, these relationships were valued by the majority, whether or not they hoped to return home.

Conclusion

Just as pathways "into" homelessness differed for young people, their experiences following the first "out of home" episode are also diverse. For a considerable number, the early phase of homelessness was characterised by periodic returns home and a number remained in, or relatively close to, their home neighbourhoods during this time (either sleeping rough or staying with friends or members of their extended family). All of these young people subsequently entered the "official" network of homeless youth following contact with the Out of Hours Service.

On leaving home or a care setting, young people entered into a world that was unfamiliar, chaotic and unpredictable. Their first and early nights out of home were traumatic and daily life in the residential settings (hostels) where they lived continued to be difficult for a large number. This is not altogether surprising since teenagers have a heightened need for privacy that is thwarted by living places that are largely communal. Hostels impose social contact with strangers and within these settings young people faced the enormous task of building new relationships. More than any other group, perhaps, teenagers are extremely sensitive to the shame associated with being homeless and they can be desperate to conceal their living situation from friends and schoolmates. Despite such hardships, a large number nonetheless appreciated the relative safety, stability and material security offered within many of the settings where they resided. This strongly suggests that life for these young people had previously been chaotic, unsafe, insecure and impoverished.

With the exception of those young people who were "newly" or recently homeless, the majority recounted a repertoire of living situations. Furthermore, entry into the city-centre "hostel scene" marked the onset of a process of detachment from their families and home neighbourhoods. Within a relatively short period of time, many had embarked on a cycle of movement between a range of "official" and "unofficial" sleeping places. A large number had experience of sleeping rough and squatting, among the most precarious of living spaces. Young people's accounts of the use of adult hostels, and the contemplations of others who faced this prospect in the near future, are particularly revealing in their portrayals of fear and uncertainty. Entry into the world of adult hostels constituted a significant crisis point and a number appeared to equate this transition with an acceptance of homelessness as a way of life.

Chapter 6

DRUGS, CRIME AND HOMELESSNESS

As documented in the previous chapter, many of the study's young people had spent months or years moving between various unstable living situations. This transience brought them into contact with other homeless youth and exposed them to a range of risk environments and behaviour. This chapter explores the consequences of this inherently unstable lifestyle with specific reference to the young people's substance use and criminal behaviour.

Drug use and/or criminality featured in the life histories of a considerable number of the young people. This finding is not altogether surprising since, as a group, homeless youth are more likely to engage in drug use and criminal activities for reasons outlined in Chapter 2. Not all of the study's young people were drug-involved, nor did all report offending behaviour. Nonetheless, drug (and alcohol) consumption came to occupy a central role in the everyday lives of a large number who were simultaneously involved, albeit at various levels, in criminal activity. The life stories of these young people constitute the major focus of this chapter. They are also the group who, in general, reported longer "careers" in homelessness.

In making sense of the drug use and criminal offences of the study's young people, the contextual significance of social and situational factors cannot be overstated. Situational factors refer to the immediate pressures in the lives of homeless youth – housing, financial situation, drug use, and so on – that impact on their social and economic activities. While uncovering several complex dimensions to their drug use and criminal activity, the accounts presented point to the instability of their living situations, and their perceptions of what they needed to survive, as key forces shaping their involvement in such activities.

Drug Use and Drug Problems: An Overview

Only seven of the 40 young people interviewed had never tried an illegal drug. Three of the non-users were young men and four were young women and, significantly perhaps, three were not Irish. One other young woman stated that she had smoked cannabis in the past but quit because her mother asked her to stop. At the time of conducting interviews, then, a total of eight young people were not using illegal drugs.

Irrespective of their drug use status, the vast majority reported high exposure to drugs and drug users within a range of settings and contexts. This level of drug exposure was not related solely to their homelessness: many had, in fact, experienced exposure to drug use in their own neighbourhoods and homes as children and young teenagers. Furthermore, almost all had experimented with at least one drug before leaving home or a care setting.

Across the sample, levels of drug involvement ranged from experimental use to episodic and recreational styles of consumption right through to heavy and problematic drug use. For the vast majority, drug and alcohol use were strongly connected. The use of prescription medicines also featured in their drug repertoires of a very considerable number.

The early age at which many of these young people initiated drug use is striking, the average being 11.5 and 13 years for young men and young women, respectively. Of the 20 young men who reported drug use, all had tried their first drug by the age of 15; seven had done so by the age of 11 and ten by the age of 13 years. Young women were older on average at the time of initiation. Nonetheless, eight of the 13 lifetime users first consumed a drug at or before the age of 14 years. The teenage years are, of course, a period of experimentation but for some young people – particularly those who are disadvantaged – drug consumption can escalate to more serious or problematic forms of use (Mayock, 2000; 2002; 2005).

Cannabis dominated as the drug of initiation, followed by inhalants. For the vast majority, first drug use took place in the company of peers, often at outdoor locations and, in fewer cases, in the home of a friend:

> *I was about, I'd say the first time I smoked hash now, I was about twelve. I was with all me mates at the time out in (a suburban location). This is goin' back years ago, you know.* — *Joe (19)*

> *The first time I smoked a joint I was about 14 and I was in my mate's gaff. I was smokin' cigarettes at the time and then he had enough hash to roll a joint. And we twisted the thing and we didn't do it properly but even then we got a bit stoned … I felt all light an' all. Yeah, I liked the buzz.* — *Gerard (16)*

A smaller number smoked cannabis for the first time in their own homes:

> *[Can you remember the first time you tried a drug?]*

> *Yeah. I was eight. You see my da smoked hash all me life, my da is a constant hash user like. So when I was a kid like me dad's box used to be around, it used to be on top of the wardrobe where we were not meant to be able to reach. But I used to just grab the chair and get up. I wasn't able to roll or anything so I'd just have one skin and I'd have a big lump of hash in it and I just didn't know anything about burning or anything like, do you know what I mean, and I'd sit there smoking away.* — *Caroline (16)*

Cannabis remained the drug of choice of a considerable number: thirteen young people nominated cannabis as their preferred drug and reports of daily use of the drug were common. By and large, cannabis smoking was viewed as an everyday activity and was used by many as a way to "chill" or relax. Many did not rate cannabis as a drug, per se, and it was frequently believed to carry fewer risks than tobacco.

Recreational Polydrug Use

As stated, a large number began to experiment with mood-
altering substances from their pre- or early teenage years. First
alcohol use overlapped with first drug use for a number, while
others were regular drinkers before using illicit substances. The
majority started to drink at or before the age of 13 and young
people almost uniformly portrayed drinking as a core leisure activity. For young men and women alike, much of this early experimentation centred on socialising with friends, usually at outdoor settings in, or close to, their home neighbourhoods. Drinking
sessions frequently involved drug use, with cannabis, ecstasy and
cocaine featuring prominently in young people's accounts of socialising and "going out". Young people rarely drank or used
drugs alone and peers were central to the enjoyment or "buzz".

[Do you usually drink and take drugs at the same time?]

*Yeah, you get a better buzz off it. You get more of a relaxation
buzz, you feel you're happy and you're relaxed. You feel you can
talk to everybody. I talk to a lot more people ... It gives you confi-
dence I suppose. — Roisín (16)*

[What do you do at the weekends?]

*Go drinking and socialising. Just around, out and about, just
anywhere. Get a few cans and walk around. Get a buzz. I get paid
on a Friday so I go out and have a few cans. — Luke (18)*

These young people built a repertoire of drug experiences relatively quickly:

*I was in secondary school and I had done me Junior Cert and I
was smoking hash when I was fifteen. And while I was doing my
Junior Cert I started doing Es at that stage. — Eoin (20)*

*I was hanging around with like, mostly young fellas that were all
17, 18, drinkin' and doin' E and, me ma knew what I was doing
E an' all and she didn't care ... Ah, in (suburban location), that's
basically where I started doin' hash and doin' E and doin' loads of*

*stuff. Was goin' out drinkin' all the time and throwin' everything
in that I could get me hands on. And, em, I started doin' coke,
then I went off the coke but I stayed on hash. — Rachel (14)*

While typical accounts of alcohol and drug use emphasised the
recreational nature of the activity, there were also many reports of
excessive consumption. Drinking to intoxication was common
and several mentioned occasions when they could not recollect
how a night of drinking ended. Many also stated openly that they
drank "a lot" or "too much" and there was strong evidence to
suggest that, at a relatively young age, a number started to use
alcohol (and other substances) to help them cope with day-to-day
problems and difficulties:

*I drink a lot. Out straight I drink a lot. I love me drink. It's the
only thing that gets me through what is going on. I know it
doesn't help you but it helps me, do you know what I mean. —
Joe (19)*

Anna, who had a difficult time both at home and at school during
her early teenage years, attributed her early heavy drinking to her
need to escape from feelings of depression:

*I'm not the tallest person as you can see, so I was quite fat and I
kind of got bullied in school and I really did hate it because they
were all so snobby and I wasn't into that, kind of money means
everything kind of thing. So I started drinking real heavily ... I
was very depressed so I just started knocking it back. — Anna (17)*

While on the one hand, young people emphasised the sociability
of drinking and drug use, many simultaneously mentioned times
when they used these substances to deal with difficult experiences
or stressful states. The alleviation of feelings of sadness or depression emerged as a prominent perceived benefit of alcohol and
drug intoxication.

Problematic Alcohol and Drug Use

Five young people – all of them young men – reported heavy drinking patterns as well as personal and legal problems arising from their alcohol consumption. Most of these young men had been drinking heavily since their early teens and most were also drug experienced. Almost all drank in street-based settings where their visibility brought a number into contact with the police. Conor told how he had engaged in daily drinking (and drug use) before his incarceration.

> *I had a drink problem now before I got locked up, that's why I was in treatment; it was my drink and my drugs. I was drinking solid for about a year and a half, every day just drinking. Every day. It was madness. I haven't drank since I got out (of prison). Not going to either. — Conor (19)*

Like Conor, a number of others were forced to address their alcohol use following arrest or incarceration. However, most resumed their former drinking routines following a period of abstinence. Fergal told how he continued to drink heavily after a short time in treatment:

> *Whenever I can get me hand on money, I fucking drink and I drink and I drink, honestly, I swear to God. But eh, when I haven't got money ... it's only generally once a week 'cos, when ya get it, it's gone on a Friday night and ya struggle through Saturday and Sunday. About Wednesday I go out to me da and brothers and get drunk off them, take what's going ... Went to St. John of Gods there in Stillorgan, but eh, only for a few weeks. Fuck, couldn't give a damn. I did it to get off three charges, just said "Oh I had a drink problem", blah blah blah, am getting treatment. But after I got off the charge I went off back to square one, wackin' the drink out of it (drinking to excess). — Fergal (18)*

As previously stated, young people rarely engaged in solitary drinking and almost always socialised with other homeless youth. The public spaces they occupied frequently attracted negative attention and made them extremely vulnerable to arrest. Following "trouble" with the police, young people sometimes reduced their alcohol consumption for a time. Few, however, expressed concern about the impact of drinking on their health and most did not plan to quit. Tony was unusual in that he gave up alcohol for health reasons.

> *[You said earlier that you were not a drinker now, when did the drinking stop?]*
>
> *At the age of 18. When I got Hepatitis and me liver started play-ing up so I stopped drinking ... I used to drink every day non-stop, knacker drinking, laneways, alleyways, just have a few cans with a bottle of vodka. Then losing your memory like and you would wake up in a field somewhere cold and soaking wet, shak-ing you know with the cold. I would say I was doing this from 16 to 18. — Tony (22)*

While alcohol featured as a problem substance for a considerable number, heroin dominated as the drug of dependence. Half of the study's young people reported lifetime use of heroin. Of these, 13 were young men and seven were young women and almost all acknowledged that their drug use was problematic to the degree that it had become a dependency. Heroin-involved youth almost always reported early drug experimentation and most had a rep-ertoire of drug experiences prior to using heroin for the first time. All reported "chasing" or smoking the drug initially and, of the nineteen who reported problematic heroin use, eleven were intra-venous users of the drug. Of these, seven were young men and four were young women. Injecting drug users (IDUs) were in their late teens or older at the time of interview. Most of these young people reported lengthy homeless "careers" and many were accessing emergency adult hostel accommodation at the time of interview. All of the study's IDUs initiated injection sub-sequent to becoming homeless and, for three, the transition to in-jecting was recent.

There are many elements in the life histories of the study's young people that prevent the production of a neat simplifying story about when precisely their heroin use began. Although heroin-involved youth had experiences that point to linkages, there was no axiomatic connection between heroin use and leaving home (or becoming homeless). This was especially apparent among those whose heroin use did not begin until after their first homeless experience. Nonetheless, the study's problematic drug users almost always reported early drug initiation.

Although the settings and situations associated with first heroin use were unique for each individual, there were nonetheless some identifiable patterns of initiation. The first of these relates to the social relationships that young people forged at an early age. Seán's account is instructive in this regard:

> I started doing E's then at 14 or 15 and, em, ecstasy satisfied me for about a year or a year and a half until I bumped into this older crowd. Well, I didn't bump into them. I wanted to bump into them. And I was complaining about needing to come down off the E and they were saying, "Well we have stuff that you will be able to take and you can go home and you can go to bed and go to sleep straight away". And, em, I started taking heroin about 6 years ago. But I wanted really to take heroin to fit in with someone because I felt like I never really got the attention off me father because he was more interested in drinking ... — Seán (21)

Seán is one of a number of young people whose transition to "hard" drug use coincided with a period of "hanging around" with older peers; he also described problems at home including economic hardship and an alcoholic father. For him, heroin was part of the "scene" and its use offered entry to an alternative and more rewarding set of experiences. Like others, he enjoyed the drug scenes of which he was a part during this early period of use but, like others, his account points to a complex mix of motives for drug use.

Paul, who was 19 at the time of interview, recounted a similar story of heroin initiation. He was in foster care from the age of one and, at the age of 13, his behaviour began to impact negatively on his placement:

I was 13. I was only a kid, hanging around with older lads and smoking hash, and just, just acting the ball. I left school, robbin' on me foster parents, and it all just built up and they had to throw me out, you know.

He went on to explain his introduction to heroin:

... well there was this fella like, that I started the gear with, like I was only 13 and he was 19. And he lived at the back of my house, you know. So I was going around to his house and we'd be smoking gear. And like he doesn't live with his da and his nanny was real sick so his ma used to be out, you know what I mean. So I was staying over there you know with him for the first while when I was kicked out. — Paul (19)

These accounts locate heroin initiation during a period of great instability in young people's lives. Drug use and early episodic homelessness were strong components of this instability but there were almost always other issues involved: household conflict, difficult family relationships or parental alcohol abuse. These young people did not report a simple cause-effect relationship between (problematic) drug use and homelessness. Emma's account similarly points to a course of initiation associated with a complex set of situations and factors:

How I kind of left home was, eh, I started on drugs. I was hanging around town, I was from (suburban locality) and I was hanging around town. I started off with taking, you know, ecstasy and fucking coke. And I met this gang and they were taking heroin so I decided to take heroin. — Emma (17)

Other accounts locate the transition to serious or "heavy end" drug use clearly during the period following their first episode of homelessness and, for a considerable number, this transition occurred shortly after accessing emergency accommodation for the first time. Tony, Eoin and Megan all came into contact with heroin scenes through the youth homeless services they accessed in the city-centre as teenagers:

[Can you remember the first time you went to a hostel?]

Yeah. It was weird, like all different people, people on gear like you know. I was sitting there like and there was a snooker room and there was seven beds. Seven for the fellas and seven for the girls, that was 14. But it was, it was horrible. I didn't know what to say like you know because I was only new. They were all friendly to me, I got to know them all then. That's when I really got into the gear. They were all strung out. That's when I got introduced to it. — Tony (22)

I stayed there (residential project) for about four months and I ended up robbin' the petty cash so I got kicked out. And I went then to (hostel) and I got kicked out of there for the same thing, trying to rob the petty cash. And I went back to (residential project) and I got kicked out of there again for being with a girl; you're not supposed to go over the girl's side and I was caught crawling out of the room. And I got kicked out of there again. And I was going back to the (hostel) and there and then I started messing around with heroin. — Eoin (19)

I was in school, I left school when I was 15 and I've been on the streets since I was 14. I was going to the Out of Hours and I was going through there and I was 15 actually when I went on drugs and I've just been going through (hostels) ever since and I was back at home there a while ago and now I'm back here (hostel). — Megan (19)

For the majority, first heroin use occurred subsequent to the initial homeless experience. Two of the study's young women were introduced to the drug by a romantic partner during a period of socialising and "hanging out", either in their local area or in the city-centre. One of these young women also reported that her relationship with her boyfriend was a factor in her home leaving.

I was very young and naïve at the time I left home. The only thing I'd ever done was drank, never smoked hash or anything like that. So that relationship progressed and we kind of, we started being with each other and we decided like, "Ah fuck it".

> *We thought we'll run away to England like ... So I kind of, over*
> *there I started learning about heroin, his cousin was saying,*
> *"You know he's an addict", an' all. And because I was so naïve at*
> *the time, I didn't understand ... I was saying like, "Why are you*
> *like that?" and "What's so important about the drugs?" So he*
> *said, "Here, you can try it". Like so that's how I started getting*
> *into drugs. — Sarah (21)*

Drug use escalated for practically all of the young people as their
"careers" in homelessness progressed and this pattern of drug
consumption was especially apparent among those who moved
constantly between hostels (targeting young people under the age
of 18) and other unstable living situations. Close proximity to
other drug users reinforced their commitment to drug scenes and
this, coupled with the ease of drug availability, allowed fledgling
habits to become entrenched. Drug use was normal in many of the
settings where young people "hung out" and provided entry to
mutually supportive peer networks.

Typical accounts of drug transitions strongly suggest that their
homeless and drug "careers" progressed concurrently. Within a
relatively short time, a substantial number had become enmeshed
in a daily routine of "scoring" and using drugs:

> *[Can you tell me about a typical day, how you'd spend your*
> *day?]*

> *Well I got up and I went down to collect me labour (social welfare*
> *payment), went off, got a fix (injected), goofed off for an hour or*
> *two, then went for me breakfast. Then I went to the drop-in-*
> *centre for a cup of tea. Then I went up to the (day centre), do you*
> *know it? I went up there for another cup of tea. Then I went for*
> *another fix, had another goof and then went out to me ma's and*
> *just sat out there 'till half 5.00, quarter to 6.00. Then I came*
> *straight home here (hostel). — Tony (22)*

Eleven of the study's young people had injected heroin, although
not all were current injectors. The transition to injecting drug use
was triggered in most cases by financial difficulties arising from

the pressures of maintaining an escalating heroin habit. The majority had not planned to inject when they first did it. This meant that they were unprepared for the event, a situation which led some to share injecting equipment with a more experienced user. Conor, who had been homeless since the age of 12, had injected heroin for the first time only a few days before he was interviewed.

> *I've been injecting since Sunday and that was my first time. I never injected until Sunday, I always smoked it and, even then, I wasn't really into it.*
>
> *[And how did that come about?]*
>
> *I don't know, it's just like ... I was feeling depressed on Sunday you know, just thinking about everything. And this mate he just said to me, "I'm going down to the (day centre). You see I got talking to him in (adult hostel) on Sunday morning and he was saying, "Come down to the (day centre) and I'll see can I get you in". So I said, "Right I'll go down". And then he said, "Well, I'll stop off and I'll have a turn on". I had no intention of going near it (heroin). So I went in with him and that's when he offered so I got tempted and I just couldn't resist. And said, "I'll try it just once". And I've been doing it since but I'm not going to do it anymore, I'll have to stop ... — Conor (19)*

By their own admission, these young people were marked by the fact that their drug use was out of control. Many expressed extreme anxiety about their situations and about their need to escape from the drugs culture that engulfed their everyday lives.

> *[What might help you, do you think?]*
>
> *If I got into a clinic, got away from the whole scene, you know. The whole drug scene yeah, away from the hostels. Just (pause) ... I don't know? It's the people you know, you bump into the wrong crowd. — Tony (22)*

As documented in the previous chapter, many of the young people in this study had few social or personal supports and were fearful or lonely in the places they resided. Those who had become immersed in street "scenes" made frequent reference to using alcohol and drugs as a way of coping with the stresses endemic to street life.

> *And now every day I'm not happy unless, unless I have something, some drugs. I don't feel happy unless I have something, something for the head like. It's bad. — Brendan (17)*

> *I'd rather drink really than do any of the drugs. I have no money to buy the drink so I have to do whatever I have. I just do what's available to me, you know. Makes the day go quicker. When you're walking around with a straight head all day you know the day just drags on. That's why I take drugs on the street, just bored. — Conor (19)*

Lawbreaking, Criminality and Incarceration

Of the 23 young men interviewed, 21 reported "trouble" with the police at some time and 20 had been charged with at least one criminal offence. At the time of interview, 19 had appeared, or were due to appear, in court in connection with one or more offences. Some had committed only a small number of crimes but others had outstanding charges from multiple transgressions for which they awaited a court date. Fourteen of the young men had served a custodial sentence at some time and three were incarcerated at the time of interview.

Young women were far less likely to report trouble with the police and far fewer had contact with law enforcement agencies. Eight had been charged with a criminal offence and a further two were enrolled in the juvenile liaison scheme (diversionary scheme operated by An Garda Síochána). In the vast majority of cases, the charges against these women were for theft. Compared to their male counterparts, their offending behaviour was more irregular and less serious, although there are exceptions. Four of the more persistent female offenders had served a custodial sentence at some time.

For the total sample then, three-quarters of the young people reported "trouble" or had been cautioned by the police, just under three-quarters had been charged with a criminal offence and almost half had been incarcerated at some time. Early offending was more common among the study's young men: seven stated that they had had contact with the police from their early teens and six (all under the age of 19 at the time of interview) had spent a period in one or more of the country's special schools for young offenders.

"Coming into Town": "Making it" in the Street Scene

The stories told by young people highlight the significance of what many described as "coming into town". This phrase was used so frequently that it merits attention. "Hanging around" town frequently coincided with young people's initial period out of home while others talked about socialising in the city-centre with peers during the period preceding their first homeless experience. More significant perhaps than the precise juncture of "coming into town" was the chain of events and experiences that this move typically set in motion. This initial period of contact with the city-centre homeless scene was a common point of initiation into a whole range of risky behaviour and activities.

> ... *I had a happy life going out with me little sister to clubs an' all and then I started taking, like smoking and drinking. Then I started on the drugs. Well, when me brother died I kind of went off me head like. Then I started smoking the heroin with me sister. And then I came into town then and badly started on the drugs, started on coke an' all. Then me mother and father found out and they just told me I can either choose the drugs or the house. And I really chose the drugs like 'cos it was hard to come off them like.*
> — *Siobhán (22)*

> *I was twelve, about twelve and a half. I ran away from me ma's into the city and just got known, got in with the wrong people, started robbing with them and then takin' drugs. Heroin was the*

second drug I took. I was just messed up from there on and kept fuckin' (pause) ... fucking up from that. — Brendan (17)

Those young people who spent much of their day socialising around town experienced high exposure to street-based drug scenes where they had close contact with other homeless youth. These early days out of home were depicted by a number as a period of excitement and new-found freedom away from stressful family situations or care settings.

> *I was excited because usually, like at twelve or thirteen or what-*
> *ever, you would have your mammy telling you what to do. In the*
> *hostels they couldn't make you do what you didn't want to do.*
> *You could walk out and say, "Yeah, I'm off", you know what I*
> *mean, "I'm going off 'till three or four in the morning". And they*
> *(staff at the hostel) would still take you back in because you were*
> *so small. So I was excited at the start, I loved it like. Everyone*
> *loved it when they first started going in (to the hostels) but it's*
> *only when they get older and then just look back at all the mess-*
> *ing and all the stupidness that you realise there's nothing to like*
> *about it. It's just, it's nasty now because I hate it now, you know*
> *what I mean. — Brendan (17)*

As newcomers to the hostel "scene", young people had to find a niche and establish an identity. Within these settings, it was important to establish a presence and to learn the parameters of "acceptable" behaviour. Being tough and independent, minding one's own business, never reporting incidents or violations to staff or the police, maintaining relationships with peers and being ever-vigilant about one's personal belongings, all became standard approaches to daily life. All of this was learned through interaction and participation. Although expectations differed by context, the following are some of the broad "rules" that young people talked about during interview:

> *... well, the rule in here (hostel) is, "don't steal from your own".*
> *And you have your kind of separate rules for inside and outside.*
> *Don't rob any of the staff, one of the staff I think got their phone*

nicked, it was returned by one of the other lads, it was taken off the person who stole it and given back and said, "If that happens again next time you won't be so lucky". You don't steal from anybody in here, whereas if you steal a phone out there, it's fine. We don't like it because it brings bad attention to the house but we're not going to kill you for it, we'll just frown on you. You mug someone outside, that's your thing. Like we'll frown upon it but we're not going to turn around and tell the staff. — Neil (20)

... the only name you'll get is being a rat. That's the only name you'll get. It's important that you never get a name like that. And it's important that you don't squeal on your own mates. I'd never squeal. I'd never do anything like that. If I did that I'd be fucked. And there's no need for it. — Declan (19)

During the early days, first impressions were important, as was integrating into the group. A critical step for some in this context was the move from "outsider" to "insider" status. Paul told how his initial anxieties faded once he got talking to "the lads". His story reveals the strain of his vulnerability and his simultaneous efforts to overcome what might well be a defining moment for his image and reputation.

I was a bit scared, you know going in (to the hostel). The lads were on the steps an' all, you know, when I was going in. I felt a bit intimidated but they weren't going to do anything, you know. You see, before that I never even left (the suburban area where he lived), I used to stay there, never came into town on me own or anything. I was in town once and that was on the hop (playing-truant) with another fella, that was about it. It was much differ-ent, it was, going into a hostel. It was crazy. But like I went in and the boys were alright. And they had a bit of hash an' all so it was just, go out the back, do a joint and just get talking to them. It was grand, you know. — Paul (19)

Cigarettes, drugs and alcohol were strong currency in these set-tings; they helped to ease tension and, as expressions of solidarity, they enabled young people to interact. Caroline maintained that hostel life was easier for smokers:

Like I've seen real quiet girl an' all come in, do you know what I mean, and they don't know what to do and they're afraid to mix with other people. And they don't smoke so they've no way of socialising with people, like you know what I mean. It's handy if you're a smoker. — Caroline (16)

The lack of structure in the lives of these young people was striking. The majority were not attending school or a training programme, nor were they accountable to a responsible or trusted adult for their whereabouts on a daily basis. As a result, their day to day lives were played out in very public environments: the street, shopping centres, parks and commercial areas where their exclusion from the mainstream was all the more conspicuous. Although many hated it and considered it a waste of time, "hanging around" became *the* major activity of the day. Within these outdoor locations, much talk and conversation centred on the drugs market: "scoring" locations, good and bad "deals" and the availability and price of various drugs. With nothing to do and nobody to account to, drinking and drug use became a way to pass the time. Instability and chaos were always difficult to cope with and validated a range of unconventional responses and activities:

[Have you ever slept rough?]

Yeah, loads of times. Hundreds of times. I've just been out all day, all night like just robbing and basically just drinking and whatever. Staying up for the whole night, then the next day, the same thing. Done it loads of times. — Christian (17)

[So most of your days you spend ...]

Robbin' and then just get a tray of drink, lump of hash and just chill out and just, just have a laugh with your mates, you know. — Paul (19)

Apart from passing the time, "hanging out" provided important street knowledge as well as insights into opportunities to earn money. Without a stable place to live, or the qualifications to secure or maintain legitimate employment, a large number started

to experiment with alternative forms of income-generation and
learned to avail of every possible opportunity to make money.
Paul explained how he and other residents of the hostel where he
lived saved and pooled their daily allowance to buy a weekly
supply of cannabis:

*In (the hostel) we had that well sussed, we did 'cos about four
days a week we were getting money for hash off them, you know.
'Cos they used to give us money you know. First we used to get
our pocket money right and that was, that was three days a week
or something. And like it wouldn't be much, it'd be, like you get
four euro. Everyone would get four euro and that. All adds up,
you know what I mean. And then we'd do a chore. So for doing
that you'd get more, you'd get four euro for that. And we were
doing that three or four days a week so we were getting up
enough for two lumps of hash, you know what I mean. Like,
probably 50 euros worth of hash. — Paul (19)*

Tricks and scams such as the one described above were usually
short-lived and several progressed to other forms of subsistence
work. Paul went on to tell of his initial forays into a world where
lawbreaking became a core strategy for financing his everyday
needs:

*When I came into town (pause) ... I was 14 or 15 when I came
into town. I was in town before that but yeah, I was scared, yeah.
I didn't know what to do. But like you're trying to fit in, you
know. Away from home town is a totally different place so you're
trying to fit in with people. You just go along with it and just
and see what happens like. Know what we used to do actually,
this is when I first started mugging people ... like we'd stand at a
bus stop, and we'd just suss out a few people, you know. Like just
get on the bus then with them and we'd be sitting behind them, in
front of them, at the side of them or whatever and we'd get the
stuff off them then and then just straight back off the bus. And
the bus would just be gone then, you know. So that was the first
few, yeah, my first few muggings.*

Paul's account illustrates just how quickly immersion in street scenes can take place. The street provided a whole range of opportunities to establish connections with people who were already involved in criminal activity and it was in these settings that he, like many others, learned techniques and strategies to enable him to survive. Paul later explained the significance of his move "into town", where he embarked on a whole new lifestyle characterised by "trouble":

> *(When I was sleeping rough in the suburbs)... I was just thinking like that I'm fucked you know like. No way that I could go around home for me dinner, no way I could go around for a shower. Nothing to do or anything, ya know, no parents now or anything. So I just had to, just had to come into town and I just stayed in town then. Just got new mates, different lifestyle altogether. It fucked me up like, the charges an' all, getting in trouble, yeah. I only got arrested twice out in (home neighbourhood) like. Then when I came in here; it's mad in here, like. Out in (suburban locality) I never done that shit before and then I come into town an' there's all this. The first phone that I snatched I took it and I ran across O'Connell Street, nearly got a bang of a bus, and I fell over some lady and it got taken off me so I didn't do that then for about a year. I says "No, I'm not doing that shit, no, fuck that", you know, because I got caught. But then I just started doing it again, and I was doin' two and three and four a day, you know, getting a good few quid. I don't know?*

Apart from providing a training ground for initiation into a wide range of alternative forms of income-generation, transient group living encouraged and facilitated bullying and victimisation. The successful negotiation of daily life meant learning to protect and defend one-self and many accounts, in fact, strongly suggest that bullying was endemic within many (though not all) hostels. Several commented on the pervasiveness of bullying and on the inability of service providers to address and deal with harassment of this kind:

[Would you say that there's bullying going on in hostels?]

Yeah, big time, big time. And like I don't know whether (pause) ... obviously the people there, the staff there are well educated, you know. But they just don't seem to know what's going on in front of their eyes, you know what I mean. This chap here a while ago, he was getting the piss took out of him, he was getting fuckin' bullied, that was what he was getting. I mean it's madness. But, I don't know, they just don't seem to cop on to what is going on around them, you know. — Seán (21)

Young people routinely feared for their personal safety and for the safety of their belongings. While most learned as time progressed to "read" the character of others as best they could – and to maintain a safe distance from potential threat – these techniques did not necessarily protect them from victimisation, as Neil's story suggests.

[What did you think of the lads (in the hostel)?]

Some of them I didn't like because, well ok, they were mean but that wasn't it. It's just (pause) ... I know when they're good. If they're bad and they pick on other people or something like that I wouldn't give them the time of day. And some of them were just mean and actually one of them there I knew I was going to have trouble with because he just took an instant disliking to me. Later on he peed in my room and tried to smother me while I was asleep. That just shows you how well I was able to pick him out. I knew I was going to have trouble with him but that's some of the things he done later ... — Neil (20)

Reports of having property stolen were common and, when such incidents did occur, young people felt powerless. Taking action meant being labelled "a rat" and the negative consequences of making a complaint to staff far outweighed the loss of clothing, footwear or money. Caroline explained:

I was going through the Out of Hours for about two weeks and I was only after buying a brand new pair of runners. They were bleedin' gorgeous, they were. I had them underneath the bed and this girl came in one night and she took them out from underneath the bed. I woke up the next morning and I said, "Where's me runners?", blah, blah, blah. I seen her wearing them,. couldn't say it to the staff obviously because that's being a rat, I would have got myself in twice as much trouble. — Caroline (16)

Being streetwise was crucial to surviving homelessness, as was the ability to defend one's property and reputation. Younger homeless people – and those who did not display a tough or macho image – were particularly vulnerable to victimisation. James, who was homeless for approximately 18 months at the time of interview, described being bullied by older and more experienced homeless youth:

There's a lot of bullying an' all going on around the street. There's fellas called Johnny and James and Richie, and they're all robbing me an' all, every time they see me. They're all a lot bigger than me like, they're all men like, do you know what I mean. Every time they see me, five or six of them grab me and rob me. They take all me money and then whatever I have on me, me jewellery or anything. — James (18)

Displays of weakness or vulnerability, according to Christian – who was something of a veteran of hostel life – presented serious risks to one's ability to survive:

I'm telling you, anybody that shows weakness on the streets is going to be fucked. If you've anything valuable of any sort, you're fucked. I've seen blokes coming in, rich little kids coming in. One night, "Bang!" — they don't know what to do. They're stripped. They don't know what's going on. "Where's me fuckin' runners?", "Where's me clothes? Oh God, somebody else is wearing them". Do you know what I mean. — Christian (17)

All of the young people who became immersed in street scenes had spent months –and, in some cases, years – moving between numerous unstable living situations. Their youth, their poverty, and the transience that had come to characterise their lives, ex-

posed them to a range of precarious alternatives. Once out of
home, the street quickly became a way of life and, with this, the
freedom that young people initially experienced on leaving home
soon turned to hostility and chaos:

> *You get sucked in to the streets too much. Like from nobody tell-*
> *ing you what to do. Do what you want, whatever you want to do,*
> *you know what I mean. The only people that stop you is the police*
> *or someone else comin' up an' killing you, you know. That's it. —*
> *Christian (17)*

Megan is one of several young people who remarked on the dramatic life changes since she first experienced homelessness.

> *[Just going back to say when you first went to the hostel, what*
> *was that like? Tell me what you were feeling ...]*

> *Well to be honest, at the start I thought, "Ah yeah, this is great".*
> *At the start like, I thought it was great. I didn't have to answer to*
> *anyone and it was just great. But after a while then, when you*
> *get used to it, it's horrible. You're walking around all day until 8*
> *o'clock at night. You're thrown out at half nine in the morning. I*
> *ended up going on drugs and it just got worse and worse, going*
> *robbing and then getting arrested. — Megan (15)*

The Street Economy

Initiation into street life was essentially a process of acculturation
into the street "scene", its resources, rules, economy and language. Young people were introduced to different niches within
the street economy and their law-breaking ranged from minor
violations to more serious criminal activity. The persistence of
their offending also varied, as did their motives for committing
crime. Many stole items to finance their immediate needs. Neil
and Rachel told about times when they had stolen everyday
goods including food and clothing. They had not been appre-
hended for these misdemeanours and neither reported more serious or persistent law-breaking:

[You mentioned there that you used to steal?]

Well that was when my dad was really, really bad, this was actually before I was in (the hostel). I would steal my food and if I needed deodorant I had to nick it and if I wanted food I had to nick it. I was just about able to get the bus fare out of the couch. Like when he (father) comes home he would fall asleep on the couch and some of the money falls down the chairs and you go hunting for it ... I just wanted it for the bus fare to get in to school in the morning. — Neil (20)

I've robbed an' all, but I haven't robbed from like anybody. Just robbed for myself ... I robbed a pair of trousers before I came in here (to the hostel) 'cos I only had a pair of jeans. So that was it like, I needed stuff like. — Rachel (14)

Unlike Neil and Rachel, others continued to engage in law-breaking as a basic subsistence strategy and, for a considerable number, crime became a primary means of generating income. In general, the repertoire of criminal activities increased as "careers" in homelessness progressed. Julian openly admitted to committing criminal acts in order to survive:

[What were you in prison for can I ask?]

Robbing cars, muggings, all that. I had to do it to survive. I mean you have to have clothes on your back, and you have to have food in your stomach. You can't go round like you see the way junkies are. I'm not like that, you know what I mean. I always have clothes on me back and I always had money like. I know I did it a stupid way but I had to survive. That's the one thing you have to do. — Julian (22)

There were different dimensions to surviving street life. Earlier discussions suggest that young people who spent time on the street had to constantly defend and protect themselves and their belongings. In addition, their lack of educational qualifications and skills training meant that they had no legitimate means of earning money. Illegal activity therefore provided an important, and very often the only, potential source of income. Young people used a vast lexicon of terms to depict the activities of the street economy: "snatching", "nicking", "mugging", "stroking" and "doing handbags".[1] While the range, type and persistence of their criminal offences varied, property theft was the most commonly reported violation:

> *[What do you do for money?]*

> *Money, I go off robbing for money. If I have to make money I have to go off and make it myself. No problem, I go off stroking. Taking whatever, like things that you know you'd make money on. Things that (pause) ... you wouldn't go into a place and rob something and then not do anything with it. You know, you go in and you know you're making a few quid out of it. — Joe (19)*

Although far less likely than their male counterparts to engage in this type of activity, a number of young women told about times when they had stolen money and goods to finance their everyday needs:

> *[How do you spend your days?]*

> *Shoplifting. Going into shops, takin' things and selling them to people. Get money and go every morning, buy drugs, go off and goof, go back to another shop and rob loads of things and keep getting drugs. — Roisín (16)*

> *[What do you do for money?]*

> *I shoplift sometimes for me smokes and that like. Just go into a shop and rob off the rich. — Megan (19)*

Emma explained the extent of her involvement in property theft and was keen to emphasise that her participation was limited:

> *Once or twice I probably robbed. Don't get me wrong, I probably robbed with (boyfriend) when I was really strung out. I probably*

---

[1] All of these terms were used in reference to stealing.

did the odd bit of robbin', you know. But I'd never be serious into it. — Emma (17)

Yet, she had considerable knowledge about many aspects of the street economy.

[What kinds of place do you go to sell a phone or clothes or whatever?]

Down there, a shop used to buy clothes off us (referring to boyfriend) and there was different places, you know. Word of mouth going around telling, "he'll buy the CDs off ya" and "that fella'll buy this off ya". You know, you just get to know them like.

Many of these young people were apprenticed into street life by older or more experienced youth, or by a romantic partner who had been on the scene for longer. Having "a suss" – or knowledge – about what was happening around town, and learning where and how to conduct "business", was critical to knowing how to survive:

We have a suss, every part of town we have a suss. If you want to sell phones we go to this person; if we want to sell laptops, we go to this person; if we want to sell bleedin' cameras go to this person, know what I mean? We have it sussed all over town, the blacks, most of the blacks, Chinese, shit like that I'll tell ya. It's good, ya know what I mean, 'cos you get rid of things (stolen property) like that instead of being caught red hot. — Fergal (18)

Although theft was the most common criminal solution in the search for necessities, it was not the only solution and a range of other unlawful activity was reported. Seán, Ronan and Sarah described the offences that brought them into contact with law enforcement agencies:

I have charges coming up in December for faking prescriptions, which is going back to the time when I was strung out on prescribed, well Valium and Dalmane. They were bogey (bogus) prescriptions that I was going in and changing. But it has landed me up in court. — Seán (21)

*I have loads of charge sheets for hitting coppers and being drunk
and disorderly, robbin' cars, snatching an' all like that. — Ronan
(17)*

*I remember goin' into my sister's office one day and I seen a
cheque book on the receptionist desk and I whipped it. I took a few
cheques out of the back of it and cashed them cheques and I think
I got about €4,000 altogether out of the cheques. And for that and
robbing, I got locked up. — Sarah (21)*

Participation in activities related to the distribution and sale of
illegal drugs was also reported. Whilst most considered the risk of
apprehension to be high, several simultaneously claimed that it
was the quickest and easiest way to make money. Brendan told
how drug selling financed his own drug use and also put a roof
over his head for a period:

*Well I was out there now, I was staying with a friend of mine for,
em, about seven or eight months. But the down side of staying in
this friend's was that I had to go out in the mornings and sell
heroin for him and I kind of messed up … the chap I was selling
for, he was getting it in quantities. You know, the half eights;
he'd be getting maybe nine, twelve or fourteen of them … so by
two o'clock the next day he'd have pulled in a thousand euro or
something. But that was no good to me. I was smokin' everything
that I was getting but he was making a good few quid. But I was
feedin' my habit and I had a place to stay so, you know what I
mean, it was handy enough for me. — Brendan (17)*

Almost all of the study's heroin users had endured periods when
their need for drugs exerted considerable control over their lives
and several openly admitted to selling drugs to support, or partly
finance, their day-to-day needs. The accounts of Megan, Eoin and
Tony capture the cycle of activity that had come to characterise
daily life.

[What are things that are hard for you at the moment?]

Walking around all day, going on drugs, robbing and goin' scoring. It's horrible. It's even horrible when you're not on drugs because you're just walking around all day, nowhere to go ... and you need money to do things. — Megan (19)

I do wake up (pause) ... Tomorrow now, I'll probably have no money for gear or Friday morning. So I'll wake up dying and walking around. Like me nerves are gone. I walk into a shop and I do be watching everything. It's hard, hard oul' work, hard oul' life it is. — Tony (22)

I am going out of here (hostel) in the morning and I have no where to go. Like I am just walking around and just robbing like ... Yeah, when I wake up in the morning, and most mornings it is just like, "Fuck this", you know, another day. It's like Ground Hog Day; the same shit, different day like. — Eoin (20)

Surprisingly few, especially among the study's younger participants, were willing to beg for money on the street. Referred to as "tapping", it was seen as degrading and several remarked on the compromises and loss of self-esteem that such activity involved. A smaller number did, however, beg for money at carefully selected city-centre locations. For Gavin, who was sleeping rough at the time of interview, "tapping" was a primary means of making money and one which he viewed as preferable to stealing:

[How did you spend yesterday, what did you do when you got up?]

Tapping. Every day the same thing, different places.

[Are there different times when you tap]

This time (3.00 pm)' till about 6.00. Then from 6.00, get a bag of heroin, get a few bags, smoke it and come back out about 11.00, stay out till about 4.00.

[And when do you go to sleep?]

About 4.00 o'clock in the morning. Wake up 8.00. We get pulled up at 8.00 in the morning, like we get ran away from the door-ways. We only get about three hours sleep.

[Are there days when you do things differently?]

Always tapping, yeah. Rob as well; snatches, phones. Don't do it all the time, I'd rather tap than rob people. I don't like robbing people because I wouldn't like it done to myself and I wouldn't like it to be done to my mother or my father, you know what I mean. They have problems of their own as well the poor people, you know what I mean, instead of me coming up robbing their phones. I only robbed one thing in my life and that was a phone.
— Gavin (15)

Someone who did not adhere to the conventional approach of sitting on the footpath asking for money was Anna. Instead, she and a friend walked a particular city-centre district where they had an established routine:

[When you were on the street at the times you lived on the streets or in squats or whatever, what did you do for money?]

Tapping. You know walking up and down the road asking people for bus fare, me and Tess used to be brilliant at that. You know Trinity, well Trinity end of Dame Street right, I'd stand on one side and she'd (Tess) stand on the other right. And we'd walk all the way up to Thomas Street, right. And we'd switch at Thomas Street, right, and we'd walk all the way back down. And by the time we'd get back down we'd have fifty, sixty euro between us. And all we'd have to do is walk straight back up again, score (buy drugs) and then smoke it and goof. She'd be turning on, she'd be injecting it. I'd be having a smoke while she'd be injecting kind of thing. But that's how we made our money, like, tapping. — Anna (17)

The majority of accounts of criminal offending suggest that young people's street involvement, and their constant movement in and out of city-centre hostels, propelled them into drug and criminal "careers". In a world of limited options, the financial benefits of scamming, pilfering and theft far outweighed the rewards of conventional work. Christian's account describes the emergence of "a life of crime" linked directly to hostel and street life:

> *It's a life of fucking crime, that's it. It's like a big circle being in the hostel. I've been in them years, you know what I mean ... Because if you're homeless, right, you're kicked out at half-nine in the morning and you can't go in 'till eight o'clock. So you've that whole day to waste, do you know what I mean. And how are you meant to be in school as well? It's very hard to be in education because like, by the time you go in at eight they see you, you know what I mean, you get placed, they bring you off somewhere, you stay there for the night, you wake up. It's very hard to get up in the morning and go to FÁS and all ... And, you know, in (the hostel) you'd wake up with six people there, you know what I mean. And they say, "I'm going off robbing" and "Where are you going?" And you're automatically sucked in to the robbing business. Rather go out and rob something, and that's what you earn in the whole week, you know what I mean, for going out robbing someone, you earn the same amount. That's it. — Christian (17)*

Most of the young people who engaged in illegal subsistence work had no formal educational qualifications; they had few skills to enable them to seek employment and, in any case, the absence of a stable home made the task of sustaining a job extremely difficult. Hostels and social services offered some money, as did training schemes and begging, but the financial rewards paled compared to the potential return from criminal activity. Put simply, non-criminal means of income-generation simply could not match the potential return from crime. Moreover, upon entering into the city-centre homeless scene, many discovered a ready-made and vibrant alternative economy. In a world of limited options, participation made practical sense for a large number of young people whose life experiences had eroded their stake in conformity.

Bullying, Violence and Victimisation

Homeless young people live in a socially predatory environment where the issues of security and defence are constant concerns.

Living or "hanging out" in public spaces exposes them to the risk of intrusion and also places them in an arena where violence is more likely to take place. Within street-based settings, many had witnessed violence, including fights, beatings, muggings and other acts of aggression. The following accounts are examples of the violent scenes to which young people were routinely exposed as observers, participants and victims:

> *There's a lot of violence on the street, yeah. There's a lot of muggings and robberies, a lot of violence, yeah, a lot of violence. A lot of shootings, a lot of stabbings.* — Declan (19)

> *I got smashed up in there (in a squat) by five blokes with bars. Cuts all over me head an' all after them beating me up in there. That's why I wouldn't stay there anymore.* — James (18)

> *Like I've seen blokes, I've done it personally myself, I've seen blokes left in fuckin' bad puddles of blood, d'you know what I mean, just for their money. It's bad.* — Christian (17)

A large number of those who "hung out" or slept on the street had been attacked and beaten since the time they left home. Fights or brawls sometimes erupted between homeless youth themselves over items and possessions, including money and drugs. The use of risky subsistence strategies also exposed young people to individuals and customers who themselves were potential victimizers. For a considerable number of street-experienced youth, violence was simply a reality "out there" that had to be dealt with.

> *Ah, I've been beaten up plenty of times and I've beaten up people plenty of times. It's the way life is out there, you know. Like there's always someone out there better than you at the end of the day.* — Declan (19)

Although more commonly reported among young men, a small number of young women were drawn into in rows over drugs, money or other possessions:

They (group of young people) saw me walking up, they were com-ing out of the Green and they saw me. And Rita literally grabbed me in a headlock and dragged me down and they were turning around and saying that I ratted on somebody for having gear ... I was supposed to have a straightener (a fight) with Rita and I had a straightener with her and then Samantha decided to put her little fucking arse in. She gave me a really bad hiding ... She was put-ting her hand up my top in to my bra to see if I had money in my bra because that's where I always kept money like and I was just like, "Oh get away from me", kind of thing. And I was like, "I don't have any money, leave me alone". And after the fight all me hair was falling out because Samantha was after pulling it out ...
— Anna (17)

The use of intimidation and violence for economic gain in the manner described by Anna was not unusual. Young people some-times used violence to defend and protect themselves or to avenge previous assaults and their tendency to seek out and cluster in groups created an increased tendency for violence to erupt.

People never robbed on me. They've tried now. One or two people have tried to rob me and I had to fucking sort them out.

[And was that physically sort them out?]

Yeah, you'd have to fight. Like it's all stupid but you'd have a fight. They all came over and tried to have a fight with me in the middle of fucking O'Connell Street of all the bleedin' places. I had to knock them out, you know. There was a few of his mates and I had a few of my mates. They came over and started swinging boxes at me, you know what I mean. I wasn't going to stand there so I grabbed and gave him a loaf (hit him), busted his eye for him, you know what I mean. And he never bothered me after it, you know what I mean. But that's the way it is. Somebody is going to always want to come up to you if they take you for a fool in any-way. And if they get the better of you you're fucked. You're genu-inely fucked, I'm telling you. — Christian (17)

Alcohol use and intoxication were also implicated in some reports of violent street-based incidents but, more than anything, the transience and unpredictability of their daily lives restricted young people's ability to engage in more conventional protective approaches. On the other hand, some young people embraced violence more readily and frequently than others. Colm's views on violence, and his perceptions of how and why it occurs, highlight how street-based living can erode young people's ties to conventional alternatives:

[Have you seen violence on the street?]

Yeah, especially when you're under eighteen. A lot of violence.

[Why would you say there's a lot of violence?]

It's just, you don't really care. You think nothing's gonna happen, all this shit. Especially when you go to the hostels. There's too many things going through your mind and you can't think straight so you wanna do drugs and you wanna be high. But when you're at home and all (pause) ... when I was living with my sister I didn't wanna do gear and stuff. I wanted to go to the pictures with me girlfriend, stay in and watch a film with her.

[And when you're on the streets ...]

You can't do it, you want to but you can't. These things don't even go through your mind. — Colm (20)

Of considerable importance in understanding the violent reactions and responses of some young people is their own personal experience of violence and victimisation. A large number were themselves victims of violence during childhood or adolescence (see Chapter 4). Homelessness itself presents significant challenges and risks, including the risk of victimisation by other youth as well as property crime and assault. Rough sleepers were particularly fearful of harassment and victimisation:

I was very paranoid, I couldn't get asleep ... I lay down to try and go to sleep at 11.00 or 12.00, like midnight. But I would say it was about half 4.00, 5.00 o'clock before I got to sleep. Because I had to try and keep one eye open because I was afraid someone would just come up and kick me out of it like. Like kicking me to death like, you know what I mean. It has happened to a few people that I know that have been basically sleeping rough and they have been kicked like. Because people who are drunk, they think it's a great laugh. They kick the homeless. — Seán (21)

Young people rarely or never reported crime against themselves to an appropriate authority and most would not consider doing so. This refusal to report crime against their person appears to be related, in some cases, to their fear of victimisation by the police. A total of ten young people – almost all young men – claimed to have been victims of police brutality and only one had made an official complaint to a relevant authority. Indeed, most considered that making any such complaint would lead to further trouble and victimisation. Others felt that they would not be believed:

Some of them (the police) were all right, some of them, they're on a mad power buzz man. They're going around kicking your head in and people don't believe it like but they do. I'm dead serious, you know, they'd whack you out of it, with the baton like. Trying to get information an' all ... and you'd get a whack of it in the head and let me tell you you'd come down after a whack of that. — Colm (20)

Homeless young people may engage in a range of strategies that have an uncertain – but almost always negative – impact on their lives and which serve to further marginalise and isolate them. Equally, in situations where they are themselves victims of violence, bullying or intimidation, most have few choices or alternatives in terms of protection, security or justice. This study's young people were frequent victims of property crime and of crime against their person, reflecting the extent to which their daily lives are played out in public places. Yet, the majority could not avail of – and considered themselves ineligible for – the protection and support that is available to the wider youth and adult population.

Detention and Prison

Engaging in deviant subsistence strategies carried significant risks, the most obvious being the risk of apprehension by the police. Homeless youth are, of course, more vulnerable to police intervention simply because they spend significant periods of time "hanging around" in public spaces. As stated earlier, 18 of the study's participants (14 young men and four young women) had experience of prison life and three (all young men) were in prison at the time of interview. The sentences served by young people ranged from a few months to two years, with the majority having served a sentence of between six and 18 months. Some – though by no means all – had previously spent a period in detention during their teenage years:

> *Did two years in (special school for young offenders) ...*
>
> *[What was that like for you?]*
>
> *It was alright, I suppose. I was wild back then; don't think it bothered me because I was used to being in places like that. —* Conor (19)
>
> *[What was (special school for young offenders) like?]*
>
> *Not hard, not really. It's grand, you know. You get used to anything like, you get used to it. —* Christian (17)

Conor and Christian had grown accustomed to moving between a whole range of settings and institutions designed to intervene at some level in their lives. Indeed, a number of the study's young men appeared to have adapted to a system of intervention which had become quite instrumental in shaping their lives and their social experiences. Ronan was one of a number who had moved constantly between living places of various kinds, including foster homes, the street and special interventions for young offenders:

> *A while ago I was locked up for eight months and before that I was homeless and before that I was in foster care.*

[Yes, you said you were with more than one foster family?]

Yeah, about twelve different houses, yeah. Then I was put in (Remand and Assessment Unit) for six months when I was only twelve or something. I was locked up for most of it, most of me teenage years. — Ronan (17)

There was a strong sense that, for at least a number, prison was simply another living situation to which they had to adjust. Young people recounted a whole range of stories about the time they spent in prison – their daily routines, relationships with other inmates, and so on – and many talked about growing accustomed to this new environment:

[What was prison like the first time you went in?]

Really scared. I didn't know what it was like, I mean, going into (place of detention), it was the first time I had been in (place of detention). I went in, it was different like. I mean you've lost your freedom and locked up, only out in the yard for an hour, that's it. And back in, back to your cell and sit there for the night. — Julian (22)

The most challenging adjustments appeared to relate to the loss of freedom of movement. Nonetheless, there were some similarities between street and prison life and, in a sense, penal institutions represented an extension of the earlier life experiences of a number:

Homeless places (hostels) are like prison like, they rob your clothes, they rob your fucking (pause) ... I can describe for you a few times I got me clothes robbed. — Julian, 22

Prison was also a place where, once again, young people had to establish an identity and find a niche. There were many reports of intimidation and bullying and having allies was important. Violence was also reported by a number of young men:

I got a bad beatin' when I was locked up. Two blokes in the prison. They were country blokes.

[How did it happen?]

I was on one wing in the prison and there was another bloke in an-
other wing. And I was after giving him a beating on the outside so
he gave two blokes two joints to give me a hiding. — Colm (20)

Like the street, prisons have drug markets and many remarked on
the ease of availability of a range of illicit substances. This provided another form of continuity since so many had been previously involved in illicit economies at street level. Many of the
young people continued to use drugs while incarcerated.

Despite these similarities, a number felt prison had provided
them with a break from the street and from drugs, in particular.
Both Eoin and Megan explained how their time "inside" enabled
them to "get off" drugs for a period.

[What is that like?]

It's not a nice place and not a good experience, like I was there
that many times. You get used to it and it is good in a way like,
because if it was not for that place I would probably be dead now.
Like that is what I think. Like if prison wasn't there I would say I
would more than likely be dead like. 'Cos it gives you time to
think an' all, like it gets you off the drugs as well and it gets your
body back into shape, and you put on a bit of weight. But like
every time you get out you just go back and do the same shit
again like. You would be, probably doing okay for a week or two
but, you go back to the same again. — Eoin (20)

[What was that experience like for you?]

It snapped me out of it a bit like from robbing and drugs and that.
When you're in prison you're clean, you get time to think about
things. I was doing so well when I was in prison. I was going to
school an' all in there and I was doing like woodwork and things.
— Megan (19)

Young women, in particular, remarked that incarceration provided them with the opportunity to return to education and skills
training:

[The whole prison experience for you, how would you describe it now?]

It got me clean, it didn't feel like a punishment to be honest with you because I got myself clean, got my head together while I was in there. I went to school, done my ECDL, I got two art and design certificates, a woodwork certificate, photography, everything, I did cookery as well. It is just like going to a treatment centre to be honest with you because at night you're in your cell, you've your own telly, do you know what I mean, it's not that bad like.
— Sarah (21)

Reports like Sarah's highlight the hardship many had experienced during the period preceding their incarceration. However undesirable in terms of limiting one's freedom and autonomy, prison was sometimes seen as providing a relatively secure environment as well as a standard of living that far exceeded what was available "on the outside". In this sense, prison offered relief and respite, even if young people did have to return to the situations they left before their imprisonment.

Conclusion

The relationship between drug use and homelessness has been debated widely in the academic literature as highlighted in Chapter 2. Likewise, crime and its relationship to homelessness has been the subject of much discussion. Less attention has focused on how drug use *and* criminal activity are related to homeless "careers", particularly in the case of young people. Much of the evidence here demonstrates the interconnectedness of homeless, drug and criminal "careers"; it also strongly suggests that homelessness exacerbates the risk of young people becoming more deeply entrenched in both drug use and criminal behaviour.

Living out of home became a hazardous experience for many of the young people and it carried significant risks. Homeless scenes – the street, emergency hostels and other unstable living situations – provided locations where rules were learned and reinforced; at the same time, young people had little control over these environments. Those who got caught up in a cycle of using crisis-oriented services and short-term hostels (for young people under the age of 18) were most at risk, not simply because of their exposure to bullying and violence, but also because they were more likely to become active participants in a culture of behaviour that further jeopardised their development, health and well-being. Indeed, much of the material presented in this chapter suggests that crisis interventions such as short-term residential settings or hostels were one of a range of State-sponsored institutions in which young people accumulated the street competency to enable them to "get by".

Chapter 7

HOMELESSNESS AND HEALTH

Homelessness clearly presents challenges and risks that the majority of housed young people do not have to confront. While becoming homeless does not decree poor health, it does increase the risk that the person will develop health problems. The combination of dangerous circumstances, psychologically debilitating experiences and high propensity for risk-taking can have dramatic health consequences for homeless young people. These risks and hazards can result in significantly higher rates of infectious diseases and serious illnesses. Homeless young people also experience exposure to stresses for which risky behaviour may represent an effective short-term coping strategy.

To understand the health-related behaviour of homeless youth it is critical to acknowledge how the social context of their lives shapes norms, expectations and opportunities to engage in risk or to avoid it. This chapter examines young people's physical and psychological health and gives specific attention to their accounts of drug and sexual risk behaviour. The findings demonstrate numerous ways in which the health and well-being of homeless young people is compromised by the absence of a stable home. Barriers and constraints to health care access are highlighted as well as ways in which their coping strategies serve, in some cases, to further jeopardise the health status of young people.

Physical Health

During interview, young people were asked about their general health and they were also encouraged to identify specific health-related difficulties or problems. As might be expected given their young age, many considered themselves to be healthy. This was typically expressed as, "I don't have health problems", "I'm healthy" or "I am fit". The study's "newly" or recently homeless rarely reported health problems and few under the age of 17 years had suffered a recent bout of ill-health.

However, the study's older respondents who typically had longer homeless "careers" frequently reported health difficulties and concerns that they had neglected or ignored for some time. Furthermore, many had grown accustomed to some level of ill-health and appeared to accept as "normal" lingering or ongoing cold and influenza symptoms, toothaches, stomach pain and generally feeling unwell. This acceptance of ill-health almost always reflected the instability of their living situations and their need to prioritise immediate needs.

Housing provides protection from the elements, as well as access to facilities to maintain personal hygiene, the opportunity to prepare and eat regular meals, and the option of an uninterrupted night's sleep. Young people who lived in short- or medium-term residential settings (hostels) targeting under-18s did have access to these facilities. There were others, however, who did not. Certainly, a large number of interviewees had experienced periods when they found it difficult to maintain their personal hygiene and to get a good night's sleep. Anna described times when she struggled to attend to these basic needs during periods of rough sleeping:

> *Sleeping on the Green was bad because it was damp like, it was cold, and you could feel the cold. It was that thing of feeling filthy, not being clean, and not having a shower. They're the things that just make your skin crawl like and that's the side to being homeless that I really can't stand ... Like we'd go in to the (public) bathrooms and we'd have like a hundred cans of spray stuff and we'd stand there for hours just spraying. — Anna (17)*

Anna took whatever measures she could to maintain some level of personal hygiene. Julian described a similar approach to taking care of himself during periods of rough sleeping:

> *I'd always brush me teeth, you know. I'd go into the McDonalds toilets, brush me teeth, wash me face. And I used to take me t-shirt off, lock the door. I used to rob fuckin' shaving foam and shaving blades and fucking all that. I'd rob deodorant and all that like. — Julian (22)*

It was extremely difficult for young people to manage their personal hygiene and health during phases of rough sleeping and several reported sustained periods of self-neglect arising from practical barriers to keeping clean and warm and/or physical and psychological "states" that prevented them from attending to basic needs. Paul's account highlights the importance of safe and secure accommodation and its impact on health and well-being:

> *[Are there any good things about staying in hostels?]*

> *Well, you've somewhere to go, it's somewhere for you to go back to, you know like. If you're tired, or you want to go asleep, you can go in there and go asleep like and get something to eat an' all like. It's much healthier as well when you're in the hostels, especially the Out of Hours, you know the Out of Hours Service? — Paul (19)*

Those who had spent months or years alternating between various unstable living situations were particularly vulnerable to malnutrition, weight loss and sleep deprivation. The health problems many reported were strongly linked to their precarious sleeping places and to their exposure to the elements. These commonly included respiratory problems such as asthma, bronchitis and pneumonia.

> *Sleeping out would make you sick, give you colds and flu' and that. That's what I got now the last night. It started coming on the other night, and then this morning I got up after sleepin' in the park and my chest was in bits. I could hardly breathe. I'm*

*used to it now, I won't get any medical. It will just go away even-
tually itself. — Conor (19)*

*Pneumonia yeah, yeah, I had it twice. When I overdosed when I
was 16 I was suffering from pneumonia and then I got double
pneumonia when I was in (adult hostel). I just woke up one
morning and I was like this crack head, I was shrunk in the face.
The three of us sat down for breakfast and me mate said, "Jesus
you are not well, I want to ring an ambulance for you". — Sean
(21)*

Heavy smoking, alcohol consumption, drug use and poor nutrition compounded the problem. Those who were homeless for
longer were more likely to report poor health and often described
multiple complications ranging from bouts of illness to persistent
ill-health. Wayne, like other dependent drug users, listed several
health difficulties:

*I have very bad bronchitis down me left side. And just all these
abscesses and shit. And I smoke. I have hep C as well. And I'm
not a very fit person. Like if I run from here to the end of the road
and I'm out of breath, do you know what I mean. I think it's because of the bronchitis. — Wayne (21)*

Five of the interviewees (three young men and two young
women) had received a diagnosis for hepatitis C. This news usually came as a shock and was always a source of great stress. On
receiving the diagnosis, most were informed of the need to take
steps to maintain good health: "I have to eat plenty of fruit and
I'm not meant to eat greasy food or anything" (Tony, 22). While
Tony and others did try to modify their lifestyles, their efforts to
do so were invariably hampered by the instability of their living
situations. Siobhán had also received a positive test result for
hepatitis C and described the difficulties she experienced during
periods of rough sleeping.

*I had kidney infections an' all and I've hepatitis C, like you know,
so ... That's hard in the cold as well like. The cold affects your
liver an' all you know like. I used to be in bits waking up in the*

mornings. I couldn't even talk or anything you know. I used to be in bits waking up, be soaking, you know, if it was raining. — Siobhán (22)

Acquired injuries – broken bones, cuts and serious abrasions – were regarded as health problems and as a reason for presenting at an accident and emergency hospital department. Tony told of a serious incident in one of the many squats where he stayed:

I broke me leg, I was staying in a squat and I fell through two storeys. I went up to casualty that night. I was in the squat and I went through two storeys and I landed on this leg and I broke me ankle and me hip and I says, "Fuck this I'm having a turn on, it will kill the pain". So I had a turn on and it killed the pain. I went up to the hospital and I was able to move it and all but I goofed off and I woke up. I fell asleep and I woke up the next morning and I was doubled up with the pain. That was the squat I used to stay in (the north inner-city), the whole thing just fell apart with me in it. — Tony (22)

Street fights and, in fewer cases, injuries sustained in young people's own homes, were also mentioned as reasons for seeking medical attention.

[Have you been to a doctor in the past year?]

I've seen doctors with me arm. I had a fractured arm, a broken wrist sort of fracture, I had. And like some cuts and scars on me head an' all so I've been seeing doctors an' all for that.

[Was that because of …?]

The beatings, yeah. On the street and with me family. — James (18)

Of critical significance are the barriers to health care access posed by homelessness. When faced with a health problem most young people did not have the support of parent(s) or family members and they had few, if any, trusted adults to turn to for advice. While many had a broad network of peers, they were usually close in age and, in any case, struggling with the same or similar health issues. It is not so surprising in this context that hospital emergency departments were the most commonly used health care interventions. A large number had visited accident and emergency rooms for one or more of the following ailments or conditions: cuts, bruises, broken bones, respiratory problems, infections and accidental overdose. More often than not, however, young people sought medical care only when the condition was acute or had progressed to intolerable levels. There were numerous reasons for this tendency to overlook or ignore physical pain or discomfort including economic constraints, fear and low expectations regarding health. Conor explained his neglect of a persistent pain in his chest.

> *I wanted to get my chest checked out earlier but it just keeps progressing and progressing. Eventually now I will have to go and get it checked out, go to the hospital. I won't be able to go to a doctor. I haven't got a medical card. So I'll have to go to the hospital. I keep putting that off.* — Conor (19)

A small number reported times when they felt so ill or in so much pain that they could not go about their daily activities.

> *I was sick when I was going through the hostels. Every day I was getting sick and I did not know what it was. And I never got it checked out until one day I got really, really bad. And I was getting sick and it was all black stuff. And I had to get my ma to come down to the flat with me girlfriend and take me up to the hospital. And that is when I found out I got the ulcer.* — Eoin (20)

Others dealt with specific health problems by deferring action in the hope that the condition would "blow over". Rough sleepers were particularly prone to this approach to health care and many had grown accustomed to ongoing states of ill-health:

> *[Did you ever get sick when you were sleeping rough?]*

It used to be very bad through the winter an' all. The cold would just go straight through you, right through your body. Horrible, choking and sneezing.

[Did you see a doctor then when you were sleeping rough?]

No, just got over it. — Megan (19)

As a chronic cause of stress, homelessness produces exceptional vulnerability to ill-health and, at the same time, hampers people's ability to attend to health problems. When homeless young people fall ill they do not have automatic access to a place to rest and recuperate. Most do not have a regular source of primary care and they rely, instead, on hospital emergency departments. In any case, some of the illegal or risky behaviour in which they engage may incur stigmatisation, thus hindering social support. Over time, some appeared to adopt an individualistic approach to dealing with daily challenges, problems and crises. It cannot be assumed, therefore, that homeless youth will seek out medical attention when they need it or that they will recognise their need for medical assistance and care.

Drug and Injecting Risk Behaviour

As demonstrated in the previous chapter, for a large number, drug use was part of a lifestyle characterised by chronic instability and high susceptibility to risk behaviour. In general, the more problematic an individual's pattern of drug use, the greater the negative impact on their health and well-being. Practically all of the study's dependent drug users reported health difficulties of one kind or another, ranging from general ill-health to more serious illness or chronic infections such as hepatitis C. These health problems were linked, in many cases, to "risky" drug use practices and to the locations where they typically consumed drugs. This section examines the risk behaviour most commonly reported by the study's "heavy end" or dependent drug users. Young people's accounts of first injection – including the situations and individuals associated with this event – provide a useful starting point for this discussion.

Responses to questions about first injection strongly suggest that the majority were unprepared for the event. Most, as noted in the previous chapter, had not planned to inject on this occasion even if they had considered doing so previously. This meant that they did not have personal injecting paraphernalia and, in several cases, their inexperience meant that they were injected by a friend or romantic partner. Emma could not recollect the detail of the event but remembered that she was injected by another person. Her account illustrates the chaos and unpredictability that frequently surrounded first injection experiences:

> *I never, never shared needles, only, well (pause) I don't know which way to put it? The first time I injected, only God knows what he (boyfriend) put into me, you know what I mean. I don't even remember myself, so after that I never used anyone else's needles, I always had clean needles ... that's why I want a test for hepatitis. But that's the only time. I never would have used after anybody else. — Emma (17)*

Other accounts of first injection scenarios draw attention to the risks to which young people were exposed in these contexts:

> *[So how did the injecting start?]*
>
> *I was in (under-18s hostel) at the time. That was when I really got introduced to heroin. I wouldn't touch it for months and months and months and then one day I just said, "Fuck it". I just got a bag, put the whole bag into the syringe and I was out of it. I couldn't walk, I was OD-ing. But the people I was with kind of snapped me out of it. We were in a squat. I lost the feeling in me whole body like you know.*
>
> *[So did you inject yourself or did someone else inject for you?]*
>
> *Someone else done it for me, I couldn't do it but I can do it now, I learned you know.*
>
> *[Did somebody use their own works?]*

No, clean works. And then I used after me mate once and that's who I caught the hepatitis off. — Tony (22)

Several of the young people described a recent illness related to their drug use and injecting drug users almost always reported physical health problems, most often abscesses from intravenous drug use. Damage to, and infection of, veins was a common result of frequent or prolonged injecting drug use:

[So you injected today, what time did you inject?]

I only injected there say about fifteen minutes before I came down to you. I'm not gonna tell you lies, I did, do you know what I mean. There's the proof (shows his arm) fuckin' blew me arm out as usual, blew the vein.

[So you're having difficulty finding a vein?]

They're all gone like from using them over the months since I started using (injecting). I'm only using a year, you know what I mean. Look, there's a scar of where I used there. That vein is gone. There's other scars see, the abscess, do you know what I mean, all them veins gone. Me hand is all blown to bits. I only done that today. Blown, see it. All blown.

[So you've had a lot of problems injecting?]

The veins are all blown. Me two feet are blown. It's not nice, you know, it causes stress like. And being homeless is not helping it, you know what I mean. — Wayne (21)

Like Wayne, other injecting drug users talked about the constraints imposed by homelessness and the impact of these constraints on their ability to manage different aspects of their drug use. For many, exposure to risk was directly related to the absence of a stable living situation. Several, for example, were routinely forced to inject in public locations – the street, derelict buildings, squats, public toilets and so on – that posed serious health risks, both to themselves and to others. Siobhán described her typical injecting routines and locations:

[And what time did you inject at?]

It was about four o'clock. In a squat.

[So what is the squat like?]

It's horrible, like there's people comin' in and out and injecting everywhere and just throwing the needles all over the place an' all like. — Siobhán (22)

Squats were frequented by a large number of drug users for the purpose of injecting and these settings were chaotic, unsanitary and often littered with used syringes. Despite the hazardous conditions, squats had the advantage of permitting social contact with other injectors. Tony explained:

[And in the morning say, where do you go to inject?]

Squats. Lots of them around here, warehouses, shops, all the shops, just climb in and inject.

[And are you usually on your own?]

A few others. I wouldn't do it on my own because in case I OD'd you know, there would be no one there to help me you know. — Tony (22)

Consuming drugs in the company of other drug users was perceived to serve an important protective function in the event of a drug overdose, as Tony's account illustrates. However, it was not without its drawbacks. He went on to explain that tensions can arise in cases where one member of the group does not have a personal supply of their drug of choice:

[So, I'm just wondering how things work? Has everyone got their own supply?]

It's awkward sometimes because just say you've only got one bag like and then someone turns around and says, "Give us some". And you say, "No I can't", and they're saying, "Ah I'd give it to you if I had it". And you feel like shite then, you know. But if I gave half I'd be still sick. I need about three, four bags a day, you know. — Tony (22)

As "careers" in drug use progressed, users sometimes adopted an isolationist approach to drug consumption. Injecting alone – a practice which carries significant risks – was reported by a number as a way to protect their personal supply of drugs and to ensure that they were not harassed by other drug users. Wayne almost always opted to inject alone. Yet, he tried to do so in a public place where he was likely to be discovered in the event of an accidental overdose.

[Do you usually inject on your own?]

Yeah, almost always.

[Is there a reason for that?]

Well, like say I score with someone, we'll go off and the two of us have a turn on out of it together, but like if I score on me own like I go off on me own, do you know what I mean. But the good thing about what I do is I go into a bathroom, like in a restaurant or somethin', and that way I'll know in five or ten minutes your man's gonna be knockin' at the door seein' what I'm up to. So if I ever did OD he's gonna obviously knock on the door, "Are you right, are you right?", do you know what I mean. If there's no answer obviously he's gonna know there's something wrong. So that's why I do that, do you know what I mean. — Wayne (21)

For the majority of the injecting drug users, the risk of overdose was perceived as a major threat and was portrayed, in many cases, as a routinised danger. This relative importance attributed to the risk of overdose was clearly a function of the likelihood of death occurring as a consequence. The high sensitivity to overdose risk was also associated with their exposure – either directly or indirectly – to overdose situations. At least two young people had witnessed a fatal drug overdose and three had themselves accidentally overdosed on at least one occasion:

I was in the hostel one of the nights. The staff came into the room, they thought I was after dying, they said I was blue. And my hands were blue and my face was blue. I was asleep all that night and didn't wake up then even the next day. Two days in the hospital and I woke up and my legs, they weren't working properly. — Brendan (17)

[Have you ever gone to an A&E in a hospital?]

Yeah, a lot of times. A couple of weeks ago I OD'd on E's.

[Okay. Who were you with at the time?]

I was with a friend and then after that I don't know. I just blacked out. — Declan (19)

There appeared to be no significant problems gaining access to sterile needles or syringes and most injectors attended a needle exchange service on a routine basis. In general, they claimed to understand the risks associated with sharing injecting equipment and few indicated that they had regularly engaged in needle sharing. Brendan's account is somewhat of an exception to what appeared to be a general rule of "no sharing".

[Have you ever shared a needle?]

I have yeah, a few times.

[And have you ever worried about that?]

I'm going to get checked when I go into this treatment place next week. I haven't done it now in a while but I did it four or five times with people more or less that I knew, you know. I wouldn't say I have anything to be honest. I wouldn't think so anyway. People I know for years have lied to me about other stuff but I wouldn't say I do. — Brendan (17)

When questioned about injecting practices, the majority of the study's intravenous drug users stated spontaneously and emphatically that they did not share injecting equipment: "I don't share", "I never shared" were typical responses. However, when probed further and asked to describe specific injecting events, there were some accounts of *one-off* or *selective* sharing. Four young people reported that they had, in fact, shared at *some time* in the past. Tony shared a syringe on one occasion and believed that it was during this injecting event that he came into contact with hepatitis C:

> I used after me mate once and that's who I caught the hepatitis off. When I was 16, the age of 16. I was saying, "Are you sure you haven't got anything?" "I'm positive, I'm positive, I'm positive" (he said). And he was the only person I used after. And then he found out he had hepatitis C so I did catch it off him. I said it to him, "You know I used after you". And he says, "Yeah". I says, "I caught that off you". Like he didn't (pause) ... just shook his shoulders, didn't have nothing to say about it. — Tony (22)

Paul told how he shared injecting equipment with his brother on several occasions:

> I got tested an' all for hep' C, all the hep' C and all that shit and I didn't have that. And you know, lucky enough I didn't have anything, yeah, 'cos I was, I was injecting for about four months like, out of the five or six years that I have been doin' gear like I was only injecting for four months. So that was alright and I was, I wasn't like being stupid or anything, like, I always had me own stuff there, you know. When I was with me brother, like I shared with me brother once or twice, you know the needle, if there was none left, like I'd share. Like I never just shared the spike with him, not a spike but shared the same barrel as him you know. Like so, I didn't get anything. So it must mean he doesn't have anything as well I suppose. — Paul (19)

It appears that statements such as "I don't share" held more diverse meanings than the single and unconditional logic they imply. More detailed accounts of injecting drug use highlight situations and contexts in which sharing did in fact take place. In Paul's case, trust and familiarity appeared to be a factor in him sharing with his brother. Desperation was another factor that emerged in accounts of one-off or episodic sharing of injecting equipment. Sarah described the first time she injected heroin:

> *I was with my ex-boyfriend and we had two bags of gear and he was saying, "I'm having a turn on, we won't get anything out of smoking this". I said, "I'm not using fucking needles". And he said, "We've no foil or anything", and he goes, "You can use it or you're getting nothing". So in the end I had to use it because I was in bits. I remember I was panicking so much. I sobbed because it was just, I hate needles, you know what I mean. So I'll never forget it like and it was all because he wanted to have a turn on and either I was getting nothing or had to inject it.*
>
> *[So he injected you?]*
>
> *Yeah.*
>
> *[With the needle he had used?]*
>
> *Yeah. — Sarah (21)*

There were also a number of reports of lending injecting syringes and at least five young people reported sharing injecting paraphernalia such as spoons and filters.

> *[Did you ever share a needle?]*
>
> *No. I caught the hep C by using the same spoon as someone. Hep doesn't, it doesn't die, it lives on the spoon even if you swab it down and all it still lives on it. But I didn't know that, I didn't know anything about all that when I started using. — Megan (19)*

The "technology" of injecting drug use was something that young people appeared to learn incrementally. This made new and novice injectors especially vulnerable because of their inexperience and lack of knowledge about health risks and how to avoid them. Even quite experienced or longer-term injecting drug users (IDUs) engaged in high-risk injecting practices and most were forced to inject in unsanitary locations and settings. While injecting drug users face a range of potential health problems, irrespective of their housing status, the absence of a stable place to live heightens all of the risks that even housed drug users can potentially face. For example, homeless heroin users are less likely to have access to safe injecting places and more likely to rush the preparation process. These and other situational factors make them vulnerable to engaging in practices that can seriously jeopardise their health. Put differently, homelessness diminishes young people's ability to manage their drug use safely by placing them in situations where they have no option but to take risks.

Sexual Risk Behaviour

Of the 40 young people interviewed, 34 were sexually active. All of the young men (except one) and the majority of the young women had experienced sexual intercourse. Relatively few were currently involved in a long-term romantic relationship and only one young man was a parent.

Levels of non-conformity to safe sex practices were extremely high across the sample. Practically all of the young men reported times when they did not use a condom to protect against sexually transmitted infections or pregnancy, and at least five stated that they had *never* used a condom. Numerous reasons for non- or inconsistent use of condoms emerged, including financial constraints, problems of access and lack of preparedness for sexual encounters. However, a number of young people appeared to have little or no awareness of the importance of safe sex practices, as Fergal's account demonstrates:

[Do you practice safe sex at all?]

No. No one does.

[Why do you think not?]

They just don't. I know 'cos, fuckin', half the people I know don't anyway, know what I mean. I don't know? Maybe posh people do. People just don't. — Fergal (18)

As the interview progressed, it became clear that Fergal had very little knowledge or understanding of HIV risk and he, like many others, relied on street lore and intuition for guidance on sexual health matters. Indeed, it appeared at times that the research interview was the first context in which some young people had ever discussed issues related to sexual behaviour and health. This led a number to openly acknowledge their lack of factual knowledge and understanding:

> *I don't know any of this shit, I'm not a fuckin' (pause) ... I did fuck-all things in school and whatever else. I don't know. It's just, I didn't learn any of this shit. — Fergal (18)*

Neil's account similarly suggests that he had little or no opportunity during his teenage years to learn about sexuality and sexual health:

> *I'm still waiting to have this talk from my parents but I don't think I'm going to get it at this age. And one of the other things is when I was in second year, I was actually in class, I was the only boy in with 12 girls so you can imagine the sex education class was extremely invigorating; "The best way to deal with menstruation problems every month". That was about it. — Neil (20)*

While young men frequently stated that they sometimes used condoms in the context of a "steady" relationship, many appeared not to do so in one-night-stand situations or in circumstances where sex came about unexpectedly:

> *[And did you have protected sex or use a condom?]*
>
> *No, not really. No. When I was living with my ex-girlfriend we did use them sometimes and sometimes we wouldn't like. It was just if they were there. I would not carry them around or anything like that. — Eoin (20)*
>
> *[Do you use protection? Condoms?]*
>
> *When I'm with my girlfriend. Yeah. After that, not really. When I'm not with my girlfriend, I don't really have time. It's just on*

the spot sort of thing. Because you are drunk, and maybe she is drunk or because you're stoned, you just get it in. With my girl-friend I always wear protection because I wouldn't want to give her anything if I did have anything. — Conor (19)

"Knowing" or having heard about sexual partners prior to the sexual encounter was a common approach to deciding on the merits or otherwise of condom use. Many believed that knowl-edge about their sexual partner's sexual "reputation" was a reli-able measure of safety and risk.

[Do you use condoms with other girls (besides girlfriend)?]

No. I am not worried. If you know about a bird then you don't need to, you know what I mean. — Gerard (16)

[Do you use protection when you have sex?]

No. To be honest with you I don't like it … like, I'm not going out sleeping with, if it was a prostitute I'd put on a Johnny, you know what I mean. But, ah no, there's clean birds out there so I wouldn't go out with just anyone. I'd pick nice birds. So, if it was a prostitute, yeah definitely. Otherwise no. — Christian (17)

A large number of the young men appeared not to fully under-stand or grasp the potential negative health consequences of un-protected sex. Yet, the adverse psychological consequences of en-gaging in unprotected sex emerged strongly from some accounts and a number had come to recognize the importance of using con-doms. This change sometimes came about following anxiety about a specific high-risk sexual encounter. Sean conveyed ex-treme anxiety when he talked about his fear of having a HIV test following unprotected sex with a young woman who he knew to be HIV positive:

I am hepatitis C positive and I have a fear now that I am HIV positive. I had unprotected sex like with a girl I know is HIV posi-tive. Em, that is the other thing that gets me down. I am afraid to go for the test because if I go for the test and it came back positive

*I would definitely, I would just (pause) ... that would be the
straw that would break the camel's back. That would be the end of
it. What is the point of living out a fuckin' existence if you are going to die anyway? You know? It's pointless.* — Sean (21)

Fewer of the study's young women were sexually active and, in
general, they reported higher levels of conformity to safe sex practices than their male counterparts. Yet, almost all reported occasions when they did not adhere to these standards or practices.
Many reports of non-use of condoms suggest that unsafe sex practices were especially likely around the time of sexual debut. Jacinta is one of a number who had not planned or anticipated her
first sexual encounter.

[How old were you when you had sex for the first time?]

*My first time, I was actually 13. It was here in town, yeah I was
13 or 14, yeah.*

[Was that with a boyfriend?]

No, he wasn't a boyfriend.

[And did you use condoms that time?]

No.

[What about now?]

*I don't do it (have sex) now. No, I'd say the last time I had it was
about a year ago and I'm damn proud of myself.*

[Ok and is there a reason for that?]

*Yeah there is. Just I had a HIV test because I had sex with a dark
fella and we never used a condom and then I was just so worried
about it after that. And I'm just afraid to have sex ever since.* —
Jacinta (16)

Jacinta's account again illustrates the stress and anxiety that frequently followed episodes of unprotected sex. Young women's

accounts also suggest that, even if they recognised the importance of condom use, many struggled to persuade their sexual partner(s) of the need to practice safe sex. While some strongly asserted that they would not consider having sex without a condom, others talked openly about their partner's resistance to condom use. Anna explained her efforts to enforce the "rule" of using condoms with her boyfriend:

> *We don't use condoms. But I brought home condoms there a couple of weeks ago and I threw them at him. Well, I didn't throw them at him, I gave them to him. And he kind of looked at me and he was like, "What are they for?" And I was like, "What do you think". And he was like, "I'm not using them". Well, I said, "You're not getting (pause) … okay, enough is enough kind of, I don't want to get pregnant". Because I've had enough pregnancy scares in my lifetime … But since I gave him the condoms we haven't had sex. — Anna (17)*

Young people had few opportunities to learn about safe sex or to discuss sexual health issues. Most had missed out on school-based sex education and, possibly also, on home-based sex education. The instability of their living situations created further barriers to learning. From their mid-teenage years, a large number had embarked upon a cycle of moving between various temporary living situations making opportunities for learning remote or impractical. In any case, the combination of their vulnerability and lack of trust in adults discouraged many from talking openly about their situations, anxieties and fears. Sarah's account highlights how concerns about privacy and confidentiality can act as a barrier to young people seeking help or advice even in a crisis:

> *To be honest with you, I thought he would have pulled out and because I was embarrassed (pause) … it was the first time with him. It was completely stupid of me now I know. But it happened so quickly, he came so fast that I didn't think. I was just so embarrassed to say anything because I'm, you know, still a bit awkward. And to be honest, part of me thinks he's a bit baby mad or something, do you know what I mean. I said to him, "Now, if I'm*

*pregnant I'll be on the boat like a shot". I don't know what kind of
decision I'd make but that was my attitude then. Because I'm too
young to have kids. I'm not ready for anything like that and I'm
not able to talk to anyone here (transitional housing unit) because, if you say it to the staff, they write it all down and I'm not
into that, do you know what I mean. So it would be easy to talk to
someone like yourself over it because a lot of the girls here you
couldn't tell because it would be all over the house, do you know
what I mean. — Sarah (21)*

In general, young people were ill-informed about many aspects of
sexual health and most were not adequately equipped to ensure
their own safety and the safety of their sexual partner(s). Significant
also is that, among the study's drug users, there was far less importance attached to the health risks associated with sexual than drug
use behaviour. While practically all recognised the risks associated
with sharing injecting equipment, relatively few appeared to understand the health consequences of unprotected sex. Indeed, unprotected sex appeared to be viewed – certainly by young men – as
a common and normal feature of heterosexual sexual relationships.
Furthermore, a large number of the study's young men appeared
not to equate non-condom use with risk, particularly in cases where
they had "screened" their sexual partners and deemed them to be
"clean".

Psychological/Emotional Health

The instability of young people's living situations impacted on
their ability to cope, as did their restricted access to basic needs
such as washing facilities, a comfortable sleeping place and a bal-
anced diet. Many expressed anxiety about their situations, past and
present, and several conveyed a profound sense of hopelessness.
Feelings of stress, sadness or depression affected young people in
numerous ways. For example, a number of young women reported
eating problems during times of acute anxiety. Melissa and Lyndsey explained:

[Did you ever feel lonely when you were living with foster families?]

Yeah, I would, especially when I moved down the country. I'd come in every day and I'd just go to my room but I wouldn't eat or nothing. I'd just stay in the room all day. I was just (pause) ... I couldn't talk to anyone down there like, that's why I'd rather be here in Dublin. The woman (foster mother) brought me to the doctor. She thought I was depressed because I wouldn't eat anything and because I came in and went straight to bed every day.
— Melissa (14)

[What about your health. Have you been sick or anything?]

No not in here (hostel), no. Before this I used to eat and I'd get a cramp in me stomach for the day. And then just before going asleep I'd end up vomiting. I don't get that here (in the hostel). But when I was in foster care, I don't know what was wrong with me, I couldn't eat and I was homesick. — Lyndsey (15)

Young people like Melissa and Lyndsey appeared to have few or no positive coping mechanisms available to them; they found it difficult to discuss their feelings and were left largely to their own devices in terms of processing and dealing with negative emotions. A small number of young women had engaged in acts of self-harm recently or in the past. Sarah reported cutting her wrists as a form of self-punishment and attributed this behaviour to feelings of dejection and despair:

I've cut me wrists, I've taken tablets and things like that, you know, and been very depressed. On anti-depressants an' all that, you know, and at times I felt there was no way out, that I was going to be strung out for the rest of me life.

[So you've tried to harm yourself by cutting your wrists?]

Yeah. A few times, just superficial. It wasn't about killing myself or anything like that, it was about hurting myself like. It was just about wanting to feel pain like. I don't know why now.
— Sarah (21)

Likewise Jacinta, who was much younger and living in short-term hostel accommodation at the time of interview, told how she had engaged in self-injurious behaviour from an early age:

> *[Ok, what kinds of things do you do when you feel stress, is there anything that helps you not to feel stressed?]*
>
> *Like hurt myself (points to arm)*
>
> *[You've cut your arms is it?]*
>
> *It's all up it and around and just around. I've done it since I was seven years old.*
>
> *[And when was the last time you cut yourself?]*
>
> *About two weeks ago.*
>
> *[What kinds of things lead you into that situation?]*
>
> *I think if I had a problem, I don't really talk to people about it, so I just, like people tell me, "Just go and hit a pillow", but it just sounds so stupid, so I just take it out on myself. — Jacinta (16)*

The majority of those who had been homeless for a considerable period appeared to struggle with feelings of confusion, sadness and despair. At the same time, many were unable to think constructively about anything other than the immediate problem of survival. The stresses in their lives were numerous, wide-ranging and related, in many cases, to everyday realities and needs:

> *Well, like living on the streets causes like, sometimes it can cause me stress. Heroin causes me stress, robbing causes me stress. — Wayne (21)*

Wayne went on to describe a particularly intense moment of despair:

> *Just you get lonely when you're on the streets. You're just sittin' there at night time and like some people cry themselves to sleep because they wanna be at home, do you know what I mean. That's*

the way I felt one night like, "Oh I wanna be at home, I don't want this anymore", do you know what I mean like. I didn't wanna live, do you know that way? That's the way I felt, like I was sayin, "Ah fuck this mate", do you know what I mean, like. What's the point like in livin? I'm only upsettin' everyone.

Conor worried about the prospect of going to prison and of remaining homeless:

[What kinds of things do you worry about?]

Prison now would be a big worry now, prison, being homeless for longer and longer you know, it's like it will never end. I can't sort myself out. — Conor (19)

These accounts conveyed a belief that the choices open to them were limited and mostly undesirable. Wayne (quoted above) was not the only young person who at times questioned "the point" of his life. Sean, who (as demonstrated earlier) was anxious about a HIV test result at the time of interview, told of his "battle" to keep his contemplation of suicide at bay:

I just want to finish my life, I just want to end me life basically. I am sick and tired of being sick and tired. Unless you have been there you can't understand what it's like to have someone say to you, "No, there is no room. There is a sleeping bag and get away from this door please". You know what I mean, your heart just sinks to the floor. Just very low at the moment, very low. And I am battling to keep thoughts out of me head ... I'd just love to get it over with, I haven't got, I haven't got the balls to slit me wrists or cut me throat, you know. So I could throw myself in the Liffey or whatever. — Sean (21)

One young person reported a suicide attempt at the age of fourteen:

I've often overdosed. Yeah, I just wanted (pause) ... just got pissed off and said, "Fuck it". Me ma was on Valium and I just took two bottles. But sure me ma walked in on top of me as I just swallowed the tablets and she started crying an' all like. I was out

*of it getting sick and all, lying on the bathroom floor. She had me
feet up in the air and I was laughing at her like but she was sitting there roaring crying, waiting for the ambulance. I was only
14 and I got pumped out.*

*[Looking back, was it that you couldn't cope with what was going
on?]*

*Just couldn't cope. I told me ma and me ma went to counselling.
Told them what me da done to me (sexual abuse) an' all. Me ma
knew he was doing something but she just couldn't prove it, you
know. Me da was a right auld scum bag, he was, I've no love for
him at all. — Tony (22)*

Tony continued to struggle with the emotional trauma of childhood sexual abuse and talked about the things that help him to
"forget":

[Would you say that your memories of childhood are all painful?]

*They are yeah. But it's good to talk about it. If you can't talk
about it I end up doing something stupid to myself like you know,
ending up in hospital you know. That's why I do the gear because
it makes me forget about it you know.*

The use of alcohol and drugs to self-medicate or as an escape
route from daily realities was particularly common among problem drug users, who were out of home for longer and currently
using adult hostels. There were also numerous reports of using
substances as a coping mechanism among young people who consumed drugs socially:

*The only thing that helps me is the hash. Helps me with all me
problems. If I've anything … I have a joint and mellow out and
I'd be alright, do you know what I mean. — Joe (19)*

The stresses and anxieties experienced by young people ranged
from everyday worries to acute anxiety about specific or ongoing
problems related to their homelessness. Those who had been out
of home for longer almost always communicated feelings of lone-

liness and depression and they had few, if any, positive coping mechanisms to help them to deal with these negative feelings.

Conclusion

During adolescence, a young person's support network usually consists of family, school, peers, neighbourhood, workplace and leisure interests and activities. Since homeless young people have restricted or no access to these supports and resources, it is more difficult for them to develop, become and remain healthy compared to their non-homeless counterparts. Homeless environments are unpredictable and the everyday challenges that young homeless people face include problems with privacy, overcrowding, theft, safety, and access to basic resources such as food, toilets and clothing. This instability affects their ability to develop the skills to deal with new situations and relationships.

Despite their youth, a large number of the study's young people reported a range of health problems. Many simultaneously had limited access to health care and several had neglected recurrent or persistent health problems. The high level of reported drug and sexual risk-taking is particularly worrying. While the study's injecting drug users had considerable knowledge and awareness of the risk of engaging in certain injecting practices, several nonetheless reported sharing, borrowing or lending injecting equipment. Indeed, their accounts highlight the complex social and relational meanings attached to what is frequently generically referred to as "sharing". There was also a high level of non-conformity to safe sex practices across the sample as well as serious deficits in young people's knowledge about sexual health more generally. Sexual risk-taking – as well as attitudes and beliefs that support unsafe sexual practices – have been documented previously among vulnerable youth (early school leavers) in an Irish context (Mayock and Byrne, 2004). The confluence of drug and sexual risk is of particular concern and is indicative of an urgent need for harm reduction messages targeting a range of risk behaviour.

Finally, many of the young people reported high levels of psychological distress, expressing sadness about their situations, past and present, while several others experienced more profound moments or periods of anxiety and depression related to their homelessness. Those who were homeless for longer were particularly prone to using drugs, alcohol or other mood altering substances as a form of escape from ongoing and painful emotional states. Internationally and in Ireland, there is evidence that substantial numbers of people who are homeless have mental health problems. Extreme care must be taken, however, not to misinterpret the nature and implications of the difficulties facing young people with respect to homelessness. While the behaviour of homeless youth may be suggestive of mental health problems, these could in fact be explained as a function of adaptive behaviour. Nonetheless, homeless young people are undoubtedly vulnerable to a variety of psychological problems not least because they have complex needs which are not easily met through conventional health services.

Chapter 8

HOMELESS YOUNG PEOPLE AND SERVICES

Despite the unique and complex service needs resulting from the high-risk lifestyles of homeless young people, relatively little is known about how they access, use and view the services available to them. Certainly, in an Irish context, there is practically no published material on this group's contact and interaction with homeless services or other helping agencies. We know from the stories presented in earlier chapters that young people accessed a range of accommodation types targeting "out of home" youth under the age of 18 years and that a considerable number had also used adult homeless services. Indeed, it was rare for interviewees *not* to refer to these services when they recounted and reflected on their life experiences. Just as young people had unique ways of responding to their homeless peers and others in their lives, they also developed modes of interaction with service providers. This point is crucial and draws attention to ways in which services shape young people's experiences and thereby potentially influence the paths they follow through homelessness.

This chapter focuses initially on young people's use and experience of services other than accommodation places including outreach, counselling, drop-in, needle exchange and drug treatment services. It then draws attention to some key features of their responses to the interventions designed to meet their needs. The final section examines the meanings young people attach to homelessness, demonstrating that their perceptions of their situations are strongly mediated by their accommodation histories and the duration of their homelessness.

Service Utilisation

As might be expected, young people varied widely in their use of services. Younger teenagers, and those who were "newly" or recently homeless, reported far less knowledge about, or contact with, services targeting young people. This is not altogether surprising since a considerable number of those under the age of 16 years had resided in only one setting since their first out of home experience. By contrast, those who were homeless for longer invariably reported contact with a large number of agencies. Table 8.1 presents summary data on the number of young people who made contact with the five most commonly used non-housing services: outreach, counselling, drop-in/day services, needle exchange and drug treatment.

Table 8.1: Number of Young People Who Reported Access/Attendance at Services*

Service	Young Men (n=23)	Young Women (n=17)	Total (n=40)
Outreach	11	5	16
Counselling	15	10	25
Drop-In/Day Services	8	3	11
Needle Exchange	6	3	9
Drug Treatment	9	7	16

* These data relate to young people's *lifetime use* of services.

The figures above are based on questions put to young people about the services they had *ever* contacted or used and provide a broad overview of patterns of service utilisation for the sample. However, they tell us nothing about the duration of their engagement with services. Some young people made contact on one occasion only while others withdrew following a period; a number attended one or more services regularly over an extended period and yet others attended intermittently.

Table 8.1 suggests that young men and women differed in their use of services, with young men far more likely to use day services and needle exchange facilities and to report contact with outreach workers. These differences undoubtedly reflect variation in their living situations (both past and current), their drug use, and the fact that young women were far less likely than their male counterparts to have experience of sleeping rough or squatting. However, it is also important to bear in mind the tendency for young women's homelessness to remain "hidden" for longer, a situation which almost certainly impacted on their awareness and use of services. Table 8.1 also indicates that a large number had attended counselling (60 per cent approximately) at some time and that there was a relatively high uptake of drug and alcohol treatment, with 40 per cent stating that they had attended a treatment setting for their drug and/or alcohol use.

Learning about Services

For many, the Out of Hours Service was the first point of contact with interventions targeting "out of home" young people. Some were taken directly to a Garda station by a parent, carer, relative or family friend. For others who slept rough in their local area for a period, learning about services was a longer process and a number (particularly young men) found out about hostels and other facilities through peer networks or close friends:

> *[Did you know what to do, how did you find out about the services?]*
>
> *Through friends.*
>
> *[On the street, like other homeless kids and stuff?]*
>
> *Yeah just by word of mouth usually. When I was 15 I slept out for a whole year. Out in (home neighbourhood) I was sleeping in the sheds. And I had loads of friends out there and they wouldn't do anything to help me. Then one friend out there told me about the Out of Hours. She says, "Go to the Garda station at 8.00 o'clock and ask for the Out of Hours". And I was saying, "What are they like?" And she said, "They'll bring you to a hostel in*

town". And that's when I went down the Garda station and they brought me to (a hostel) then. — Tony (22)

Word of mouth was a common mechanism for learning about services and those who began to "hang out" in the city-centre appeared to learn quickly about the range available to them. Brendan had considerable experience of the homeless "scene" and felt that news about services and how to access them spread quickly on the street.

I'd say you'd have people that probably sleep rough in the cars and that they wouldn't know all the hostels that are in town. But I reckon, the majority of them, they'd find out soon enough, through their social workers and that, that there are places to phone and places to stay. — Brendan (17)

Knowing about services did not mean that young people used them regularly, or at all, for that matter. There were, in fact, several reports of one-off visits and some refused to engage with certain services. This issue will be discussed in greater detail later in the chapter.

Outreach Services

In general, only those young people who had experience of sleeping rough reported contact with outreach workers. Almost half of the young men, compared to just under one-third of the young women, were familiar with the work of outreach teams. Young people differed in their perceptions of the role and benefits of outreach services. Some, for example, understood the role of the service solely in terms of the provision of food, blankets and other basic needs.

Ah the soup, yeah, I would have met them (outreach workers) on the soup run. At Stephen's Green and Custom House, I've got soup and sandwiches off them and blankets, just in case you wouldn't get a hostel, you know. — Tony (22)

The majority who had contact with outreach workers perceived them to be helpful and caring and a number appeared to have built a relationship with one such worker over time. Individual outreach workers were often praised, not simply because they offered basic needs such as food and hot drinks, but also because they provided advice on how to access temporary accommodation, social assistance, employment or other services. Aoife described how one outreach worker helped her to access drug treatment:

> *I met (outreach worker) and she was helping me, she was working with me and she got me on the clinic (drug treatment) like. She's very good and she helped me like, you know. I'm on the clinic and hopefully I'll be with my mother soon and get off the drugs. — Aoife (19)*

A smaller number of young people expressed scepticism about outreach workers and about their capacity to provide them with meaningful help or support. Seán felt that the outreach worker he encountered did very little to help him:

> *I was outside (adult hostel) sleeping and the outreach worker wanted to talk to me. I didn't want to talk to him because like, I says, "Can you offer me accommodation?" No. "Have you any food even?" No. "Have you any fuckin' tea or drinks?" No. "Well good luck to you, go away". I just didn't want to talk to him. — Seán (21)*

Although Julian acknowledged the efforts of outreach workers to provide help and support, he protested the intrusive nature of their questions:

> *Like someone comes down (to the street) to make sure you're okay and all. I just tell them, "I'm doing grand", just not to worry. I used to hate them. They were asking me questions and all that. I hate being asked mad questions. — Julian (22)*

Outreach work is clearly an important component of efforts to provide homeless young people with basic subsistence needs and, for more resistant or "difficult to reach" groups, it plays a critical role in the process of engaging them with services. Young people over the age of seventeen years were far more likely than younger teenagers to be familiar with the work of outreach teams and they were also more likely to express indifference or resentment towards these workers. Indeed, antipathy towards services and service providers was almost always stronger among young people who had been homeless for longer. This acted, in many cases, as a barrier to their seeking and accepting help.

Counselling Services

Almost two-thirds of the young people had attended counselling at some time, making it the most commonly accessed service (apart from accommodation). For some, this counselling took place during childhood or early adolescence, either in a school or care setting, while others had attended counselling subsequent to their first homeless experience. Several who had accessed drug treatment services had also received counselling at the treatment centre they attended. A small number of the study's young men had or were currently attending anger management sessions and their attendance was sometimes a mandatory condition imposed by the courts.

Only a small minority of young people depicted counselling as a constructive and positive intervention. Tony was unusual in that he appeared to value the opportunity to talk about personal issues:

[Is there anything that helps you with stress?]

I go to me counsellor. I go to her every fortnight when I have a chance. If I need to talk to her, get things off my chest, I can have a cry and I feel great after it, after having a talk about it you know. — Tony (22)

Those who depicted counselling as helpful were almost always older and had attended the service over an extended period. This allowed them to build a positive relationship with their counsellor and to feel sufficiently confident to discuss personal issues. Younger teenagers were generally resistant and often asserted that counsellors were pushy and intrusive. This negative perception of the role and benefit of counselling appeared to stem from prior negative encounters with adult authority figures and State interventions. Resistance to counselling (and indeed other interventions) was particularly strong among young people with a care history, who held strong misgivings about the State's "system" of intervention. This suspicion was fuelled by anger and resentment in many cases. Ronan, who was taken into care at a young age, harboured strong resentment about his separation from his parents and siblings:

> *[Do you remember what it (care) was like?]*
>
> *It was horrible ... 'Cos me ma was over in the mental hospital and I got put in a home for two years, a resident's bed for young children. — Ronan (17)*

Likewise, Fergal's distrust of State intervention was related to his experiences in care. He believed that social workers and other professionals constantly tried to shift blame for his situation and behaviour towards him and his family.

> *Any time they'd take me down to the manager or counsellor or (pause) ... they're always asking why am I angry, why am I so angry. "Is it your ma, is it your da?" You know, twisting it. And I'd tell them, "No, it's you". They're the ones that fucked me life up, know what I mean? — Fergal (18)*

Negative experiences of counselling as children left others feeling sceptical about its benefits as teenagers. Caroline told how she was forced to attend counselling as a child:

> *I hate counselling because of the amount of time I got sent to it when I was a kid. And I hated it. Do you know what I mean, they were bastards. I wanted to beat them up so I just won't do it now. I won't. — Caroline (16)*

It must be remembered that a sense of tremendous loss overshadowed the lives of many of the young people interviewed. As highlighted in previous chapters, most had learned painful lessons about the hazards, as they saw it, of trusting others. Adults and, in particular, those adults who acted as wardens of the State were perceived as threatening. Young people often stated that they preferred to talk to a close friend or family member about their problems and some feared that staff in the places they resided would impart their private "business" to other authorities – the police, the courts or a social worker. Apart from feeling sceptical about the motives of interventionists, many also found the prospect of talking about their childhood and adolescent experiences to be daunting. This was certainly the case for Christian who was reluctant to open up old wounds:

> *I wouldn't blab about my past or anything to people, you know, about my childhood or anything, not about that. I'd talk about things that have happened over the last couple of years, but not about my family or anything. I don't want to talk to myself about that, you know what I mean. Just the fact that I hate it, you know.*
> — *Christian (17)*

Young people's accounts of the experience of counselling highlight their vulnerability and their profound lack of trust in the individuals and agencies charged with meeting their needs. While misgivings about counselling were particularly strong, these sentiments applied equally to other services and appeared to be rooted in their negative experiences of a range of State interventions. A large number had lost faith in the systems of intervention designed to meet their needs and some of the young people who had been homeless for longer felt that the services aimed at resolving their difficulties were at least partly responsible for their present situations.

Drop-In/Day Services

There are three day services in the city-centre of Dublin: one targets homeless young people under the age of 18 years, a second targets a slightly older group of homeless youth and the third targets drug users. Day services generally open from ten o'clock in the morning and remain open until early or late evening. They aim to provide a safe and supportive environment for young people and offer shower and laundry facilities, a place to prepare food, as well as computer and recreational facilities. Regular users of the Out of Hours Service learned quickly about the day centre for young people under the age of 18 and most who used this service did so for practical purposes: as a way to access shelter, food, storage and laundry facilities. Aiming to provide respite from the street, particularly during unfavourable weather conditions, these services also afford opportunities to socialise and to forge new social relationships and a considerable number of young people spoke positively about them. James recalled how the service had helped him to stay "away from trouble". Like others, he singled out an individual member of staff who he found to be particularly supportive:

[Why do you think it (day service) is a good place?]

Because it gets you away from trouble ... the staff in there are sound. There is one guy (name) he's sound he is. I like him, he's alright. — James (18)

Having only recently started to use one of the day services, Eoin's account again draws attention to the use of such services as a way to access basic needs, pass the time and "hang out":

The last few weeks I have just been getting up and going to the (day centre). I would probably get my lunch there and then they close up for an hour and half from 1.00 to 2:30. And I would go off then and maybe go back later. Just hang around, yeah. They have a pool table and they have lockers, and washing facilities and showers and it is a drop-in centre so you can stay all day like. — Eoin (20)

Siobhán identified one city-centre facility as her preferred choice because of the personal support she received:

They help you a lot like, they do help you a lot like. If you need to talk they're there for you; if you need phone calls, you can; they get you tea and sandwiches. They're good like. If they see you down or anything they come over and try to cheer you up or ask do you want to talk. They ask is there anything wrong like that you wanna talk about and all. They're great. — Siobhán (22)

Day services certainly offer young people an alternative to the streets and were valued for the opportunities they provided for social interaction. They also brought a degree of structure and predictability to daily life, which otherwise involved walking the streets and "hanging around" town. As might be expected, young people liked to discuss their activities and the latest news from the street when socialising in these settings. However, the young people claimed that these discussions were discouraged and, in some cases, forbidden by staff. Christian, who had stopped using day services, recalled the responses of staff members to street talk:

It's a place where you get away from the streets, that's what the staff say. Well, of course it's a place to get away from the streets, it's inside, isn't it? But they don't let you talk about anything that happens outside. — Christian (17)

Christian continued to voice his opposition to this rule, claiming that it did not accord with the reality of young people's daily lives. Trying to discourage verbal exchange related to street life was unrealistic because those who attended did not have "constructive" alternatives, he argued:

They want you to talk constructive. These people that are in the hostels, they don't fucking know constructive. The only thing they know is fucking just a life of shite, you know what I mean. So how are they meant to talk? There's nothing else to talk about. I never use it now. I hate it. Never use it. I have used it before ... You're not allowed to talk about the streets, you're not allowed to talk about crime, about women. You're not allowed to talk about anything. But these are the things that these people talk about everyday, d'you know what I mean. Once they go outside they talk about these things. — Christian (17)

Declan was also critical of the rules that some day services tried to enforce:

> *[When you were under 18 did you ever go to (day centre for under 18's)?]*
>
> *Yeah.*
>
> *[What was it like?]*
>
> *It was all right, it wasn't too bad. They were very strict up there, I didn't like that about it. They were like, you couldn't do anything, you know what I mean, they'd kick you out over a stupid thing, like even if you were bleeding cursing or anything like that. Ah they were very strict for the younger age, you know, so I didn't really like that place. — Declan (19)*

Finally, a number of young people depicted city-centre day services as undesirable social settings because of their close proximity to street-based drug "scenes" and to well-known "scoring" locations. For young people who were trying to curb their drug intake, attending day services meant meeting and socialising with other drug users. Exposure to drug offers was therefore an inevitable part of participation, a situation which presented challenges and difficulties for those who were trying to "stay clean":

> *The odd time I would go to the (drop in centre for 18-25 years olds) but I wouldn't stay long in it because it just done me head in. I was trying to stay clean at the time and they were coming in offering heroin like. (City-centre) Street is the main sort of street to get gear in Dublin and like they would come down to the (drop in centre) offering, they would be saying, "Are you looking for gear?". So that was annoying. — Seán (21)*

To a considerable extent, young people's accounts of attending city-centre-based day services draw attention to their multiple needs and to the difficulties such designated services are likely to face in meeting these needs. It is clearly a challenge for service providers to strike a balance between recognising and respecting young people's social and cultural worlds and, at the same time, setting rules that help to protect younger and less experienced youth and ensure that the service environment does not simply become an extension of street life.

Needle Exchange and Drug Treatment Services

All of the study's intravenous drug users were regular users of needle exchange facilities. They usually learned about these services from outreach workers or networks of peers and appeared to understand the importance of having access to clean needles. Their accounts also strongly suggest that they felt comfortable and willing to attend needle exchange programmes. A considerable number valued the broader supports available to them in these settings and there was strong evidence to suggest that young people perceived needle exchange facilities as non-judgemental and non-threatening environments. Indeed, if anything stands out from their accounts of attending needle exchange facilities, it is the relief that young people expressed about not having to conceal their activities in these settings.

Of the 19 young people who stated that they had a drug problem, 16 had attended a drug treatment service at some time, indicating a high uptake of these services. All of the young women (seven in total) and nine of the 13 heroin-using men had sought and presented for treatment. However, first attempts to "get off" rarely, if ever, worked and practically all reported multiple relapse episodes.

The vast majority of the study's dependent drug users expressed a desire to address the problem of their drug consumption and most identified drug treatment as their most pressing need. However, the aim of quitting drug use was constantly hampered by a range of practical and psychological barriers. As highlighted in Chapter 6, young people's drug intake usually increased – sometimes quite dramatically – following a period of homelessness and this shift was strongly associated with their immersion in street scenes. Typical reports of failed drug treatment attempts suggest that these same factors impacted negatively on their ability to quit drug use. Those who had outgrown services targeting young people under the age of 18 years and currently resided in adult hostels made frequent reference to a range of situational factors that constantly impacted on their efforts to curb their drug intake and/or abstain from drugs.

[Of all the services that you have used, have you found one to be really good?]

The hostel (for 16-21 year olds) and that. The staff are nice and that and it's not a bad environment. It's only bad because I am trying to stay away from drugs. 'Cos if you are clean and you are coming in here sometimes, you would be sitting there looking at someone goofing off and, you know, they would be stoned and they would offer you. "Do you want anything?" or "Have you got any?" And that gets you thinking then, like, probably would do it. — Eoin (20)

Young people almost always talked about the need to distance themselves from drug using peers and from the broader hostel scene that supported drug use and made abstinence extremely difficult.

[And what do you think would help you now?]

To stay away from the people I'm hangin' around with and that, that's the biggest problem, in the hostels. If I got a flat I'd be able to stay away from them, I'd be able to get a job and work. — Colm (20)

The conviction that the transience, poverty, poor health and criminal activities associated with *being* homeless made relapse inevitable, was widespread among the group:

[Is there anything that might help you now?]

You know like when you're on the drugs you've a lot of tension … I'd like to go into treatment and just detox and then just get a life, you know and get a flat.

[Is having your own flat important?]

It is yeah because I'd settle down like. Because at least you could go home when you want, go to bed when you want. But being in here in this hostel, you're out all day like and it'd drive you to drugs. — Siobhán (22)

Aoife was extremely pessimistic about her ability to abstain from drug use without a stable place to live, and did not expect to be in a position to do so without the support of her mother:

I won't be giving the drugs up until I'm with me mother because there's nothing else for me to do in the day, do you know what I mean. I need to be staying at home with me mother like and then I'd like, then I'd be off the drugs. When I'm not with my mother, there's nothing else for me to live for, do you know what I mean. — Aoife (19)

By contrast Anna, who had recently moved home, explained the positive side of drug treatment:

[How do you feel now about drug treatment now?]

Very hopeful. Because you see the methadone has kind of given me that little bit of space to realize that I can't be getting stoned everyday. And it's given me that bit of time to disassociate myself from all the people I was hanging around with. — Anna (17)

Later in the interview, she compared her own situation with that of others who do not have the benefit of a home and supportive parents:

You see, when you are on the streets it's very, very difficult to get yourself together ... it's easier to be stoned when you're out on the street because it takes everything away I suppose. I don't even know how to explain it but you just, you can't get yourself to-gether because you don't have a bed to sleep in, you don't have anywhere warm and comfortable. When you go through with-drawals it isn't pleasant, it's the furthest thing from pleasant and if you haven't got a nice warm bed to go to when you're going

> *through withdrawals then it's too hard. And like they're the peo-*
> *ple that get stuck, do you get me? They're the people that fall*
> *through the hole kind of, that have no chance … I was lucky*
> *enough to have parents who loved me no matter what, and that*
> *are there for me. — Anna (17)*

While finding it difficult to address the problem of their drug use without a stable place to live, equally their drug dependence prevents them from accessing accommodation. Homeless drug dependent youth therefore frequently find themselves in a difficult bind. Several identified the absence of a stable place to live, coupled with their hopelessness and lack of motivation to quit, as leading barriers to them accessing treatment. Indeed, a number remained relatively disconnected from drug treatment services, even if they had enrolled in a programme. Others who had been out of home for longer felt powerless to change their situations. Sarah's story reveals the potential of secure housing to increase the capacity of young homeless people to resolve drug and other problems. At the time of interview, Sarah was living in a transitional housing unit which, she claimed, enabled her to look beyond "survival mode" to consider longer-term issues related to employment, training and education.

> *Ever since I've been here a lot of stuff has happened. And this is*
> *the only place that's actually worked for me. I'm seven months*
> *clean now and in that seven months I've had one relapse and I*
> *think that's brilliant, that I've only had one. I've started a course*
> *as well to get a diploma so I'm still in that course and I'm after*
> *starting college as well. — Sarah (21)*

Young People Responding to Homeless Services

Young people are not passive recipients of the services designed to meet their needs; rather, they interact with adults and young people within these settings and much of this interaction influences their everyday and longer-term experiences and outcomes. Earlier sections have drawn attention to young people's suspicion of many of the professionals charged with meeting their needs and to their reluctance, in some cases, to engage with services. This distrust was often deep-seated and had its origin in their frequently negative early experiences of agencies and individuals who intervened in their lives. However, young people had other reasons for not attending services, prominent among these, a fear of bullying and intimidation. Many who were well-acquainted with street scenes claimed that bullying was pervasive in these contexts and that younger groups were particularly vulnerable. A number stated that they tried to avoid other homeless youth who were well-known for their use of aggressive tactics:

> *There's a lot of bullying, yeah, with little kids. Yeah, there is. Big people bullying little kids, there's a lot of it.*
>
> *[What would they bully them to do?]*
>
> *To snatch, rob, drugs. Anything, anything. Yeah, it happens in the hostels, it happens down the street. It happens everywhere. —* Declan (19)

Bullying was implicated in the non-use of certain services including hostels, day centres and drop-in centres, and this appeared to be a particular problem among the under-18s. James told how he did not use hostels because of his fear of other residents.

> *[What worries you about life at this present time?]*
>
> *Sleeping on the streets, I want to get off the streets now.*
>
> *[What about the hostels?]*
>
> *No I wouldn't. I don't like using them because there's people in there that gives me hidings (beatings) as well like, do you know what I mean. That's why I wouldn't stay there, you know what I mean. —* James (18)

Linked to the problem of bullying were a number of strongly held ideas and beliefs about the users of these services. Anna had never accessed city-centre hostel accommodation because she associated it with youth who were dangerous and undesirable:

> *All the youth hostels I knew now, all the little knackers that I*
> *didn't want to be around, all the scumbags that kept taking our*
> *phones and everything slept in those hostels so I never used them.*
> — *Anna (17)*

Significant also is that older youth, in particular, appeared to suffer from service fatigue. A number had grown tired of engaging with services which did not, as they saw it, help them to get their lives "back on track". Others felt strongly that some of the services they accessed had served to further diminish their stake in mainstream society. Several, for example, who were homeless for longer claimed that their constant movement between city-centre services had resulted in their becoming fully absorbed into a life of survival.

> *I wouldn't be here if I didn't come into town, I know I wouldn't.*
> *Out there (home neighbourhood) like, I probably could have*
> *something like a robbed car charge, but I wouldn't have, you*
> *know, the serious bad charges I have now. I wouldn't say so any*
> *way. Just in town, it's much different, it's totally different than*
> *the suburbs. When you come into the city, like, it's much differ-*
> *ent.* — *Paul (19)*

Paul went on to explain how he and others were drawn into a cycle of drug use and criminal activity during the years they spent commuting between city-centre services:

> *Since I was twelve I have been in hostels. Anyone that's been*
> *there has picked up charges with the police, has messed with coke,*
> *dabbled with tablets. They drink, smoke hash, rob, mug people.*
> *Like, they've done all them things ... Some mornings like you*
> *could leave the hostel and the drop-in centre wouldn't be open for*
> *an hour or two or it could be weekends and it's not open at all.*
> *And we'd just be saying, "Well, what will we do now?" Drugs*
> *are the only thing you think of doing. It's just the buzz you get*
> *off them for the day, you just think about it that way. And you go*
> *off robbing then.* — *Paul (19)*

Colm gave an all but identical account of how young residents of city-centre hostels become progressively and more heavily involved in drug use and criminal activity:

> *They should have better places. Like the people that come through the Out of Hours, yeah, 99.99 per cent of them is gonna be doing gear no matter what. Going through hostels for under eighteens and the Out of Hours hostels, 99.999 is gonna do gear ... If they start hanging around with the people that are in the hostels they're gonna do heroin, they're gonna start beating people up on the streets for their phones and their money. That's the way it is.*
> — Colm (20)

The services that homeless young people accessed came to occupy a distinctive place in their social worlds. This is not surprising since services are themselves social environments which, over time, influence how they position and view themselves within wider society. Furthermore, young people attach meanings and ultimately make sense of the services they access in the course of their own development. It appears that many with longer histories of homelessness felt that the services they accessed over several years were at least partly responsible for their situations, and there were strong claims that current systems of intervention had worked in the opposite direction to enmesh them in street scenes.

The Meaning of "Homelessness"

A key objective of this book is to draw attention to the experiences and perspectives of young homeless people, including how they perceive and construct their own situations. Much of the data presented in this and earlier chapters suggest that a significant number framed their status and situation as "homeless". This was evident when they talked about their daily lives, social networks and peer relationships and also from how they referenced the services they accessed.

Nonetheless, not all of the young people considered themselves to be homeless and their reasons varied. Christian did not equate his situation with "homelessness", although he had lived out of home for a number of years.

> *[How would you define your situation? Do you see yourself as homeless?]*

> *This isn't homelessness. Homelessness is sleeping on the street. Nowhere to live. Things like that. Adult hostel people, they are homeless; sometimes they get a bed in a hostel. This is not home-less, right. You don't even need to lift your fingers, you know what I mean. There's a chef, there's fucking (pause) ... they wash your clothes, they buy you your clothes. That's not home-less. How can you call that homeless for fuck sake? Do you know what I mean? You go out and you look and see someone that's homeless and you see the difference, you know what I mean. That's it. It's just living away from home.* — Christian (17)

For Christian, homelessness meant "sleeping on the street" and having "nowhere to live", a status which, as he perceived it, could not be applied to himself. He was living in a residential setting (hostel) for under-18s at the time of interview and viewed his situation as fundamentally different to that of adult hostel users. The line he draws between homelessness and living away from home centres largely on the material goods (food, clothing and so on) that are available to him and not to individuals who live on the street or in adult hostels. Like Christian, Luke and Brendan did not believe themselves to be homeless and felt that their situa-tions were best defined as "living away from home":

> *[How would you define your situation?]*

> *A person that's livin' away from home.*

> *[Alright. Are you homeless then?]*

> *Well I would be, I'd be homeless without this place (under-18s hostel) so it could be worse.* — Luke (18)

I'd say I'm a person living out of home, I'd say, because I don't even like the thought of someone that's homeless. I don't like the thought of that. — Brendan (17)

Several other users of services targeting under-18s shared this reluctance to apply the term "homeless" to their situations. This is not altogether surprising since homelessness is a deeply stigmatising status. The study's "newly" or recently homeless rarely defined their situations in terms of homelessness and a considerable number rejected any suggestion of *being* homeless. This perspective was particularly strong among young women. Rachel did not consider herself to be homeless because she had somewhere to stay but did state that she had experienced homelessness in the past. Like many others, she interpreted homelessness narrowly as "sleeping out" or sleeping rough.

[Do you consider yourself to be homeless?]

No, not in here (hostel for under-18s). No, I consider homeless as going to a Garda station of a night.

[Would you say that you've experienced homelessness?]

Yeah.

[But you're not homeless now?]

Not any more. — Rachel (14)

Jacinta had also been living in a short-term hostel (residential setting) for a considerable period of time and sometimes visited her parents at weekends. Like Rachel, she did not identify with the term homeless because she had shelter.

[Some people in your kind of situation would describe themselves as homeless …?]

I don't. No. I don't know? No, I think I'm lucky, yeah.

[You're lucky to have a place like here is it?]

No. I'm just lucky to have a shelter. I'm lucky because of half the shit that I ever did, like. There was mates that used to always try and be there for me and try and help me through things and I think if they weren't there for me I wouldn't have like came as far as this. And I think that the school as well and them as well, the teachers, everyone in there in that school, they all helped me through everything. — Jacinta (16)

It is significant, nonetheless, that when questioned about where she deemed to be "home", Jacinta considered neither the hostel where she lived, nor her parent's house, to be "home".

[So where do you consider ... where would you call home?]

Well sometimes I say I'm going home for the weekend and then I say to my ma and da, "I'm going home again". I don't really class either of them as home. I don't class them as that, they're not my home.

Likewise, Olivia did not see herself as homeless but did not perceive the hostel where she lived to be a home.

[Ok, so some people who live in a situation like this call themselves homeless, do you feel that you're homeless?]

In a way but in general I don't think of it that way.

[How do you think about it?]

Like I live in a house.

[You live in a house ok. Would you call this your home, yeah?]

It's a house yeah, but I call my sisters house home. — Olivia (15)

The references young people made to "home" are strongly suggestive of emotional as well as physical dimensions to their understating of what constitutes a home. While residents of short- or medium-term hostels targeting under-18s did not generally self-identify homeless, many also stated that they did not have a home and this produced its own anxieties. Melissa – one of the study's youngest participants – did not equate her situation with home-lessness but also worried about being perceived as "different" by her peers. She was clearly not "at home" with her situation:

[What about friends now at the moment, do you have … ?]

Yeah like I have loads of friends in school because they're all me old friends out of me sixth class and fifth class and stuff. But I won't bring any of them back here (to the hostel). I just, I wouldn't be able for that. Only a few of my friends know I live here and if that gets around like everyone will know, you know, and I don't want that.

[So would that be embarrassing for you?]

Yeah.

[Do you think they'd treat you different?]

Its not that they'd treat you different but like some people will say stuff to you, you know. If I go, "I live in a hostel", they think like something like refugees, that's what they're going to think be-cause they don't know anything about these places. Like if I say a hostel they'll think I'm living with like other people from other countries. That's what they think a hostel is. They don't think it's just a normal house that has kids. — Melissa (14)

As the account above suggests, those who did not embrace the term homeless were often simultaneously aware of their "out-sider" status and of the assumptions and judgements of others. In a general sense, the responses of younger participants reveal their efforts to come to terms with their new situations. Equally, how-ever, they highlight their rejection of the notion of *being* homeless.

There were many others, however, who had fully embraced a homeless identity. The following are examples of how young people integrated the notion of *being* homelessness into their ac-counts of everyday life.

Being homeless is not a nice thing to be, you know, it's not. — Declan (19)

But there's no top dogs with us in the homeless group. Every-body's their self and that's it. — *Joe (19)*

You're homeless like, that's what it's like out there. You always have to think ahead of yourself. — *Julian (22)*

Then I ended up homeless from the drugs, you know. Then I ended up coming through the hostels. — *Tony (22)*

I just don't want to be homeless but I'd nothing else to do with me life so I got like to mix around in bad company and I got on drugs like. I want to get off them now but it's actually too late now at the moment to get off them. I'm gone to far. — *Megan (19)*

You are better off just keeping it to yourself, yeah. But when you are homeless you need company. — *Eoin (20)*

Several others explicitly self-identified as homeless: for these young people homelessness was clearly part and parcel of how they saw their situation and their everyday lives.

Homeless, I'm a person that's homeless. Nowhere to go, homeless. — *Ronan (17)*

I would see myself as a homeless person, yeah. — *Declan (19)*

Conor, who also described himself as homeless, considered the street to be his "second home":

[And when it's a nice night would you sleep outside rather than come in or ...?]

Yeah, I like being out there. I don't like being inside (i.e. in hos-tels). I'm used to being outside, it's like my second home. Well it is my home, you know, because I haven't got a home, that's about it. I prefer being on the streets to going into hostels. — *Conor (19)*

It is significant that the vast majority of those who applied the term homeless to themselves were over the age of 18 years. Most has spent a number of years moving between unstable living situations and practically all were past or current users of adult homeless services. Life had changed quite dramatically for these young people since they first left home and several also identified a progressive downward spiral in their lives:

> *I just got it now this year, I got the sense of it that I'm deep in now.* — Brendan (17)

There was also evidence to suggest that young people's perceptions of their situation can change in the opposite direction. Julian found himself out of home as a young teenager and had extensive experience of rough sleeping, squatting and using hostels. During this time he self-identified as homeless and *being* homeless was part and parcel of his everyday life. However, at the time of interview, he was living in a transitional housing unit. His account underscores the role of accommodation in determining how young people perceive and interpret their situations.

> *[Back then would you have identified yourself as being a homeless person?]*
>
> *Yeah, a homeless person.*
>
> *[What about now?]*
>
> *Not really, no, because I have a home.* — Julian (22)

Homelessness is clearly not an absolute category and relates to various socially defined categories and to ideas about home (Johnson et al., 1991). Young homeless people, like all social actors, bring a variety of different meanings to social situations. Furthermore, the personal identities that homeless people construct and avow change with the passage of time (Snow and Anderson, 1987).

Conclusion

It appears that services work for some young people and not for others. Overall, young people appeared to have relatively high levels of awareness of the services available to them and, in line with other research (Fountain and Howes, 2002; Wincup et al., 2003), the longer the period of homelessness, the greater their knowledge and use of available services.

Homeless youth are a difficult group to serve and their experiences, both prior and subsequent to becoming homeless, impact on their willingness to use and benefit from such amenities. The absence of appropriate services in suburban areas of Dublin city is clearly a problem and one which leads to young people converging on the city-centre to avail of services. It was in these very settings that several of the study's young people claimed to have learned behaviour and responses that served to further entrench them in homelessness, drug use and criminal activity. The findings presented certainly suggest that at least some of the interventions designed to meet the needs of homeless youth may have inadvertently facilitated their descent into a "subculture" of homelessness.[1]

Homeless young people are a highly diverse group with complex needs that vary depending on their age, experiences, health-related behaviour and the duration of their homelessness. The barriers they face in terms of obtaining the services and supports they require are significant and appear to be compounded – certainly for those who remain homeless for longer – by a sense of hopelessness and a perception that the "system" has failed them in their efforts to make positive changes in their lives.

Not all of the young people interviewed considered themselves to be homeless even if they had lived out of home for several weeks or months. The stigma young people perceive in being homeless may make them unwilling to apply the label to themselves (Fitzpatrick, 2000). Moreover, people may attempt to dis-

---

[1] This use of the term "subculture" follows Snow and Anderson (1993: 39) where the term is used to describe "a fairly distinctive mélange of behaviors, artifacts, and cognitive elements that together characterize a way of life of a set of individuals and distinguish them from other groups or aggregations within the larger society". A subculture need not be founded on shared values and beliefs, but may arise from a common predicament and associated survival problems.

tance themselves from the label "homeless" to bolster their sense of self-respect (Osborne, 2002). However, the longer young people remained without stable accommodation the more likely they were to adopt a homeless identity. The move from under-18s services appeared to constitute a significant turning point in terms of how they perceived their situations. This finding is noteworthy since exiting homelessness may become harder the more the individual becomes entrenched in the homeless identity (Snow and Anderson, 1993).

Chapter 9

CONCLUSION

This book set out to explore the lives of homeless young people in Dublin at the beginning of the twenty-first century. Dublin, and indeed Ireland, has changed almost beyond recognition over the past decade or so. A prolonged period of economic growth, enhanced economic prosperity, and high levels of inward migration have all contributed to this change (Fahey et al, 2007). In the midst of such prosperity, homeless young people appear somewhat incongruous. This research did not attempt to estimate the extent of youth homelessness in Dublin. As highlighted in Chapter 2, such an exercise is fraught with difficulties and is also of limited utility in understanding youth homelessness. Rather, this work has attempted to bring about a greater understanding of the *processes* involved in becoming and remaining homeless.

In this final chapter, we first consider a number of key aspects of the problem of youth homelessness in Dublin based on the findings documented in the five preceding chapters. Young people's homeless pathways are then discussed with reference to a model of youth homeless "careers". The chapter then reflects on how youth homelessness is conceptualised in both Europe and North America, with particular reference to public policy interventions. We conclude by highlighting the challenges facing policy makers in Ireland in delivering the necessary range of services to ensure that young people exit homelessness at the earliest possible juncture.

The Study

The approach to the conduct of this research was shaped by the core objective of accessing the first hand accounts of homeless youth through the conduct of detailed life history interviews with 40 young people between 14 and 22 years. All of the study participants had lived in Dublin in the six months prior to interview and were currently or had recently experienced homelessness.

It is important to emphasise that the research did not target young people "at risk" of homelessness.[1] The study's participants had, in most cases, already entered into the official network of services targeting homeless young people in Dublin. This point is significant for a number of reasons. Firstly, the "newly" or recently homeless young people interviewed represent the views and experiences of a group whose futures are uncertain. Some, for example, may find a stable placement in the future and there may be others who find that they are in a position to return home. Only with the benefit of follow-up data will a clearer picture of their pathways through homelessness emerge. Secondly, a large number of the study's young people were quite experienced users of services targeting homeless youth. Several were over the age of 18 and had a relatively lengthy history of homelessness. These accounts help to illustrate the consequences of longer "careers" in homelessness and they highlight the challenges young people face when they are no longer eligible for services targeting the under-18s. There is a risk, however, that the life histories of these young people produce a picture of youth homelessness that is particularly bleak. The study's sample certainly included a number whose problems and difficulties span a whole range of areas and for whom interventions have proven largely unsuccessful.

These issues should be borne in mind when considering the possible spectrum of young people who experience homelessness

---

[1] Although this group are potentially important to understanding young people's routes "into" homelessness (as well as possible points of prevention and early intervention), their inclusion in the study would have required a different approach to recruitment and, indeed, a substantially altered research design.

and how this study's findings may reflect the type and range of issues and problems facing homeless youth more broadly. While the sampling strategy targeted a diverse range of participants – and certainly succeeded in capturing the city-centre youth homeless scene – it may well be that a proportion of the young people interviewed represent the "sharpest" end of the youth homeless spectrum. Earlier chapters have demonstrated, for example, that the needs of many of these young people are at least partly attributable to the duration of their homelessness.

Homelessness, Marginality and Risk

The majority of the study's young people identified major changes in their lives since they first left home or care and these changes were almost always related to negative social and personal experiences. Young people were often able to identify when and how different problems arose and how these impacted on their lives, suggesting that they had a developmental perspective on their situations. The theme of dislocation was strong within many stories of leaving home and the negative impact of this displacement intensified following young people's entry into hostel life. In general, daily life within hostels (residential settings) for young people under the age of 18 years was portrayed as difficult. Transience within these settings limited young people's opportunities to form stable and reliable relationships and also made daily life unpredictable. Indeed, many of the relationships they forged within hostel and street-based settings pushed them towards activities which served to further alienate them from mainstream society. There was also a profound stigma attached to hostel life. Young people were aware of the judgements of others and of what several claimed to be a negative public perception of homeless youth.

The risks that accompany homelessness were most obvious among the study's longer-term homeless. Many of these young people had spent months or years commuting between various unstable living situations. Several were drug dependent and a considerable number reported criminal activity and contact with law enforcement agencies. As time progressed, many engaged in behaviour that had a negative impact on their lives and ultimately served to further marginalise and isolate them.

Drug and Criminal "Careers"

Levels of drug use were extremely high across the sample and approximately half of the study's young people had become seriously involved in "heavy end" drug use. Although the onset of heroin use is complex, typical accounts suggest that few initiated use prior to their first homeless experience. The transition to injecting occurred for all of the study's intravenous drug users subsequent to their becoming homeless.

Street life can be "criminogenic" in that it fosters both the opportunity and necessity for criminal behaviour (McCarthy and O'Hagan, 1991). For many who had spent months or years out of home, law-breaking became a means of generating income, reflecting young people's need to adopt unconventional and illegal strategies in order to survive. For those who found other avenues and options closed, the street economy became a primary means of obtaining money. Young people engaged in a range of illegal and quasi-illegal money-making strategies, with property theft being the most commonly reported offence. It is significant that a considerable number were reluctant to engage in begging or "tapping" because it was a demeaning display of their poverty and vulnerability. Both drug use and criminal activity led to many unintended consequences. Drug dependence propelled at least a number into daily criminal activity, making them extremely open to arrest and subsequent incarceration, and a considerable number had been incarcerated for their crimes. The relationship between homelessness, drug use and crime is clearly complex and cannot be fully unravelled in this book. However, we can tentatively observe that few young people were heavily involved in drug use and even fewer had records of offending at the time of leaving home. Both drug use and criminality certainly escalated for the majority following their first out-of-home experience.

Violence and Victimisation

Violence and victimisation were significant problems among the study's young people. The street emerged as a highly competitive environment where young people often experienced threat and many found themselves in situations where they felt the need to protect themselves and to defend their personal possessions. Within street-based settings young people were also regular observers of violence and several admitted to having engaged in violent behaviour at some time, particularly in self-defence. Others stated that they had used physical force as an outward show of strength or as a way to communicate harsh messages to other youth. Homelessness may erode young people's ties to conventional society and gradually destroy inhibitions restricting violent behaviour (Baron and Hartnagel, 1997). Equally, however, it simultaneously places young people in locations where violence is more likely. Young people understood the dangers of living on the street and they harboured many associated fears. A large number were, in fact, themselves victims of intimidation or violence, and bullying was as a significant problem among young people under the age of 18, in particular. Some were bullied into relinquishing personal possessions, others had been forced by others to commit criminal acts and a large number had been attacked, beaten or intimidated on at least one occasion. It is significant that when young people were victims of violence, they rarely or never reported crime against themselves to an appropriate authority, suggesting that they considered themselves ineligible for protection, help or support.

Homelessness and Health

While the vast majority of the study's younger participants did not report health problems, this picture changed dramatically for young people over the age of 17. Rough sleepers were particularly prone to infection and almost all reported respiratory problems including asthma, bronchitis and pneumonia. Heavy smoking, poor nutrition, alcohol and drug consumption and exposure to the elements all combined to make a large number of the study's respondents prone to ill-health. Unsurprisingly, given their precarious lifestyles, many reported mishaps and accidents that led to broken bones, cuts, bruises and serious abrasions. Finally, five of the study's young people (all injecting drug users) had received a diagnosis for hepatitis C.

As stated earlier, overall levels of drug use were high across the sample. There was also strong evidence to suggest that housing instability played a pivotal role in young people's exposure to drug-related risk as well as being a formidable challenge to their ability to manage these risks. Young people were routinely forced to use drugs in unsanitary locations such as squats, alley ways and public toilets. Although practically all of the study's IDUs were well-informed about the risks associated with sharing injecting equipment, several nonetheless reported episodic or selective sharing (i.e. sharing with a relative or romantic partner). Finally, levels of non-conformity to safe sex practices were extremely high across the sample. This finding is consistent with the international consensus that homeless young people engage in sexual practices that place them at high risk of contracting sexually transmitted infections.

The Meaning of "Homelessness"

Not only did the homeless experience vary between young people, but they also attributed different meanings to their situations and not all subscribed to the notion of *being* homeless. This is not altogether surprising since homelessness is a deeply stigmatising status and one which young people may well reject. Most of the participants in this study defined homelessness quite narrowly as "sleeping out" or "sleeping on the street" and the majority of those who lived in hostels for the under-18s did not apply the label "homeless" to themselves. In contrast, adult hostel users talked about *being* homeless and they used the term explicitly and routinely to describe various aspects of their daily lives. Across the sample, young people perceived the transition to adult hostels as more than simply a crisis of accommodation: as a symbol of *real* homelessness, entry to adult hostels denoted a crisis of identity for those who had, or were about to, make this transition.

Young People's Homeless Pathways

The notion that individuals experience differentiated pathways through homelessness is central to this book. At its most simple definition, a pathway through homelessness would describe the route of an individual into homelessness, their experience of homelessness and their route out of homelessness into secure housing. At the most complex level, a unique pathway could be ascribed to all those who have ever experienced homelessness.

Consistent with recent international research on homelessness, the findings of this study demonstrate that homelessness cannot be attributed to a single cause. It was rare for young people to identify one factor in isolation and, in general, a number of factors combined to produce vulnerability to homelessness. For many, the event precipitating homelessness was closely related to other issues or home situations and, even if a specific crisis acted as a catalyst, their leaving home was most often the end point of a prolonged period of disruptions and difficulties. The following three pathways or routes into homelessness were identified:

- Pathway 1: Care history

- Pathway 2: Household instability and family conflict

- Pathway 3: Negative peer associations and problem behaviour.

Although not mutually exclusive, these pathways point overwhelmingly to poverty and social deprivation, difficult family situations and strained relationships with parents and carers as key factors precipitating homelessness. An important finding arising from the identification of the three pathways relates to the early age at which the stability of their home situations were undermined, making them vulnerable to homelessness. Almost half of the study's young people experienced homelessness for the first time at or before the age of 14. Another significant finding relates to the very considerable number who experienced some combination of emotional, physical or sexual abuse. While the processes related to becoming homeless are clearly multifaceted and complex, it is nonetheless clear that many of the study's young people had endured years of hardship and trauma prior to their leaving home.

Amid the diversity and idiosyncrasy of individual cases across the sample, it was possible to devise a model of youth homeless "careers" based on young people's biographical accounts of the homeless experience (Figure 9.1).

Figure 9.1: Model of the Youth Homeless "Career"*

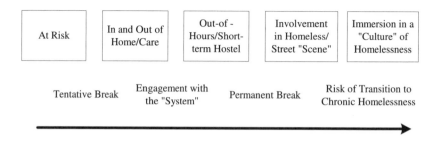

*Adapted from Chamberlain and McKenzie (1998: 71).

Tentative Break

During the early days, weeks or months out of home (or care) some young people occupied one or a number of *unofficial* sleeping places (that is, they stayed with friends, extended family, or slept rough). This phase could be said to constitute a *tentative break* from the family home or care setting. These initial days, weeks or months were frequently characterised by periodic returns to the family (or foster home), highlighting young people's reluctance to make a more enduring break from home. Indeed, this study's analysis of early homeless pathways highlights a "window of opportunity" for intervention between parents and their children that is all too frequently missed. None of the young people who fell into this broad "category" resolved their home-based difficulties. For some, a period of sleeping rough in their local area ensued and most moved between a number of unstable living situations (friends, romantic partners, extended family) before making contact with the Out of Hours Service.

Engagement with "The System"

Upon making contact with the Out of Hours Service, young people entered into a system of intervention that was quite distinctive and the ensuing period saw many *engaging* with this system in numerous complex ways. At the point of moving into a hostel for the first time, they had to familiarise themselves with their new surroundings and with the people who already occupied the living space they now shared. This was largely a process of "sounding out" and learning. Furthermore, they faced the challenge of negotiating new relationships and there was also considerable pressure to conform to the expectations of peers who were more established within the hostel "scene".

Not surprisingly, the study's "newly" or recently homeless reported fewer living situations since the time they left home and most had little or no contact with a network of street-based homeless youth. The weeks or months since they had left home had been difficult and most experienced loneliness and anxiety following their separation from family and/or home neighbourhood. All considered the hostel where they lived to be a short-term arrangement and hoped to move to a more stable living situation in the near future. A number expressed a desire to return home, even if their home situation could not realistically provide a safe and secure environment. This group had not become immersed in street scenes, most were not heavily involved in drug use and they usually attended school, either in their home neighbourhood or in one close to the hostel. The future is unpredictable for these young people and follow-up interviews will provide additional information on their homeless pathways. Some may move to a medium- or long-term accommodation or to an alternative care setting, while others may return home. It is worth pointing out, however, that at the time of interview, a number of the study's younger women (under-18 years) had lived in a short-term hostel for a considerable period, ranging from several months to two years. The relative stability of living in a single setting enabled them to participate in conventional daily activities. Nonetheless, there was a profound stigma attached to hostel life and the transience and unpredictability that characterised these settings was a source of considerable stress for residents.

For those young people who had longer histories of homelessness, coupled with a history of multiple living situations (hostels, rough sleeping, squatting, staying with relatives or friends), there are a number of identifiable patterns and trends. A large number started on a path of alternating between various emergency and short-term accommodation types and, for many, this pattern extended over a period of years. This style of engagement with *the system* (i.e. city-centre services for homeless youth) is striking for a number of reasons. The move "into town" initially conferred feelings of freedom and independence; there were few or no adult authority figures and such relocation offered the possibility of a whole new "life". During this period, many started to develop strong connections with a street-based youth homeless scene where they were exposed to a range of risky behaviour and activities. A considerable number (probably a majority) being already experienced drug users at this juncture, almost all further expanded their drug repertoires and several made the transition to heroin use. This period also saw many resuming, extending or embarking for the first time on behaviour and activities that brought them into contact with law enforcement agencies and, for a large number, breaking the law was directly related to their efforts to finance everyday needs including food, clothing, alcohol and drugs.

Permanent Break and the Risk of Transition to Chronic Homelessness

Those whose involvement in street scenes continued over an extended period moved incrementally towards making a more *permanent break* from home, family and community. Many who described this pathway through homelessness had become entrenched in heavy or problematic drug or alcohol use and they almost always reported a history of "trouble" with the police. Their ability to manage their daily lives was hampered by the absence of a stable place to live and, for a considerable number, by physical health and psychological problems. While the majority of the study's participants could not be described as chronically homeless, a large number were heavily immersed in a subculture of homelessness and some are clearly at risk of making the transition to adult homelessness. As highlighted above, there is nothing fixed or absolute about youth homeless "careers" and no inevitable progression to more chronic homeless states. Nonetheless, this study demonstrates just how rapidly "careers" in homelessness can progress and highlights patterns that suggest that homelessness can become a progressive decline for some young people. Those whose participation in homeless street scenes extended for longer periods moved incrementally towards making a more permanent break from home, family and community. Their life stories also point to the services they accessed as teenagers – and their interactions with and responses to these services – as a significant and, all too often, negative turning point. The concentration of services targeting youth in crisis in city-centre locations appears problematic and may well facilitate young people's entry to street life.

Not Only Homeless ...

This research clearly demonstrates that homelessness was not the only problem facing the young people interviewed. The majority came from impoverished family backgrounds and they described extremely difficult home and family situations. Most experienced problems at school which led, in many cases, to their leaving the educational system without formal qualifications. Several of the young people had experienced separation from their parents and siblings, either because of problems in their homes or because of a death or tragedy in the family, whilst others had endured high levels of conflict within their homes. In addition, a considerable number had become involved in serious or problematic drug use, while others had come into contact with law enforcement agencies, and/or had spent time in prison or places of detention. Finally, a significant minority suffered from ill-health and these health problems were a direct consequence of living on the street and in other precarious situations.

Across the sample, a combination of poverty, deprivation and childhood adversity emerged as factors common to the majority. Despite this observation, we are cognisant that transitions to adulthood are unique and that there is not one single, uniform way of growing up with such adversity (MacDonald and Marsh, 2006). Moreover, this research broadly affirms an interpretation of homelessness as a complex and dynamic process that is subject to change over time. It is arguably this complexity that affirms the need for an understanding of young people's homeless pathways. A pathways approach can help to coherently and accurately identify the confluence of factors that lead to homelessness. Furthermore, since youth homelessness can result in patterns that extend to adulthood, the identification of pathways can highlight points of intervention that mitigate the likelihood of longer-term homelessness.

It is perhaps important in this context to reiterate some of the observations in Chapter 1 concerning the evolution of youth homelessness in Ireland. Most notably, what constitutes youth homelessness is itself variable and only in recent years has a legal definition held ascendancy as a consequence of the *Child Care Act, 1991*. Defining the "young", as opposed to "adult", homeless as those under-18 years may provide a degree of legal and bureaucratic certainty. However, it does not reflect the reality of the lives of homeless young people or the fact that housing instability can be an ongoing challenge for many who experience homelessness during their teenage years. On reaching the age of 18, young people who remain homeless or in unstable living situations have little or no option but to enter into services and interventions targeting adults where they face great uncertainty, as well as the prospect of becoming enmeshed in homeless street scenes.

Understanding Youth Homelessness

Gaetz and O'Grady (2002) have argued that much of the research on youth homelessness in Europe has interpreted the phenomenon as the extreme manifestation of a growing number of young people – sometimes referred to pejoratively as an "underclass" – who are socially, economically and culturally marginalised from mainstream society. Research on youth homelessness in North America, on the other hand, has been undertaken primarily by criminologists who seek to understand why crime is so prevalent amongst this population. In relation to research into adult homelessness, Fitzpatrick and Christian (2006) note that researchers of this topic in Britain tend to have academic backgrounds in social policy and housing whereas, in the US, academic backgrounds in psychology and medicine tend to dominate. Methodologically, this situation has broadly resulted in quantitative methods dominating US research, with qualitative methods featuring most prominently within British studies. These shifting and differing theoretical and methodological approaches have resulted in differing understandings of homelessness. Explanations for homelessness in the US, particularly for families with children, highlight structural factors, specifically the role of the housing market and the lack of affordability of rental housing, over individualist explanations. In Britain, a move is evident that highlights the individual support needs of homeless persons alongside a clear policy message that homelessness is more than simply a housing problem.

In the broader European context, the European Observatory on Homelessness has provided a range of largely secondary data on aspects of homelessness over the past 15 years but, again, a theoretical consensus has remained elusive. As Fitzpatrick (1998: 206) has observed when reviewing the early reports of the Observatory: "[v]irtually all commentators acknowledge that both structural and individual factors are relevant to the production of homelessness. But it is notable that various ... correspondents placed a radically different emphasis on one or the other as the key to explaining homelessness in their countries". Attempts to relate the extent of homelessness in different European countries to the nature of the welfare regimes have proven equally problematic. As Daly (1999: 327) has observed, "[p]rovision and policy for homelessness does not follow in any simplistic way from social policies writ large".

In Ireland, at a public policy level in general, there is little evidence of the emergence of an American-style "underclass" (Nolan and Whelan, 2000). While there is some evidence of the rhetoric associated with US-style debates on the underclass, particularly in the media (Saris and Bartley, 2002; Saris et al, 2002), there is no evidence that this occasional rhetoric has influenced policy makers and rarely has the debate on youth homelessness in Ireland been framed within such a paradigm. The relatively limited literature on the subject in Ireland tends to follow the theoretical and policy model that is practised in the UK rather than in the US. This is not particularly surprising given the close interaction across the two jurisdictions between both academics and practitioners in this area.

Whilst it is not possible to resolve the conceptual and methodological difficulties evident within both research and policy based on the content of the eight preceding chapters, this work can constructively contribute to the ongoing debate on homelessness. Acknowledging the diversity of strongly and sincerely held viewpoints on homelessness does not necessarily result in policy paralysis, although the absence of a clear-cut consensus about the causes and, hence, the solution to homelessness can be frustrating. However, as we have argued, homeless experiences are complex, fluid and diverse and are mediated by the systems of intervention that pertain at a particular point in time.

As demonstrated in previous chapters, how both the State and voluntary agencies understand and respond to youth homelessness in Ireland has changed considerably over the past 40 years. Initially viewed as a consequence of maladjustment on the part of the young person, homelessness is now increasingly viewed as stemming from the inability of the various services to meet the needs of such children. Although a range of initiatives and thoughtful proposals have been advanced in recent years, coupled with considerable additional funding, homelessness amongst the young remains a reality in twenty-first century Dublin. Nonetheless, it would be churlish not to acknowledge the positive changes that have occurred over this period. These changes include the passing of the *Child Care Act, 1991*, the provision of an enhanced range of residential and non-residential services and a more substantial investment in preventative services. The responsibility of the State to meet the needs of these children was clarified during the 1990s in a series of bruising encounters between the Superior Courts and the Health Boards, primarily the Eastern Health Board, over the interpretation of Section 5 of the *Child Care Act, 1991*. From a situation where a range of voluntary agencies operated a relatively limited range of services with inadequate statutory funding, services are now operated either directly by, or in partnership with, the State. Nonetheless, while the State has taken primary responsibility for the "categorisation" of, and provision of services to young homeless people, this research demonstrates that considerable difficulties and challenges remain.

Concluding Remarks

At the beginning of the twenty-first century, the key issue is how the various statutory and voluntary agencies organise their services in a manner that ensures that young people exit homelessness at the earliest possible juncture. To a considerable extent, the findings documented in this book suggest that this is not necessarily an easy task, but it should nonetheless be more than simply an aspiration. Many of the young people interviewed for the purpose of this study were known to various agencies of the State – including the child care, youth homeless and criminal justice systems – from a young age and over an extended period. This finding points to failures within numerous systems of intervention and at various junctures in children's and young people's lives. All of the young people whose stories are recounted in this book had the common experience of leaving home prematurely. Just as the events precipitating their leaving home varied, so too did their experiences following the initial days and weeks out of home. This diversity of experience, coupled with their varied histories and differing chronologies of life events, posed genuine challenges to the analysis and representation of their life stories. However, these challenges are themselves illuminating and demonstrate that there is not a single set of circumstance or experiences that defines homelessness among the young.

Appendix I

GLOSSARY OF TERMS

Bang	Administer a drug intravenously
Bird	Young woman/Girlfriend
Chasing/chasing the dragon	Smoking heroin
Coke	Cocaine
Copper	Police officer
Da	Father
E	Ecstasy
Gaff	House/Own home or home of other person
Goof/Goof off	Term used to describe person who appears sedate and listless as a result of drug intake
Hiding	Beating
Johnny	Condom
Joint	Street term for a cannabis cigarette

Junkie	Heroin addict
Knacker drinking	Drinking outdoors
Ma	Mother
OD	Drug overdose
On the hop	Playing truant
Score/Scoring	The process of obtaining illicit drugs
Stroking	Stealing
Strung out	Addicted to a drug, usually heroin
Suss/having a suss	Street term for knowing about/having knowledge
Tapping	Begging
Turn on	Episode of drug-taking which is considered pleasurable by the drug user
Using (drugs)	Often used in reference to injecting drugs as distinct from other modes of administration
Works	Injecting equipment

Appendix II

MEASURING ADULT HOMELESSNESS IN IRELAND

Before proceeding to examine the data on adult homelessness collected by statutory authorities, it is useful to consider the following statement by Cloke et al. (2001: 275):

> Counts of homeless people are not straightforward, objective facts open to unambiguous interpretation, but rather social constructs the production and analysis of which throws up a whole host of questions and potential difficulties surrounding what is being enumerated, by whom, how and to what end.

Following the *Housing Act, 1988*, Local Authorities are legally obliged to carry out assessments of their homeless populations. Under Section 9 of the Act, each Local Authority is required to carry out, at periods not exceeding three years, assessments of the need for the provision by them of adequate and suitable accommodation for people (a) who the housing authority have reason to believe, require, or are likely to require, accommodation from the authority (or voluntary body); and (b) who, in the opinion of the authority, are in need of such long term accommodation and are unable to provide it from their own resources. The first assessment took place at the end of March 1989 and, to date, seven assessments have taken place. The three initial assessments provided relatively little detail on the characteristics of those households deemed by the Local Authorities to require accommodation from statutory or voluntary housing bodies but, in each successive assessment since 1996, more detailed information has been published, with the 2005 assessment providing the most detailed set of data to date.

Households, Housing and Homelessness

The number of households[1] deemed by Local Authorities to have a housing need has increased from 19,376 in the initial assessment in 1989 to 43,684 in the most recent assessment of 2005. A particularly sharp increase was recorded between 1996 and 2002 at the height of the "Celtic Tiger", but a 9.8 per cent decrease was recorded between 2002 and 2005.[2] The 43,684 households recorded in 2005 comprised 87,635 individuals, of whom 41 per cent were child dependants, down from 45 per cent in 2002 and 46 per cent in 1999. The last decade saw a substantial increase in the Irish population and this needs to be taken into account when measuring housing need. The number of households included in the assessment declined over the same period from 36 per 1,000 households in 2002 to 30 in 2005, while the number of individuals included in the assessment declined from 28 per 1,000 population to 21.2 (for further details, see O'Sullivan, 2004, 2006a, 2006b).

While nationally the number of households assessed and recorded as having a housing need increased by some 60 per cent between 1996 and 2005, considerable variations are evident. For example, 21 authorities recorded a decrease in the number of such households over this period. In some cases, the decrease was relatively slight but, in others, it was significant. In the 2005 Assessment of Housing Need, 2,399 households were categorised as

---

[1] The use of the term "household" in this context may seem incongruous, given that such "*house*holds" are either in need of housing or homeless, but this is the nomenclature used in the assessments.

[2] One part of the explanation for the decrease between 2002 and 2005 is the more rigorous eliminating of multiple registered households, i.e. households registered with more than one Local Authority. There were 3,833 multiple registrations in 2005 compared with 3,288 in 2002.

homeless,[3] down marginally on the 2002 figure.[4] These households comprised 2,571 adults and 460 child dependants. Disaggregated data are not available for the 2002 assessment but, in comparison with the 1999 assessment, a striking decline in the number of child dependants in homeless headed households is observed. This is largely explained by the decline in the use of bed and breakfast-type accommodation for homeless families over this period.

Of particular interest in the context of the current study is the category "Young Persons Leaving Institutional Care or Without Family Accommodation".[5] This category displays some unusual patterns. In 2005, 31 per cent of households in this category were residing in Sligo County Council, a largely rural area, with no residential services for young people. One such household was identified in 2002 and none prior to that date. Similarly, Louth County Council, which in the first five assessments recorded no households in this category, recorded 34 in 2005. Just over 11,000 households were headed by a head of household aged between 18

---

[3] Section 9 (2) of the Housing Act, 1988 stipulates that a housing authority in making an assessment of housing need shall have regard to the need for housing of persons who—(*a*) are homeless, (*b*) are persons to whom *section 13* applies i.e. persons belonging to the class of persons who traditionally pursue or have pursued a nomadic way of life, (*c*) are living in accommodation that is unfit for human habitation or is materially unsuitable for their adequate housing, (*d*) are living in overcrowded accommodation, (*e*) are sharing accommodation with another person or persons and who, in the opinion of the housing authority, have a reasonable requirement for separate accommodation, (*f*) are young persons leaving institutional care or without family accommodation, (*g*) are in need of accommodation for medical or compassionate reasons, (*h*) are elderly, (*i*) are disabled or handicapped, or (*j*) are, in the opinion of the housing authority, not reasonably able to meet the cost of the accommodation which they are occupying or to obtain suitable alternative accommodation.

[4] In the 2005 assessment, 57.3 (25,045) of all households were categorised as "unable to afford existing accommodation", compared to 14.5 per cent in 1989.

[5] The guidance issued to the local authorities to assist them in completing the assessment states, "These would normally be single persons over the age of 18 years; those under 18 being the responsibility of the relevant health board. Married or cohabiting young persons generally fit into other categories".

and 25 years. Of these households, nearly 30 per cent were in the greater Dublin region.

Commencing with the 1991 Assessment of Housing Need, a separate, but parallel Assessment of Homelessness was conducted by Local Authorities. A key rationale for this was to ensure that homeless households not registered for Local Authority housing would be recorded for the purposes of enumerating the homeless population in Ireland. A total of 2,399 households were categorised as homeless in the 2005 assessment, a figure which is down marginally from 2002, but is considerably higher than the figures during the 1990s. Of these households, 2,078 were one-person households, with the remaining 321 incorporating more than one person. This translated into 2,571 adults and 460 child dependants, or a total of 3,031 individuals. It would appear that, for the 2005 Assessment, *all* households deemed to be homeless were registered for Local Authority housing. Thus, the figure of 2,399 households listed above is comparable with the assessments of homelessness between 1991 and 2002. The most common manner in which these data are presented, particularly by NGOs, is to identify the number of homeless persons recorded. However, this figure includes child dependants and should be distinguished from the number of homeless adults. On all units of measurement, a substantial decline can be observed between 1999 and 2005.

As is the case with the Assessments of Housing Need, considerable variation is evident between the Local Authorities in respect of the recording of homeless households in their functional areas. Between forty and fifty per cent of Local Authorities at each assessment recorded no homeless households, with 20 per cent recording, on average, less than 10 homeless households. More significantly, no less than 10 Local Authorities have ever recorded a homeless household or individual in any of the assessments of homelessness to date and 45 per cent of all Local Authorities in 2005 did not record a homeless household.

A striking feature of the data recorded during both the assessments of housing need and homelessness is the inconsistent recording, either from assessment to assessment or between the

Local Authorities. This is likely to reflect different priorities, but also very different interpretative practices. Consequently, the aggregate data are subject to an unusually high degree of caveat. The different recording systems operated by the Local Authorities, while they may reflect some degree of internal logic or consistency, appear so disparate as to engender a high degree of scepticism over the usefulness of the data at a national or aggregate level. More robust data are available in the greater Dublin region where, since 1999, a tri-annual assessment of the extent of homelessness is conducted by the Homeless Agency. The survey, conducted by the Homeless Agency on behalf of the four Local Authorities in the Greater Dublin region, is part of their obligations under the *Housing Act, 1988*. Consequently, it only seeks information on those households for which the Local Authorities have statutory responsibility.

In 1999, the Economic and Social Research Institute (ESRI) conducted an assessment of the extent of homelessness on behalf of the Homeless Initiative (renamed the Homeless Agency in 2001) using a significantly improved approach to enumeration than was used in previous Local Authority assessments.[6] This study found a total of 3,890 homeless persons in the Dublin, Kildare and Wicklow area, of whom 2,900 were adults (1,850 male and 1,050 female), with a total of 990 dependent children (Williams and O'Connor, 1999). The assessment also found that there were 275 people sleeping rough in the Dublin, Kildare and Wicklow areas in March 1999.

The average age of homeless males was just over 39 years while that of females was seven years younger at 32 years. A second assessment in 2002 (again conducted by the ESRI on behalf of the Homeless Agency) showed virtually no increase in the num-

---

[6] This and the two subsequent assessments (Williams and O'Connor, 1999; Williams and Gorby, 2002, Wafer, 2006) were carried out during one selected week of the year and are based on: (a) those individuals who use homeless services during that week and; (b) those who are accepted as homeless by a local authority but who do not have contact with any service during the week of the count. In addition, a count of rough sleepers is carried out.

ber of homeless individuals between 1999 and 2002 (when 2,920 homeless individuals were recorded), but a marginal decrease in the number of homeless households was recorded (Williams and Gorby, 2002). Both the 1999 and 2002 assessments found that single person households were the dominant homeless type in Dublin, with 7 out of 10 of all households falling into this category. Single person households were also found to be overwhelmingly male (81 per cent of the total in 2002). However, in the three years since the first ESRI assessment, the percentage share of single person households has decreased by 6 percentage points and, as this share decreased (by 270), households with children and couple-only households increased by 100 and 40, respectively.

In 2005, a further assessment was conducted by the Homeless Agency (Wafer, 2006). However, because it utilised a somewhat different methodology to that employed in 1999 and 2002, a comparison across all categories is not strictly possible. The single most significant change was the removal of a substantial number of households who, in previous assessments, were described as on the Local Authority waiting list only, i.e. not recorded as utilising homeless services. In 1999, 1,550 households were recorded in this category, 1,090 in 2002 and only 44 in 2005. In effect, 707 households were de-activated in the 2005 assessment when, as a consequence of validating their homeless status on the housing waiting list, it was determined that these were no longer active cases. Examining only service users, the number of households declined only marginally between 1999 and 2005, from 1,350 to 1,317.

Of those households using services, in 2005 63 per cent were male compared to 75 per cent in 1999, with the majority of households headed by a single person (77 per cent), down from the 1999 figure of 87 per cent. 43 per cent of service-using households were homeless for more than three months at the time of the 2005 survey, compared with 41 per cent in 1999. Significantly, the numbers recorded as sleeping rough declined from 312 in 2002 to 185 in 2005, a decrease of 41 per cent. Of those sleeping rough in 2005, 70 per cent were male, 50 per cent were aged between 21 and 39 and nearly half had been sleeping rough for more than two years.

In broad terms, it would appear from the existing, albeit inadequate, data sources that the number of households experiencing homelessness and, in particular, those households sleeping rough, have declined over the past number of years. A number of factors including an enhanced strategic focus on providing a co-ordinated response to homelessness, particularly in Dublin, and a substantial increase in the funding of homeless services are contributory factors to this apparent decrease.

BIBLIOGRAPHY

Ad-hoc Committee on the Homeless (1984) *Report*. Dublin: Department of Health.

Adler, C. (1991) "Victims of violence: The case of homeless youth". *Australian and New Zealand Journal of Criminology*, 24, 1, 1-14.

Alexander, K. and Ruggieri, S. (1998) *Changing Lives*. London: CRISIS.

Anderson, I. (2001) *Pathways through Homelessness: Towards a Dynamic Analysis*. Research Seminar, 27th March, 2001. Scotland: Housing Policy and Practice Unit, University of Stirling.

Anderson, I. (2003) "Synthesising homelessness research: Trends, lessons and prospects". *Journal of Community and Applied Social Psychology*, 13, 2, 197-205.

Anderson, I. and Christian, J. (2003) "Causes of homelessness in the UK: A dynamic analysis". *Journal of Community and Applied Social Psychology*, 13, 2, 105-118.

Anderson, I. and Tulloch, D. (2000) *Pathways through Homelessness: A Review of the Research Evidence*. Edinburgh: Scottish Homes.

Anderson, I., Kemp, P. and Quillars, D. (1993) *Single Homeless People*. London: HMSO.

Anderson, J., Cheney, R., Clatts, M., Faruque, S. Kipke, M., Long, A., Mills, S. Toomey, K. and Wiebel, W. (1996) "HIV risk behaviour, street outreach, and condom use in eight high-risk populations". *AIDS Education and Prevention*, 8, 3, 191-204.

Appelbaum, R.P. (1990) "Counting the homeless". In Momeni, J. (Ed) *Homelessness in the United States: Data and Issues*. Westport: Praeger. pp.1-16.

Archard, P. (1979) *Vagrancy, Alcoholism and Social Control*. Basingstoke: Macmillan.

Auerswald, C.L. and Eyre, S.L. (2002) "Youth homelessness in San Francisco: A life cycle approach". *Social Science and Medicine*, 54, 10, 1497-1512.

Avramov, D. (Ed) (1998) *Youth Homelessness in the European Union*. Brussels: FEANTSA.

Ayerst, S.L. (1999) "Depression and stress in street youth". *Adolescence*, 34, 135, 567-575.

Bailey, S.L., Camlin, C.S. and Ennett, S.T. (1998) "Substance use and risky sexual behaviour among homeless and runaway youth". *Journal of Adolescent Health*, 23, 6, 378-388.

Ballintyne, S. (1999) *Unsafe Streets: Street Homelessness and Crime*. London: Institute for Public Policy Research.

Barnes, J. (1989) *Irish Industrial Schools 1868 – 1908*. Dublin: Irish Academic Press.

Baron, S.W. (2003) "Street youth, violence and victimisation". *Trauma, Violence and Abuse*, 4, 1, 22-44.

Baron, S.W. (2007) "Street youth, gender, financial strain, and crime: Exploring Broidy and Agnew's extension to General Strain Theory". *Deviant Behavior*, 28, 3, 273-302.

Baron, S.W. and Hartnagel, T.F. (1997) "Attributions, affect and crime: Street youths' reactions to unemployment". *Criminology*, 35, 3, 409-434.

Becker, H. (1970) *Sociological Work*. Chicago: Aldine.

Becker, H. (1998) *Tricks of the Trade*. Chicago: University of Chicago Press.

Becker, H.S. (1963) *Outsiders: Studies in the Sociology of Deviance*. New York: The Free Press of Glencoe.

Beer, A., Delfabbro, P., Natalier, K., Oakley, S., Packer, J. and Verity, F. (2006) "Homelessness amongst young people in rural regions of Australia". In Milbourne, P. and Cloke, P. (Eds) *International Perspectives on Rural Homelessness*. London: Routledge. pp. 231-246.

Bell, J. (1989) *Women and Children First. A Report by The National Campaign for the Homeless on Homeless Women and Their Children In Dublin*. Dublin: National Campaign for the Homeless.

Berkman, L. and Kawachi, I. (2000) "A historical framework for social epidemiology". In L. Berkman and I. Kawachi (Eds) *Social Epidemiology*. New York: Oxford University Press. pp. 3-12.

Bessant, J., Coupland, H., Dalton, T., Maher, L., Rowe, J. and Watts, R. (2003) *Heroin Users, Housing and Social Participation: Attacking Social Exclusion Through Better Housing*. Melbourne: Australian Housing and Urban Research Institute.

Bhreatnach, A. (2006) *Becoming Conspicuous: Irish Travellers, Society and the State 1922-70*. Dublin: UCD Press.

Brandon, D., Wells, K., Francis, C. and Ramsay, E. (1980) *The Survivors: A Study of Homeless Newcomers to London and the Responses Made to Them*. London: Routledge Kegan Paul.

Breugel, I. and Smith, J. (1999) *Taking Risks: An Analysis of the Risks of Homelessness for Young People in London*. London: Safe in the City.

Brooke, S. (2004) *Housing Problems and Irish Children: The Impact of Housing on Children's Well-being*. Dublin: Children's Research Centre.

Brooks-Gunn, J. and Rotheram-Borus, M.J. (1994) "Rights to privacy in research: Adolescents versus parents". *Ethics and Behaviour*, 4, 2, 109-121.

Buchner, J.C., Bassuk, E.L. and Zima, B.T. (1993) "Mental health issues affecting homeless women: Implications for intervention". *American Journal of Orthopsychiatry*, 63, 3, 385-399.

CARE (1972) *Children Deprived – The CARE Memorandum on Deprived Children and Children's Services in Ireland*. Dublin: CARE.

Care and Accommodation for Young People at Risk or Homeless in Dublin. A Report by a Group of Social Workers and Members of Voluntary Organisations. Dublin: April 1986.

Carlen, P. (1994) "The governance of homelessness: Legality, lore and lexicon in the agency-maintenance of youth homelessness". *Critical Social Policy*, 41, 2, 18-35.

Carlen, P. (1996) *Jigsaw – A Political Criminology of Youth Homelessness*. Buckingham: Open University Press.

Carlson, H. (1990) "Women and homelessness in Ireland". *Irish Journal of Psychology*, 11, 1, 69-76.

Chamberlain, C. and Johnson, G. (2001) "The debate about homelessness". *Australian Journal of Social Issues*, 36, 1, 35-50.

Chamberlain, C. and Johnson, G. (2003) *The Development of Prevention and Early Intervention Services for Homeless Youth: Intervening Successfully*. Melbourne: Australian Housing and Urban Research Institute.

Chamberlain, C. and MacKenzie, D. (1994) "Temporal dimensions of youth homelessness". *Australian Journal of Social Issues*, 29, 1, 1-25.

Clapham, D. (2002) "Housing pathways: A post modern analytic framework". *Housing, Theory and Society*, 19, 2, 57-68.

Clapham, D. (2003) "Pathways approaches to homeless research". *Journal of Community and Applied Social Psychology*, 13, 2, 119-127.

Clare, L. and Byrne, D. (1976) *Children Sleeping Rough and Children Begging*. Dublin: An Coisde Cuspoiri Coiteann.

Clarke, M. and Cooper, M. (2000) *Homeless Youth: Falling between the Cracks: An Investigation of Youth Homelessness in Calgary.* Youth Alternative Housing Committee.

Clatts, M., Davis, W. R., Sotheran, J.L. and Atillasoy, A. (1998) "Correlates and distribution of HIV risk behaviours among homeless youths in New York City: Implications for prevention and policy". *Child Welfare,* 77, 2, 195-207.

Clatts, M.C. and Davis, W.R. (1999) "A demographic and behavioural profile of homeless youth in New York City: Implications for AIDS outreach and prevention". *Medical Anthropology Quarterly,* 13, 3, 365-374.

Clatts, M.C., Davis, W.R. and Atillasoy, A. (1995) "Hitting a moving target: The use of ethnographic methods in the evaluation of AIDS outreach programs for homeless youth in NYC". *Qualitative Methods in Drug Abuse and HIV Research.* NIDA Research Monograph 157, 117-135.

Clatts, M.C., Goldsamt, L., Yi, H., and Viorst Gwandz, M. (2005) "Homelessness and drug abuse among young men who have sex with men in New York City: A preliminary epidemiological trajectory". *Journal of Adolescence,* 28, 2, 201-214.

Clatts, M.C., Hillman, D.J., Atillasoy, A. and Davis, W.R. (1999) "Lives in the balance: A profile of homeless youth in New York City". In J. Blustein, C. Levine and N. Neveloff Dubler (Eds) *The Adolescent Alone: Decision-Making in Health Care in the United States.* Cambridge: Cambridge University Press. pp.139-159.

Clatts, M.C., Welle, D., Goldsamt, L.A. and Lankenau, S. E. (2002) "An ethno-epidemiological model for the study of trends in illicit drug use: Reflections on the 'emergence' of crack injection". *International Journal of Drug Policy,* 13, 4, 285-295.

Clear, C. (1993) "Homelessness and youth in nineteenth century Ireland: Some observations". In M. Clancy, J.F. Cunningham, and MacLochlainn, A. (Eds) *Growing Up Poor.* Galway: Galway Labour History Society. pp. 5-18.

Clear, C. and Flanagan, P. (1986) *Report on Young Homeless People Sleeping Rough in Dublin.* Dublin: Dublin Simon Community.

Cleary, A. and Prizeman, G. (1998) *Homelessness and Mental Health: A Research Report.* Dublin: Homelessness and Mental Health Action Group.

Cleary, A., Corbett, M., Galvin, M. and Wall, J. (2004) *Young Men on the Margins.* Dublin: Katherine Howard Foundation.

Clements, K., Gleghorn, A., Garcia, D., Katz, M. and Marx, R. (1997) "A risk profile of street youth in Northern California: Implications for gender-specific human immunodeficiency virus prevention". *Journal of Adolescent Health,* 20, 5, 343-353.

Cloke, P., Johnsen, S. and May, J. (2005) "Exploring ethos? Discourses of 'charity' in the provision of emergency services for homeless people". *Environment and Planning* A, 37, 3, 385-402.

Cloke, P., Milbourne, P. and Widdowfield, R. (2001) "Making the homeless count? Enumerating rough sleepers and the distortion of homelessness". *Policy and Politics*, 29, 3, 2590-79.

Cloke, P., Milbourne, P. and Widdowfield, R. (2003) "The complex mobilities of homeless people in rural England". *Geoforum*, 34, 1, 21-35.

Coghlan, H., Schickle, W. and Chance, F. (1976) *Children Sleeping Rough: The Problem and our Proposals.* Dublin: HOPE.

Cohen, C.I. and Sokolovsky, J. (1989) *Old Men of the Bowery: Strategies for Survival among the Homeless.* New York: The Guildford Press.

Collins, B. and McKeown, K. (1992) *Referral and Settlement in the Simon Community.* Dublin: Simon Community (National Office).

Commander, M., Davis, A., McCabe, A. and Stanyer, A. (2002) "A comparison of homeless and domiciled young people". *Journal of Mental Health*, 11, 5, 557-564.

Costello, L. and Howley, D. (1999) *Under Dublin's Neon: A Report on Street Drinkers in Dublin City.* Dublin: CentreCare.

Cox, G. and Lawless, M. (1999) *Wherever I Lay my Hat: A Study of Out of Home Drug Users.* Dublin: Merchant's Quay Project.

Craig, T., Hodson, S., Woodward, S. and Richardson, S. (1996) *Off to a Bad Start: A Longitudinal Study of Homeless Young People in London.* London: The Mental Health Foundation.

Crane, M. (1997) *Homeless Truths: Challenging the Myths about Older Homeless People.* London: Help the Aged and Crisis.

Crane, P. and Brannock, J. (1996) *Homelessness Among Young People in Australia: Early Intervention and Prevention.* Hobart, Tasmania: National Clearinghouse for Youth Studies.

Crawley, M. and Daly, M. (2004) *Heroin – The Mental Roof Over Your Head: Links Between Homelessness and Drug Use.* Dublin: Tallaght Homeless Advice Unit.

Dachner, N. and Tarasuk, V. (2002) "Homeless 'squeegee kids': Food insecurity and daily survival". *Social Science and Medicine*, 54, 7, 1039-1049.

Daly, M. (1990) "New perspectives on homelessness". In J. Blackwell, B. Harvey, M. Higgins and J. Walsh (Eds) *Housing: Moving Into Crisis?* Dublin: Combat Poverty Agency and National Campaign for the Homeless. pp. 18-31.

Daly, M. (1999) "Regimes of social policy in Europe and the patterning of homelessness". In D. Avramov (Ed) *Coping with Homelessness: Issues to be Tackled and Best Practices in Europe.* Aldershot: Ashgate. pp. 309-330.

Davies, J., Lyle, S., Deacon, A., Law, I., Julienne, L. and Kay, J. (1996) *Discounted Voices: Homelessness among Young Black and Minority Ethnic People in England.* Leeds: School of Sociology and Social Policy, University of Leeds.

De Rosa, C., Montgomery, S., Kipke, M., Iverson, E., Ma, J. and Unger, J. (1999) "Service utilisation among homeless and runaway youth in Los Angeles, California: Rates and reasons". *Journal of Adolescent Health*, 24, 3, 190-200.

Denzin, N. (1989) *Interpretive Biography.* London: Sage.

Department of an Taoiseach (2005) *Sustaining Progress 2003-2005. Final Report on Special Initiatives.* Dublin: Stationery Office.

Department of Education (1994). *School Attendance/Truancy Report.* Dublin: Department of Education.

Department of Environment and Local Government (2000) *Homelessness – An Integrated Strategy.* Dublin: Department of Environment and Local Government.

Department of Environment and Local Government, Department of Health and Children, Department of Education and Science (2002) *Homeless Preventative Strategy: A Strategy to prevent homelessness: Patients leaving hospital and mental health care, adult prisoners and young offenders leaving custody and young people leaving care.* Dublin: Stationery Office.

Department of Health and Children (2000) *National Children's Strategy.* Dublin: Stationery Office.

Department of Health and Children (2001) *Youth Homelessness Strategy.* Dublin: Stationery Office.

Department of Health. *Survey of Children in Care of Health Boards. Various Years.* Dublin: Child Care Division, Department of Health.

Dey, I. (1993) *Qualitative Data Analysis.* London: Routledge.

Dibblin, J. (1991) *Wherever I Lay My Hat: Young Women and Homelessness.* London: Shelter.

Dillon, B., Murphy-Lawless, J. and Redmond, D. (1990) *Homelessness in County Louth.* A Research Report by SUS Research for Dundalk Simon Community and Drogheda Homeless Aid.

Dillon, C. (1993) *A Survey of Youth Homelessness in Co. Clare – Nov/Dec 1992.* Ennis: Ennis Youth Centre.

Donohue, F. (1988) "The role of the Eastern Health Board in providing services for the homeless". In J. Blackwell, and S. Kennedy (Eds) *Focus on Homelessness: A New Look at Housing Policy.* Dublin: Columba Press. pp.95-111.

Dublin Diocesan Welfare Committee (1974) *Vagrancy – a Report of the Dublin Diocesan Welfare Committee. Presented to His Grace Most Reverend Dr. Dermot Ryan,* May 1974.

Duggan, C. (1989) *A Place to Stay and Time to Think: An Evaluation of the Catholic Social Services Conference Project for Boys.* Dublin: Catholic Social Service Conference.

Dunlap, E., Johnson, B.D., Sanabria, H. Holliday, E. Lipsey, V., Barnett, M., Hopkins, W., Sobel, I., Randolph, D. and Chin, K. (1990) "Studying crack users and their criminal careers: The scientific and artistic aspects of locating hard-to-reach subjects and interviewing them about sensitive subjects". *Contemporary Drug Problems,* 17, 1, 121-144.

Dunne, J. (1979) *Residential Care Services for Deprived Children (other than offenders) in Ireland.* Dublin: Department of Social Studies. Mimeo.

Durcan, G. (1997) "Secure accommodation in the child care system: The legal background". In Children's Legal Centre (Ed) *Secure Accommodation in Child Care.* Dublin: Children's Legal Centre. pp.3-10.

Dworsky, A.L. and Piliavin (2000) "Homeless spell exits and returns: Substantive and methodological elaborations on recent studies". *Social Service Review,* 74, 2, 193-213.

Eastern Health Board (1987) *Homeless Young People.* Dublin: Eastern Health Board. Unpublished.

Eastern Health Board (1994) *Youth Homelessness in the Eastern Health Board.* Dublin: Eastern Health Board.

Eastern Health Board (1997) *Report of Working Party on Children in Prostitution.* Dublin: Eastern Health Board.

Edgar, B. and Doherty, J. (2001) *Women and Homelessness in Europe: Pathways, Services and Experiences.* Bristol: Policy Press.

Edgar, B. and Meert, H. (2006) *Fifth Review of Statistics on Homelessness in Europe.* Brussels: FEANTSA.

Ensign, J. (2003) "Ethical issues in qualitative health research with homeless youths". *Journal of Advanced Nursing,* 43, 1, 43-50.

Ensign, J. and Bell, M. (2004) "Illness experiences of homeless youth". *Qualitative Health Research,* 14, 9, 1239-1254.

Ensign, J. and Gittelsohn, J. (1998) "Health and access to care: Perspectives of homeless youth in Balitmore City, USA". *Social Science and Medicine,* 47,12, 2087-2099.

Ezzy, D. (2000) "Illness narratives: Time, hope and HIV". *Social Science and Medicine,* 50, 5, 605-617.

Fahey, T., Russell, H. and Whelan, C.T. (Eds) (2007) *Best of Times? The Social Impact of the Celtic Tiger.* Dublin: Institute of Public Administration.

Feeney, A., McGee, H.M., Holohan, T. and Shannon, W. (2000) *The Health of Hostel-Dwelling Men in Dublin.* Dublin: Royal College of Surgeons in Ireland and Eastern Health Board.

Ferguson, H. (2007) "Abused and looked after children as 'moral dirt': Child abuse and institutional care in historical perspective". *Journal of Social Policy,* 36, 1, 123-139.

Fetterman, D.M. (1989) *Ethnography: Step by Step.* Newbury Park, CA: Sage.

Fitzgerald, J., Dovey, K., Dietze, P. and Rumbold, G. (2004) "Health outcomes and quasi-supervised settings for street injecting drug users". *International Journal of Drug Policy,* 15, 4, 247-257.

Fitzgerald, S.T., Shelley, M.C. and Dail, P.W. (2001) "Research on homelessness: Sources and implications of uncertainty". *The American Behavioural Scientist,* 45, 1, 121-148.

Fitzpatrick Associates (2006) *Review of Implementation of Homeless Strategies.* Dublin: Department of the Environment, Heritage and Local Government.

Fitzpatrick, K. and LaGory, M. (2000) *Unhealthy Places: The Ecology of Risk in the Urban Landscape.* New York: Routledge.

Fitzpatrick, K.M., LaGory, M.E. and Ritchey, F.J. (1999) "Dangerous places: Exposure to violence and its mental health consequences for the homeless". *American Journal of Orthopsychiatry,* 69, 4, 438-447.

Fitzpatrick, S. (1998) "Homelessness in the European Union". In M. Kleinman, W. Matznetter and M. Stephens (Eds) *European Integration and Housing Policy.* London: Routledge. pp.197-214

Fitzpatrick, S. (1999) *Pathways to Independence: The Experience of Young Homeless People.* Edinburgh: Scottish Homes.

Fitzpatrick, S. (2000) *Young Homeless People.* Basingstoke: Macmillan.

Fitzpatrick, S. (2005) "Explaining homelessness: A critical realist perspective". *Housing, Theory and Society.* 22, 1, 1-17.

Fitzpatrick, S. and Christain, J. (2006) "Comparing homelessness research in the US and Britain". *European Journal of Housing Policy,* 6, 3, 313-333.

Fitzpatrick, S. and Clapham, D. (1999) "Homelessness and young people". In S. Hutson and D. Clapham (Eds) *Homelessness: Public Policies and Private Troubles*. London: Continuum. pp. 173-190.

Fitzpatrick, S. and Jones, A. (2005) "Pursuing social justice or social cohesion?: Coercion in street homelessness policies in England". *Journal of Social Policy*, 34, 3, 389-406.

Fitzpatrick, S., Kemp, P. and Klinker, S. (2000) *Single Homelessness: An Overview of Research in Britain*. Bristol: Policy Press.

Flemen, K. (1997) *Smoke and Whispers: Drugs and Youth Homelessness in Central London*. London: Hungerford Drug Project.

Focus Ireland (1995) *Here, There and Nowhere: A Study of Youth Homelessness in Tallaght*. Dublin: Focus Ireland.

Focus Point and the Eastern Health Board (1989) *Forgotten Children – Research on Young People who are Homeless in Dublin*. Dublin: Focus Point.

Forum on Youth Homelessness (2000) *Report of the Forum on Youth Homelessness*. Dublin: Northern Area Health Board.

Fountain, J. and Howes, S. (2002) *Home and Dry? Homelessness and Substance Use*. London: Crisis.

Gaetz, S. (2004) "Safe streets for whom? Homeless youth, social exclusion and criminal victimisation". *Journal of Criminology and Criminal Justice*, 46, 4, 423-455.

Gaetz, S. and O'Grady, B. (2002) "Making money: Exploring the economy of homeless workers". *Work, Employment and Society*, 16, 3, 433-456.

Gaetz, S., O'Grady, B. and Vaillancourt, B. (1999) *Making Money: The Shout Clinic Report on Homeless Youth and Unemployment*. Toronto: Central Toronto Community Health Centres.

Geber, G. (1997) "Barriers to health care for street youth". *Journal of Adolescent Health*, 21, 5, 287-290.

Gilligan, R. (1992) "Can the Child Care Act, 1991 be effective in addressing the problem of youth homelessness". In *The Child Care Act, 1991 and Youth Homelessness. An Opportunity for Progress*. Papers from a conference jointly organised by the National Campaign for The Homeless and Barnardos. pp. 11-27.

Glaser, B. and Strauss, A. (1967) *The Discovery of Grounded Theory*. Chicago: Aldine.

Goffman, I. (1961) *Asylums*. Harmondsworth: Penguin.

Government of Ireland (1985) *In Partnership with Youth: The National Youth Policy*. Dublin: Stationery Office.

Gowan, T. (2002) "The nexus: Homelessness and incarceration in two American cities". *Ethnography*, 3, 4, 500-534.

Greene, J.M., Ennett, S. T. and Ringwalt, C.L. (1997) "Substance use among run-away and homeless youth in three samples". *American Journal of Public Health*, 87, 2, 229-235.

Greene, J.M. and Ringwalt, C.L. (1996) "Youth and familial substance use's association with suicide attempts among runaway and homeless youth". *Substance Use & Misuse*, 31, 8, 1041-1058.

Gubrium, J. and Holstein, J. (2002) "From the individual interview to the interview society". In J. Gubrium and J. Holstein (Eds) *Handbook of Interview Research: Context and Method*. Thousand Oaks, CA: Sage. pp. 3-32.

Habermas, T. and Bluck, S. (2000) "Getting a life: The emergence of the life story in adolescence". *Psychological Bulletin*, 126, 5, 748-769.

Hagan, J. and McCarthy, B. (1992) "Streetlife and delinquency". *British Journal of Sociology*, 43, 4, 533-561.

Hagan, J. and McCarthy, B. (1997) *Mean Streets: Youth Crime and Homelessness*. Cambridge: Cambridge University Press.

Hagan, J. and McCarthy, B. (2005) "Homeless youth and the perilous passage to adulthood". In D.W. Osgood, E.M. Foster, C. Flanagan and G.R. Ruth (Eds) *On Your Own Without a Net: The Transition to Adulthood for Vulnerable Populations*. Chicago: University of Chicago press. pp. 178-201.

Hall, T. (2003) *Better Times than This: Youth Homelessness in Britain*. London: Pluto Press.

Hall, T. (2006) "Out of work and house and home: Contested youth in an English homeless hostel", *Ethnos- Journal of Anthropology*, 71, 2, 143-163.

Hall, T. and Montgomery, H. (2000) "Home and away: 'Childhood', 'youth' and young people", *Anthropology Today*, 16, 3, 13-15.

Halpenny, A.M., Greene, S., Hogan, D., Smith, M. and McGee, H. (2001) *Children of Homeless Mothers: The Daily Life Experience and Well-being of Children in Homeless Families*. Dublin: Children's Research Centre/The Royal College of Surgeons in Ireland.

Halpenny, A.M., Keogh, A.F. and Gilligan, R. (2002) *A Place for the Children? Children in Families Living in Emergency Accommodation: The Perspectives of Children, Parents and Professionals*. Dublin: Children's Research Centre/Homeless Agency.

Hammersley, R., Morrison, V., Davies, J.B. and Forsyth, A. (1990) *Heroin Use and Crime: A Comparison of Heroin Users and Non-Users In and Out of Prison*. Edinburgh: Scottish Office.

Hart, I. (1978) *Dublin Simon Community 1971-1976: An Exploration*. Dublin: Economic and Social Research Institute.

Harvey, B. and Menton, M. (1989) "Ireland's young homeless". *Children and Youth Services Review*, 11, 1, 31-43.

Hatty, S.E., Burke, S. and Davis, N. (1996) "No exit: Violence, gender and the streets". In C. Sumner, M. Israel, M. O'Connell and R. Sarre (Eds) *International Victimology: Selected Papers from the 8th International Symposium: Proceedings of a Symposium held 21-26 August, 1994*. Canberra: Australian Institute of Criminology.

Health Advisory Service (2001) *The Substance of Youth Needs*. London: Health Advisory Service.

Health Service Executive (2005) *Hidden Homelessness among Young People Aged 16-21 Years*. Dublin: Health Service Executive.

Helleiner, J. (1998a) "Contested childhood: The discourse and politics of traveller childhood in Ireland". *Childhood*, 5, 3, 303-324.

Helleiner, J. (1998b) "For the protection of the children: The politics of minority childhood in Ireland". *Anthropological Quarterly*, 71, 2, 51-62.

Helleiner, J. (2003) "The politics of traveller 'child begging' in Ireland". *Critique of Anthropology*, 23, 1, 17-33.

Hickey, C. (2002) *Crime and Homelessness*. Dublin: Focus Ireland and PACE.

Hickey, C. and Downey, D. (2003) *Hungry for Change: Social Exclusion, Food Poverty and Homelessness in Dublin*. Dublin: Focus Ireland.

Higgins, M. (2001) *Shaping the Future: An Action Plan on Homelessness in Dublin, 2001-2003*. Dublin: Homeless Agency.

Higgins, M. (2002) Counted in 2002. *Cornerstone – the magazine of the Homeless Agency*, 14, 14-15.

Hill, R.P. and Stamey, M. (1990) "The homeless in America: An examination of possessions and consumption behaviours". *Journal of Consumer Research*, 17, 3, 303-321.

Holohan, T. (1997) *Health Status, Health Service Utilisation and Barriers to Heath Service Utilisation among the Adult Homeless Population of Dublin*. Dublin: Eastern Health Board.

Homeless Agency (2004a) *Making it Home: An Action Plan on Homelessness in Dublin 2004-2006*. Dublin: Homeless Agency.

Homeless Agency (2004b) *Homelessness Directory 2004/2005*. Dublin: Homeless Agency.

HOPE (1979) *Out in the Cold: A Report of Unattached Youth in Dublin in the Winter of 1978/79*. Dublin: HOPE.

Houghton, F.T. and Hickey, C. (2000) *Focusing on B&B's: The Unacceptable Growth of Emergency B&B Placement in Dublin*. Dublin: Focus Ireland.

Houghton, F.T. and Hickey, C. (2001) *Caught in a Trap: The Long-term Homeless – A Profile of Needs and Service Use*. Dublin: Focus Ireland.

Houghton, F.T., Kelleher, P. and Kelleher, C. (2001) "Children out-of-home in Ireland". In A. Cleary, M. Nic Ghiolla Phadraig and S. Quin (Eds) *Understanding Children. Vol.1: State, Education and Economy*. Cork: Oak Tree Press. pp. 79-98.

Howley, D.A.M. (2000) *An Outstretched Hand – A Sociological Insight into Street Begging in Dublin City*. University College Dublin: Unpublished Ph.D. Thesis.

Hubbard, G. (2000) "The usefulness of indepth life history interviews for exploring the role of social structure and human agency in youth transitions". *Sociological Research Online*, 4, 4, http://www.socresonline.org.uk/4/4/.html

Hutson, M. and Liddiard, M. (1994) *Youth Homelessness: The Construction of a Social Issue*. London: Macmillan.

Hutson, S. and Liddiard, M. (1997) "Youth homelessness: Marginalising the marginalised?" In H. Jones (Ed) *Towards a Classless Society?* London: Routledge. pp. 96-119.

Ireland's Young Homeless 1985. Report of the First Survey on Homelessness Among Young People in Ireland, with Analysis and Recommendations.

Jacobs, K., Kemeny, J. and Manzi, T. (1999) "The struggle to define homelessness: A constructivist approach". In S. Hutson and D. Clapham (Eds) *Homelessness: Public Policies and Private Troubles*. London: Cassell. pp. 11-28.

Johnson, B., Murie, A., Naumann, L. & Yanetta, A. (1991) *A Typology of Homelessness*. Edinburgh: Scottish Homes.

Jones, A. (1999) *Out of Sight, Out of Mind? The Experiences of Homeless Women*. London: CRISIS.

Jones, G. (1993) *Young People In and Out of the Housing Market Research Project*. Edinburgh: Centre for Educational Sociology, University of Edinburgh and Scottish Council for Single Homeless.

Jones, G. (1995) *Leaving Home*. Buckingham: Open University Press.

Keane, C. and Crowley, G. (1990) *On My Own: Report on Youth Homelessness in Limerick City*. Limerick: Mid-Western Health Board and Limerick Social Service Centre.

Kearns, K.C. (1984) "Homelessness in Dublin: An Irish urban disorder". *American Journal of Economics and Sociology*, 43, 2, 217-233.

Kelleher, P., and Kelleher, C. (1998) *Left Out on Their Own: Young People Leaving Care in Ireland*. Dublin: Focus Ireland.

Kelleher, P., Kelleher, C. and Corbett, M. (2000) *Left Out on Their Own: Young People Leaving Care in Ireland*. Dublin: Focus Ireland/Oak Tree Press.

Kellett, P. and Moore, J. (2003) "Routes to home: Homelessness and home-making in contrasting societies". *Habitat International*, 27, 1, 123-141.

Kennedy, S. (1985) *But Where Can I Go? Homeless Women in Dublin*. Dublin: Arlene House.

Kennedy, S. (Ed) (1987) *Streetwise. Homelessness among the Young in Ireland and Abroad*. Dublin. The Glendale Press.

Kipke, M., Montgomery, S., Simon, T., Unger, J. & Johnson, T. (1997) "Homeless youth: Drug use patterns and HIV risk profiles according to peer affiliation". *AIDS and Behavior*, 1, 4, 247-259.

Klee, H. and Reid, P. (1998) "Drug use among the young homeless: Coping through self-medication". *Health*, 2, 2, 115-134.

Krippendorf, K. (1980) *Content Analysis: An Introduction to its Methodology*. Beverly Hills, CA: Sage Publications.

Lankenau, S.E., Clatts, M.C., Welle, D., Goldsamt, L.A., and Gwandz, M.V. (2005) "Street careers: Homelessness, drug use, and sex work among young men who have sex with men (YMSM)". *International Journal of Drug Policy*, 16, 1, 10-18.

Latkin, C.A., Forman, V., Knowlton, A. and Sherman, S. (2003) "Norms, social networks, and HIV-related risk behaviours among urban disadvantaged drug users". *Social Science and Medicine*, 56, 3, 465-476.

Lawless, M. (2003) "Private lives – public issues: An investigation of the health status of female drug users". In *Pieces of the Jigsaw: Six Reports Addressing Homelessness and Drug Use in Ireland*. Dublin: Merchant's Quay Ireland. pp. 1-70.

Lawless, M. and Corr, C. (2005) *Drug Use Among the Homeless Population in Ireland: A Research Report for the National Advisory Committee on Drugs*. Dublin: Stationery Office.

Lee, B.A. and Schreck, C.J. (2005) "Danger on the streets: Marginality and victimisation amongst homeless people". *American Behavioral Scientist*, 48, 8, 1055-1081.

Lempens, A., van de Mheen, D. and Barendregt, C. (2003) "Homeless drug users in Rotterdam, the Netherlands: Profile, way of life, and the need for assistance". *Substance Use and Misuse*, 38, 3-6, 339-375.

Levin, R., McKean, L., and Raphael, J. (2004) *Pathways to and from Homelessness: Women and Children in Chicago Shelters*. Chicago: Centre for Impact Research.

Levine, R. J. (1995) "Adolescents as research subjects without permission of their parents or guardians: Ethical considerations". *Journal of Adolescent Health*, 17, 5, 287-297.

Lewis, C., Johnson, B., Golub, A. and Dunlap, E. (1992) "Studying crack abusers: strategies for recruiting the right tail of an ill-defined population". *Journal of Psychoactive Drugs*, 24, 4, 323-336.

Lewis, M. and Sullivan, W.M. (1996) *Emotional Development in Typical Children.* Erlbaum, New Jersey.

Liddiard, M. and Hutson, S. (1991). "Homeless young people and runaways - agency definitions and processes". *Journal of Social Policy*. 20, 3, 365-388

Lister, D. (2004) "Young people's strategies for managing tenancy relationships in the private rented sector". *Journal of Youth Studies*, 7, 3, 315-330.

Lister, D. (2006) "Unlawful or just awful? Young people's experience of living in the private rented sector in England". *Young: Nordic Journal of Youth Research*, 14, 2, 141-155.

MacDonald, R. and Marsh, J. (2006) *Disconnected Youth? Growing up in Britain's Poor Neighbourhoods*. Basingstoke: Macmillan Palgrave.

MacKenzie, D. and Chamberlain, C. (2003) *Homeless Careers: Pathways In and Out of Homelessness*. Swinburne and RMIT Universities.

MacLean, M.G., Embry, L.E., and Cauce, A.M. (1999) "Homeless adolescents' paths to separation from family: Comparison of family characteristics, psychological adjustment, and victimisation". *Journal of Community Psychology*, 27, 2, 179-187.

Maher, L. and Dixon, D. (1999) "Policing and public health: Law enforcement and harm minimisation in a street-level drug market". *British Journal of Criminology*, 39, 4, 488-512.

Maher, L., Sargent, P., Higgs, P., Crofts, N., Kelsall, J. and Le, T. (2001) "Risk behaviours of young Indo-Chinese injecting drug users in Sydney and Melbourne". *Australian and New Zealand Journal of Public Health*, 25, 1, 50-54.

Mallet, S., Edwards, J., Keys, D., Myers, P. and Rosenthal, D. (2003) *Disrupting Stereotypes: Young People, Drug Use and Homelessness*. Melbourne, Victoria: The Centre for Women's Health in Society, University of Melbourne.

Martens, W.H.J. (2001) "Homelessness and mental disorders: A comparative review of populations in various countries". *International Journal of Mental Health*, 30, 4, 79-96.

May, J. (2000) "Housing histories and homeless careers: A biographical approach". *Housing Studies*, 15, 4, 613-638.

May, J., Cloke, P. and Johnsen, S. (2005) "Re-phasing neoliberalism: New Labour and Britain's crisis of street homelessness". *Antipode*, 37, 4, 703-730.

May, J., Cloke, P. and Johnsen, S. (2006) "Shelter at the margins: New Labour and the changing state of emergency accommodation for single homeless people in Britain". *Policy and Politics*, 34, 4, 711-729.

May, J., Cloke, P. and Johnsen, S. (2007) "Alternative cartographies of homelessness: Rendering visible British women's experience of 'visible' homelessness". *Gender, Place and Culture*, 14, 2, 121-140.

Mayock, P. (2000) *Choosers or Losers? Influences on Young People's Choices about Drugs in Inner-City Dublin.* Dublin: Children's Research Centre, Trinity College, Dublin.

Mayock, P. (2002) "Drug pathways, transitions and decisions: The experiences of young people in a Dublin inner-city community". *Contemporary Drug Problems*, 29, 1, 117-156.

Mayock, P. (2005) "'Scripting risk': Young people and the construction of drug journeys". *Drugs: Education, Prevention and Policy*, 12, 5, 349-368.

Mayock, P. (2007) "A 'career' in youth homelessness?" *Cornerstone – the magazine of the Homeless Agency*, 30, 20-22.

Mayock, P. and Byrne, T. (2004) *A Study of Sexual Health Issues, Attitudes and Behaviours: The Views of Early School Leavers.* Dublin: Crisis Pregnancy Agency.

Mayock, P. and Vekić, K. (2006) *Understanding Youth Homelessness in Dublin City: Key Findings from the First Phase of a Longitudinal Cohort Study.* Dublin: Stationery Office.

McCarthy, B. and Hagan, J. (1991) "Homelessness: A criminogenic situation?" *British Journal of Criminology*, 31, 4, 393-410.

McCarthy, B. and Hagan, J. (1992) "Surviving on the street: The experiences of homeless youth". *Journal of Adolescent Health*, 7, 4, 412-430.

McCarthy, B., Felmlee, D. and Hagan, J. (2004) "Girl friends are better: Gender, friends and crime among school and street youth". *Criminology*, 42, 4, 805-835.

McCarthy, D., Argeriou, M., Huebner, R.B. and Lubran, B. (1991) "Alcoholism, drug abuse and the homeless". *American Psychologist*, 46, 11, 1139-1148.

McCarthy, P. (1991) *At What Cost? A Research Study on Residential Care for Children and Adolescents in Ireland.* Dublin: Streetwise National Coalition/Resident Managers Association.

McCarthy, P. and Conlon, E. (1988) *A National Survey on Young People Out of Home in Ireland.* Dublin: Streetwise National Coalition.

McCullagh, C. (1992) *Reforming the Juvenile Justice System: The Examination of Failure*. Paper presented to the Conference on the State of the Irish Political System, University College Cork, May, 1992.

McKenzie, D. and Chamberlain, C. (2003) *Homeless Careers: Pathways in and out of Homelessness*. Swinburne and RMIT Universities.

McKeown, K. (1999) *Mentally Ill and Homeless in Ireland: Facing the Reality, Finding the Solutions*. Dublin: Disability Federation of Ireland.

McVerry, P. (2001) "Absolutely brilliant but are we talking about this planet?" *Cornerstone – the magazine of the Homeless Agency*, 10, 8-9.

McVerry, P. (2003) *The Meaning is in the Shadows*. Dublin: Veritas.

Meade, M.A. and Slesnick, N. (2002) "Ethical considerations for research and treatment with runaway and homeless adolescents". *The Journal of Psychology*, 136, 4, 449-463.

Metraux, S. and Culhane, D.P. (2004) "Homeless shelter use and reincarceration following prison release". *Criminology and Public Policy*, 3, 2, 139-160.

Milbourne, P. and Cloke, P. (Eds) (2006) *International Perspectives on Rural Homelessness*. London: Routledge.

Milburn, N.G., Rosenthal, D., Rotheram-Borus, M.J., Mallet, S., Batterham, P., Rice, E. and Solorio, R. (2007) "Newly homeless youth typically return home". *Journal of Adolescent Health*, 40, 6, 574-576

Molnar, B.E., Shade, S.B., Kral, A.H., Booth, R.E. and Watters, J.K. (1998) "Suicidal behaviour and sexual/physical abuse among street youth". *Child Abuse & Neglect*, 22, 3, 213-222.

National Campaign for the Homeless (1985) *Ireland's Young Homeless, 1985*. Dublin.

National Youth Policy Committee (1984) *Final Report* Dublin: Stationery Office.

Neale, J. (1997a) "Theorising homelessness: Contemporary sociological and feminist perspectives". In R. Burrows, N. Please and D. Quilgars (Eds) *Homelessness and Social Policy*. London: Routledge. pp. 35-49.

Neale, J. (1997b) "Homelessness and theory reconsidered". *Housing Studies*, 12, 1, 47-61.

Neale, J. (2001) "Homelessness amongst drug users: A double jeopardy explored". *International Journal of Drug Policy*, 12, 4, 353-369.

Netto, G. (2006) "Vulnerability to homelessness, use of services and homeless prevention in Black and minority ethnic communities". *Housing Studies*, 21, 4, 581-601.

Nolan, B. and Whelan, C.T. (2000) "Urban housing and the role of underclass processes: The case of Ireland". *Journal of European Social Policy*, 10, 1, 5-21.

Northern Area Health Board (2000) *Report of the Review Group on Crisis Intervention Services for Children*. Dublin: Northern Area Health Board.

Novac, S., Brown, J. and Bourbonnais, C. (1996) *No Room of Her Own: A Literature Review of Women and Homelessness*. Ottawa: Canadian Mortgage and Housing Corporation.

Novac, S., Serge, L., Eberle, M. and Brown, J. (2002) *On Her Own: Young Women and Homelessness in Canada*. Ottawa: Canadian Housing and Renewal Association.

O'Brien, J. (1988) "Youth homelessness". In J. Blackwell and S. Kennedy (Eds) *Focus on Homelessness: A New Look at Housing Policy*. Dublin: Columba Press. pp. 45-53.

O'Brien, J. (1993) "The need for alternative forms of accommodation for young people in Ireland". In Focus Point *The Foyer System: A European Perspective on Accommodating, Training and Supporting Young People Towards Independence*. Dublin: Focus Point. pp. 15-29.

O'Brien, J., Waldron, A.M., Perot, S. and Pigott-Glynn, L. (1999) *The Mental and Physical Health and Well-being of Homeless Families in Dublin: A Pilot Study*. Dublin: Focus Ireland, the Mater Hospital and the Northern Area Health Board.

O'Cinneide, S. and Mooney, P. (1972) *Simon Survey of the Homeless*. The Simon Community of Dublin supported by the Medico-Social Research Board.

O'Connell, M.E. (2003) "Responding to homelessness: An overview of US and UK policy interventions". *Journal of Community and Applied Social Psychology*, 13, 2, 158-170.

O'Donnell, A.M. (1990) "An investigation of youth homelessness with particular reference to educational needs – Part 1. *Irish Home Economics Journal*, 1, 1, 3-7.

O'Donnell, A.M. (1992) An investigation of youth homelessness with particular reference to educational needs – Part 2". *Irish Home Economics Journal*, 1, 2, 46-53.

O'Flaherty, B. (2004) "Wrong person and wrong place: For homelessness, the conjunction is what matters". *Journal of Housing Economics*, 13, 1, 1-15.

O'Grady, B. and Gaetz, S. (2004) "Homelessness, gender and subsistence: The case of Toronto street youth". *Journal of Youth Studies*, 7, 4, 397-416.

O'Mahony, B. (1988) *A Capital Offence. The Plight of the Young Single Homeless in London*. London: Routledge/Barnardos.

O'Sullivan, D. (1979) "Social definition in child care in the Irish Republic: Models of child and child care intervention". *Economic and Social Review*, 10, 3, 209-230.

O'Sullivan, E. (1993) "Identity and survival in a hostile environment: Homeless men in Galway". In C. Curtin, H. Donnan and T. Wilson (Eds) *Irish Urban Cultures*. Belfast: Institute of Irish Studies. pp. 161-180.

O'Sullivan, E. (1995a) "Section 5 of the Child Care Act 1991 and youth homelessness". In H. Ferguson and P. Kenny (Eds) *On Behalf of the Child: Child Welfare, Child Protection and the Child Care Act 1991*. Dublin: A&A Farmar. pp. 84-104.

O'Sullivan, E. (1995b) "Homeless children and the problematics of social work". *Irish Social Worker*, 13, 3, 4-6.

O'Sullivan, E. (1996a) "Adolescents leaving care, leaving home and child care provision in Ireland and the UK: A critical view". In M. Hill and J. Aldgate (Eds) *Child Welfare Services: Developments in Law, Policy, Practice and Research*. London; Bristol; Penn.: Jessica Kingsley Publishers. pp. 212-224.

O'Sullivan, E. (1996b) *Homelessness and Social Policy in the Republic of Ireland*. Occasional Paper No. 5, Department of Social Studies, University of Dublin, Trinity College.

O'Sullivan, E. (1998) "Aspects of youth homelessness in the Republic of Ireland". In D. Avramov (Ed) *Youth Homelessness in the European Union*. Brussels: FEANTSA. pp. 250-261.

O'Sullivan, E. (2001a) "'Mercy unto thousands': Constructing the institutional child". In A. Cleary, NicGiolla Phadraig, M. and Quinn, S. (Eds) *Understanding Children. Volume One: Education, Support and the Role of the State* Dublin: Oak Tree Press. pp. 45-78.

O'Sullivan, E. (2001b) "Laudable objectives but a fatal flaw". *Cornerstone – the magazine of the Homeless Agency*, 10, 10-11.

O'Sullivan, E. (2004) "Welfare regimes, housing and homelessness in the Republic of Ireland". *European Journal of Housing Policy*, 4. 3, 323-343.

O'Sullivan, E. (2006a) "Homelessness". In D. Redmond and M. Norris (Eds) *Housing Contemporary Ireland: Economy, Society, Space and Shelter*. Dublin: Institute of Public Administration. pp. 245-267.

O'Sullivan, E. (2006b) "Homelessness in rural Ireland". In Cloke, P. and P. Milbourne (Eds) *International Perspectives on Rural Homelessness*, London, Routledge, pp188-207.

O'Sullivan, E. and Higgins, M. (2001) "Women, the welfare state and homelessness in the Republic of Ireland". In B. Edgar, J. Doherty and A. Mina-Couell (Eds) *Women and Homelessness in Europe*. Bristol: Policy Press. pp. 77-90.

O'Sullivan, E. and O'Donnell, I. (2007) "Coercive confinement in Ireland: The waning of a culture of control". *Punishment and Society: The International Journal of Penology*, 9, 1, 27-44.

Office for Social Inclusion (2007) *National Action Plan for Social Inclusion 2007-2016.* Dublin: Stationery Office.

Osborne, R.E. (2002) "'I may be homeless, but I'm not helpless': The costs of identifying with homelessness". *Self and Identity*, 1, 1, 43-52.

Park, J.M., Metraux, S., Brodbar, G. and Culhane, D.P. (2004) "Public shelter admission among young adults with child welfare histories by type of service and type of exit". *Social Service Review*, 78, 2, 284-303.

Patton, M.Q. (1990) *Qualitative Evaluation and Research Methods* (2nd ed.). Newbury Park, CA: Sage Publications.

Perris, A. (1999) *Youth Homelessness in Clondalkin: A Community Perspective.* Dublin: Clondalkin Area Partnership.

Petersen, A.C. and Leffert, N. (1995) "Developmental issues influencing guidelines for adolescent health research: A review". *Journal of Adolescent Health*, 17, 5, 298-305.

Piliavin, I., Sosin, M., Westerfelt, A.H. and Matsueda, R.L. (1993) "The duration of homeless careers: An exploratory study". *Social Service Review*, 67, 4, 576-598.

Pleace, N. (2000) "The new consensus, the old consensus and the provision of services for people sleeping rough". *Housing Studies*, 15, 4, 581-594.

Pleace, N. (2005) *State, Trait or Something Else? The Need for a New Definition of Homelessness in the UK.* HSA Conference Workshop Paper, April.

Pleace, N. and Quilgars, D. (1999) "Youth homelessness". In J. Rugg (Ed) *Young People, Housing and Social Policy.* London: Rougledge. pp. 93-108.

Pleace, N. and Quilgars, D. (2003) "Led rather than leading? Research on homelessness in Britain". *Journal of Community and Applied Social Psychology*, 13, 2, 187-196.

Power, B. (1971) "The young lawbreaker – A sociological and pastoral investigation of crime among the young in a city area". *Christus Rex*, 25, 4, 56-79.

Randall, G. and Brown, S. (1996) *From Street to Home: An Evaluation of Phase 2 of the Rough Sleepers Initiative.* London: Stationery Office.

Randall, G. and Brown, S. (1999) *Prevention is Better than Cure.* London: Crisis.

Randall, G. and Brown, S. (2001) *Trouble at Home: Family Conflict, Young People and Homelessness.* London: Crisis.

Reid, P. and Klee, H. (1999) "Young homeless people and service provision". *Health, Social Care and Community*, 7, 1, 17-24.

Report on Industrial Schools and Reformatories (The Kennedy Report). (1970) Dublin: The Stationery Office.

Rew, L., Taylor-Seehafer, M. and Thomas, N. (2000) "Without parental consent: Conducting research with homeless adolescents". *Journal of the Society of Pediatric Nurses*, 5, 3, 131-138.

Rhodes, T. (2002) "The 'risk environment': A framework for understanding and reducing drug-related harm". *International Journal of Drug Policy*, 13, 2, 85-94.

Ringwalt, C.L., Greene, J.M. and Robertson, M.J. (1998) "Family backgrounds and risk behaviours of youth with thrownaway experiences". *Journal of Adolescence*, 21, 3, 241-252.

Robins, J. (1980) *The Lost Children: A Study of Charity Children in Ireland 1700-1900.* Dublin: Institute of Public Administration.

Rooney, J.F. (1980) "Organizational success through program failure: Skid row rescue missions". *Social Forces*, 58, 3, 904-924.

Rosenbert, A.A., Solarz, A.L., and Bailey, W.A. (1991) "Psychology and homelessness: A public policy and advocacy agenda". *American Psychologists*, 46, 11, 1239-1244.

Saris, A.J. and Bartley, B. (2002) "The arts of memory: Icon and structural violence in a Dublin 'underclass' housing estate". *Anthropology Today*, 18, 4, 14-19.

Saris, A.J., Bartley, B., Kierans, C., Walsh, C. and McCormack, P. (2002) "Culture and the state: Institutionalizing 'the underclass' in the new Ireland". *City*, 6, 2, 173-191.

Schiff, L.R. (2003) "The power to define: Definitions as a site of struggle in the field of homelessness". *Qualitative Studies in Education*, 16, 4, 491-507.

Seale, C. (1999) *The Quality of Qualitative Research.* London: Sage.

Seymour, M. and Costello, L. (2005) *A Study of the Number, Profile and Progession Routes of Homeless Persons before the Court and in Custody.* Dublin: Government of Ireland.

Sherman, S.G. and Latkin, C.A. (2002) "Drug users' involvement in the drug economy: Implications for harm reduction and HIV prevention programs". *Journal of Urban Health*, 79, 2, 266-277.

Shinn, M., Knickman, J.R., and Weitzman, B.C. (1991) "Social relationships and vulnerability to becoming homeless among poor families". *American Psychologist*, 46, 11, 1180-1187.

Shlay, A. and Rossi, P. (1992) "Social science research and contemporary studies of homelessness". *Annual Review of Sociology*, 18, 1, 129-160.

Simpson, M. (2003) "The relationship between drug use and crime: A puzzle inside an enigma". *International Journal of Drug Policy*, 14, 4, 307-319.

Smith, J. (2005) "Risk, social change and strategies of inclusion for young homeless people". In Barry, M. (Ed) *Youth Policy and Social Inclusion: Critical debates with young people*. London: Routledge.

Smith, J., Gilford, S., and O'Sullivan, A. (1998) *The Family Background of Homeless Young People*. London: Family Policy Studies Centre.

Smith, M., McGee, H.M. and Shannon, W. (2001) *One Hundred Homeless Women: Health Status and Health Service Use of Homeless Women and their Children in Dublin*. Dublin: Health Services Research Centre, Department of Psychology and Department of General Practice, Royal College of Surgeons in Ireland.

Snow, D.A. and Anderson, L. (1987) "Identity work among the homeless: The verbal construction and avowal of personal identities". *American Journal of Sociology*, 92, 6, 1336-1371.

Snow, D.A. and Anderson, L. (1993) *Down on Their Luck: A Study of Homeless Street People*. Berkeley, CA: University of California Press.

Snow, D.A., Baker, S. G. and Anderson, L. (1988) "On the precariousness of measuring insanity in insane contexts". *Social Problems*, 35, 2, 192-196.

Stein, M. (2006) "Research review: Young people leaving care". *Child and Family Social Work*, 11, 3, 273-279.

Stephens, J. (2002) *The Mental Health Needs of Homeless Young People*. Cardiff: Barnardos.

Stockley, D., Canter, D. and Bishopp, D. (1993) *Young People on the Move*. Guildford: Psychology Department, University of Surrey.

Study Group on Homelessness (1993) *Homelessness*. Council of Europe Press.

Tallaght Homeless Advice Unit (1994) *Out of the Gaff. A Report on Homelessness in Tallaght*.

Task Force on Child Care Services (1980) *Final Report*. Dublin: Stationery Office.

Third, H. (2000) "Researching homelessness and rough sleeping in the Scottish context". *Social, Policy and Administration*, 34, 4, 448-464.

Thrane, L.E., Hoyt, D.R., Whitbeck, L.B. & Yoder, K.A. (2006) "Impact of family abuse on running away, deviance, and street victimisation among homeless rural and urban youth". *Child Abuse & Neglect*, 30, 10, 1117-1128.

Tuairim (1966) *Some of our Children – A Report on the Residential Care of the Deprived Child in Ireland*. Tuairim: London.

Tyler, K.A. and Johnson, K.A. (2004) "Victims and offenders: Accounts of paybacks, invulnerability and financial gain among homeless youth". *Deviant Behavior*, 25, 5, 427-449.

Tyler, K.A. and Johnson, K.A. (2006) "Pathways in and out of substance use among homeless-emerging adults". *Journal of Adolescent Research*, 21, 2, 133-157.

van der Ploeg, J. and Scholte, E. (1997) *Homeless Youth*. London: Routledge.

van der Ploeg, J.D. (1989) "Homelessness: A multidimensional problem". *Children and Youth Services Review*, 11, 1, 45-56.

Wafer, U. (2006) *Counted In, 2005*. Dublin: Homeless Agency.

Wagner, D. (1993) *Checkerboard Square: Culture and Resistance in a Homeless Community*. Oxford: Westview Press.

Waldron, A., Tobin, G. and McQuaid, P. (2001) "Mental health status of homeless children and their families". *Irish Journal of Psychiatric Medicine*, 18, 1, 11-15.

Wallace, S.E. (1968) "The road to skid row". *Social Problems*, 16, 1, 92-105.

Ward, P. (1995) "Homeless children and the Child Care Act, 1991". *Irish Law Times*, 13, 19-21.

Warnes, A.M. and Crane, M. (2006) "The causes of homelessness among older people in England". *Housing Studies*, 21, 3, 401-421.

Wasson, R.R. and Hill, R.P. (1998) "The process of becoming homeless: An investigation of female-headed families living in poverty". *The Journal of Consumer Affairs*, 32, 2, 320-342.

Watson, S. (1984) "Definitions of homelessness: A feminist perspective". *Critical Social Policy*, 4, 11, 60-73.

Watson, S., and Austerberry, H. (1986) *Housing and Homelessness: A Feminist Perspective*. London: Routledge and Kegan Paul.

Watters, J.K. and Biernacki, P. (1989) "Targeted sampling: Options for the study of hidden populations". *Social Problems*, 36, 4, 416-430.

Whelan, D.T. (1973) *Report on Unattached Youth: Part I – Dublin Area*. Dublin: Simon Ireland.

Whitbeck, L.B. and Simons, R.L. (1990) "Life on the streets: The victimization of runaway and homeless adolescents". *Youth and Society*, 22, 1, 108-125.

Whitbeck, L.B. and Simons, R.L. (1991) "A comparison of adaptive strategies and patterns of victimization among homeless adolescents and adults". *Violence and Victims*, 8, 2, 135-152.

Whitbeck, L.B., Hoyt, D. R., and Bao, W. (2000) "Depressive symptoms and co-occurring depressive symptoms, substance abuse, and conduct problems among runaway and homeless adolescents". *Child Development*, 71, 3, 721-732.

Whitbeck, L.B., Hoyt, D. R., and Yoder, K.A. (1999) "A risk-amplification model of victimisation and depressive symptoms among runaway and homeless adolescents". *American Journal of Community Psychology*, 27, 2, 273-296.

Whyte, G. (2002) *Social Inclusion and the Legal System: Public Interest Law in Ireland.* Dublin: Institute of Public Administration.

Williams, J. and Gorby, S. (2002) *Counted in 2002: The Report of the Assessment of Homelessness in Dublin.* Dublin: Homeless Agency and Economic and Social Research Institute.

Williams, J. and O'Connor, M. (1999) *Counted in: The Report of the 1999 Assessment of Homelessness in Dublin, Kildare and Wicklow.* Dublin: Economic and Social Research Institute/Homeless Initiative.

Williams, M. and Cheal, B. (2001) "Is there any such thing as Homelessness? Measurement, explanation and process in 'homelessness' research". *Innovation: The European Journal of Social Sciences*, 14, 3, 239-253.

Wincup, E., Buckland, G. and Bayliss, R. (2003) *Youth Homelessness and Substance Use: Report to the Drugs and Alcohol Research Unit.* London: Home Office Research Study 258.

Wong, Y.I. and Piliavin (1997) "A dynamic analysis of homeless-domicile transitions". *Social Problems.* 44, 3, 408-423.